[redacted]

CLIVE BARKER'S THE THIEF OF ALWAYS™

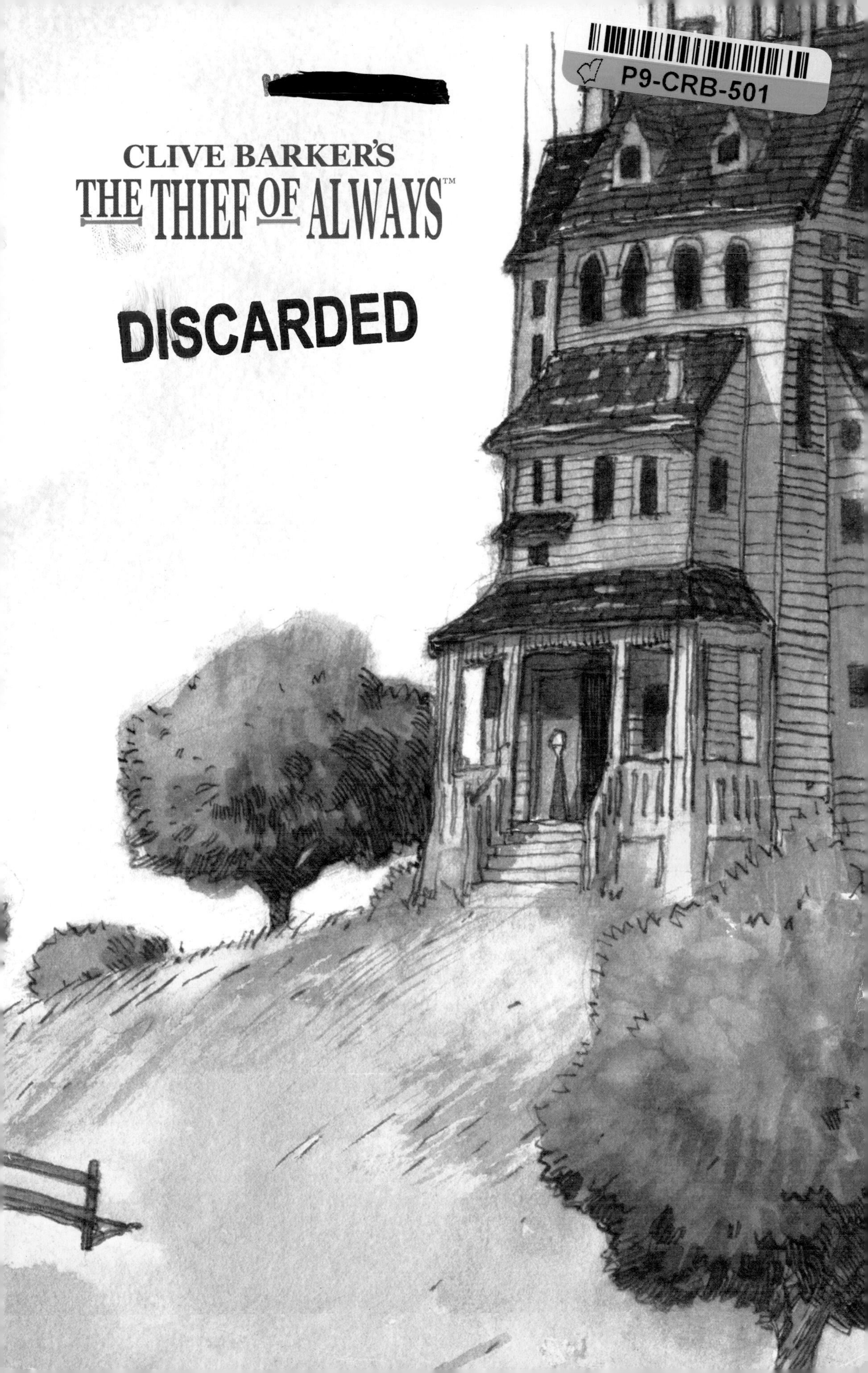

www.idwpublishing.com

SOFTCOVER ISBN: 1-933239-38-7
HARDCOVER ISBN: 1-933239-17-4
08 07 06 05 1 2 3 4 5

CLIVE BARKER'S THE THIEF OF ALWAYS. September 2005. FIRST PRINTING. IDW Publishing, a division of Idea + Design Works, LLC. Editorial offices: 4411 Morena Blvd., Ste. 106. San Diego, CA 92117. The Thief of Always ©1992 by Clive Barker. Adaptation © 2005 Idea + Design Works, LLC. All Rights Reserved. Originally published as The Thief of Always #1-3. The IDW logo is registered in the U.S. Patent and Trademark Office. Any similarities to persons living or dead are purely coincidental. With the exception of artwork used for review purposes, none of the contents of this publication may be reprinted without the permission of Idea + Design Works, LLC. Printed in Korea.

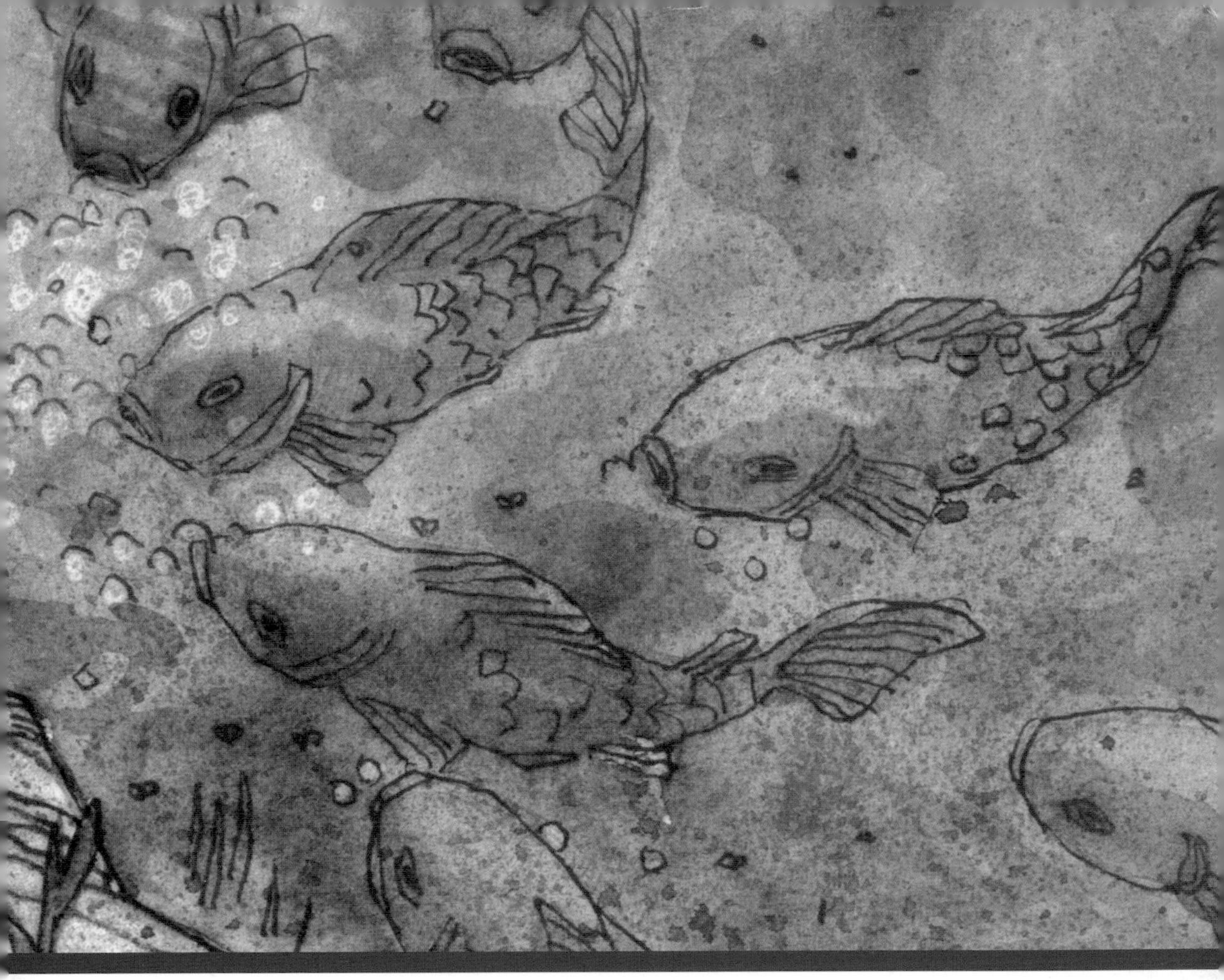

Clive Barker's

The Thief of Always

Adaptation by

Kris Oprisko

Illustrated by

Gabriel Hernandez,

Sulaco Studios

Lettered by

Robbie Robbins & Tom B. Long

Design by

Robbie Robbins

Edited by

Chris Ryall & Alex Garner

CLIVE BARKER'S
THE THIEF OF ALWAYS™

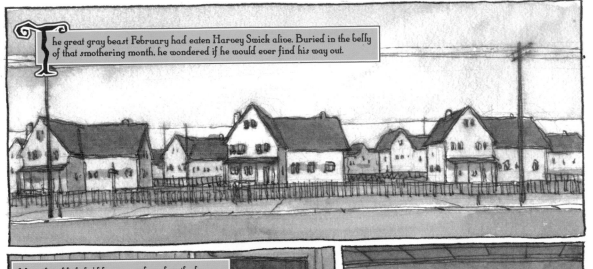

The great gray beast February had eaten Harvey Swick alive. Buried in the belly of that smothering month, he wondered if he would ever find his way out.

More than likely he'd become so bored as the hours crawled by that one day he'd simply forget to breathe.

His demise would become a celebrated mystery, which wouldn't be solved until some great detective decided to re-create a day in Harvey's life.

The detective would follow Harvey's dismal routine—from home, to school, and back again...

...finally rendering the obvious verdict.

HARVEY SWICK WAS EATEN BY THE GREAT GRAY BEAST FEBRUARY.

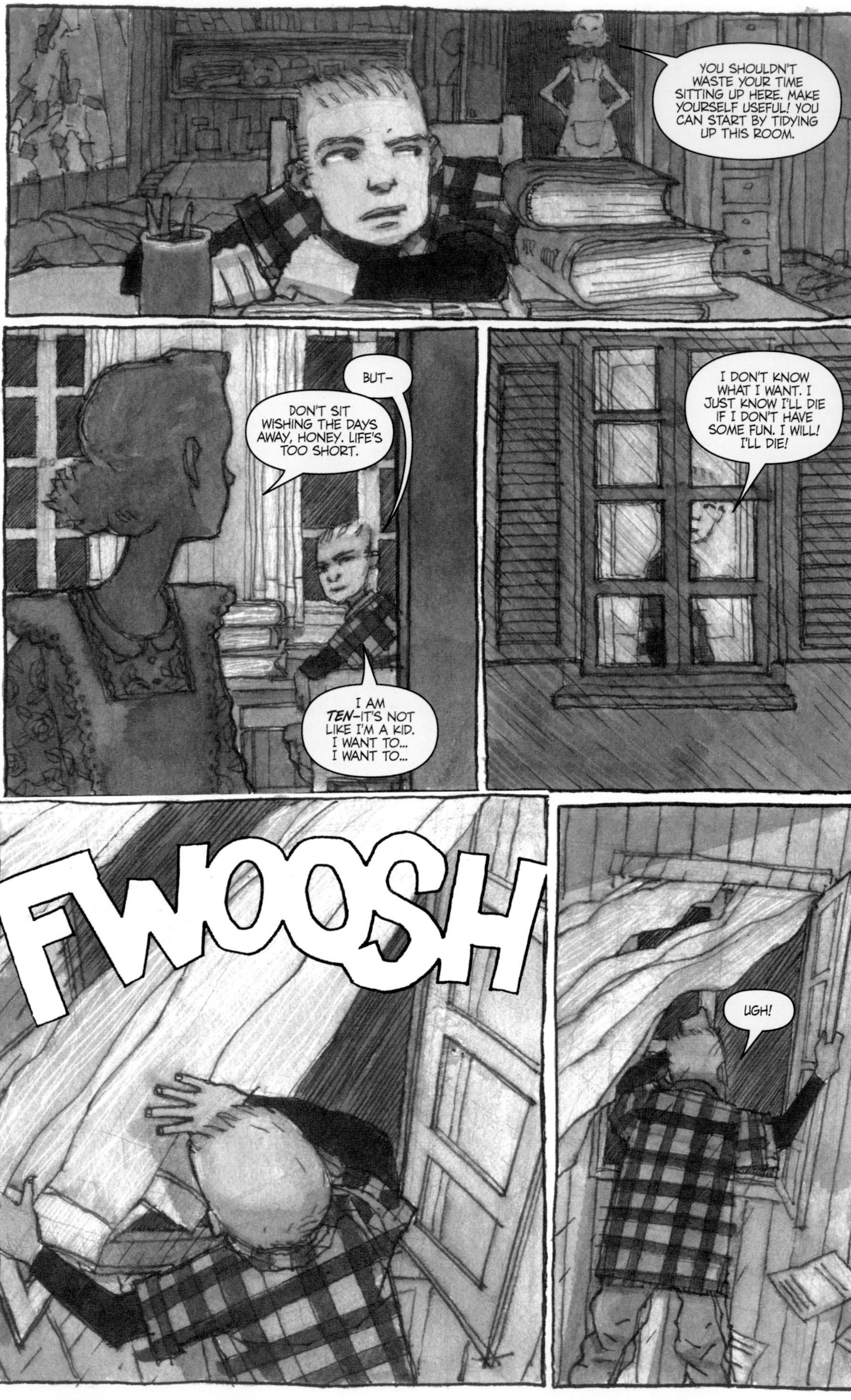
YOU SHOULDN'T WASTE YOUR TIME SITTING UP HERE. MAKE YOURSELF USEFUL! YOU CAN START BY TIDYING UP THIS ROOM.
BUT-
DON'T SIT WISHING THE DAYS AWAY, HONEY. LIFE'S TOO SHORT.
I AM *TEN*-IT'S NOT LIKE I'M A KID. I WANT TO... I WANT TO...
I DON'T KNOW WHAT I WANT. I JUST KNOW I'LL DIE IF I DON'T HAVE SOME FUN. I WILL! I'LL DIE!
FWOOSH
UGH!

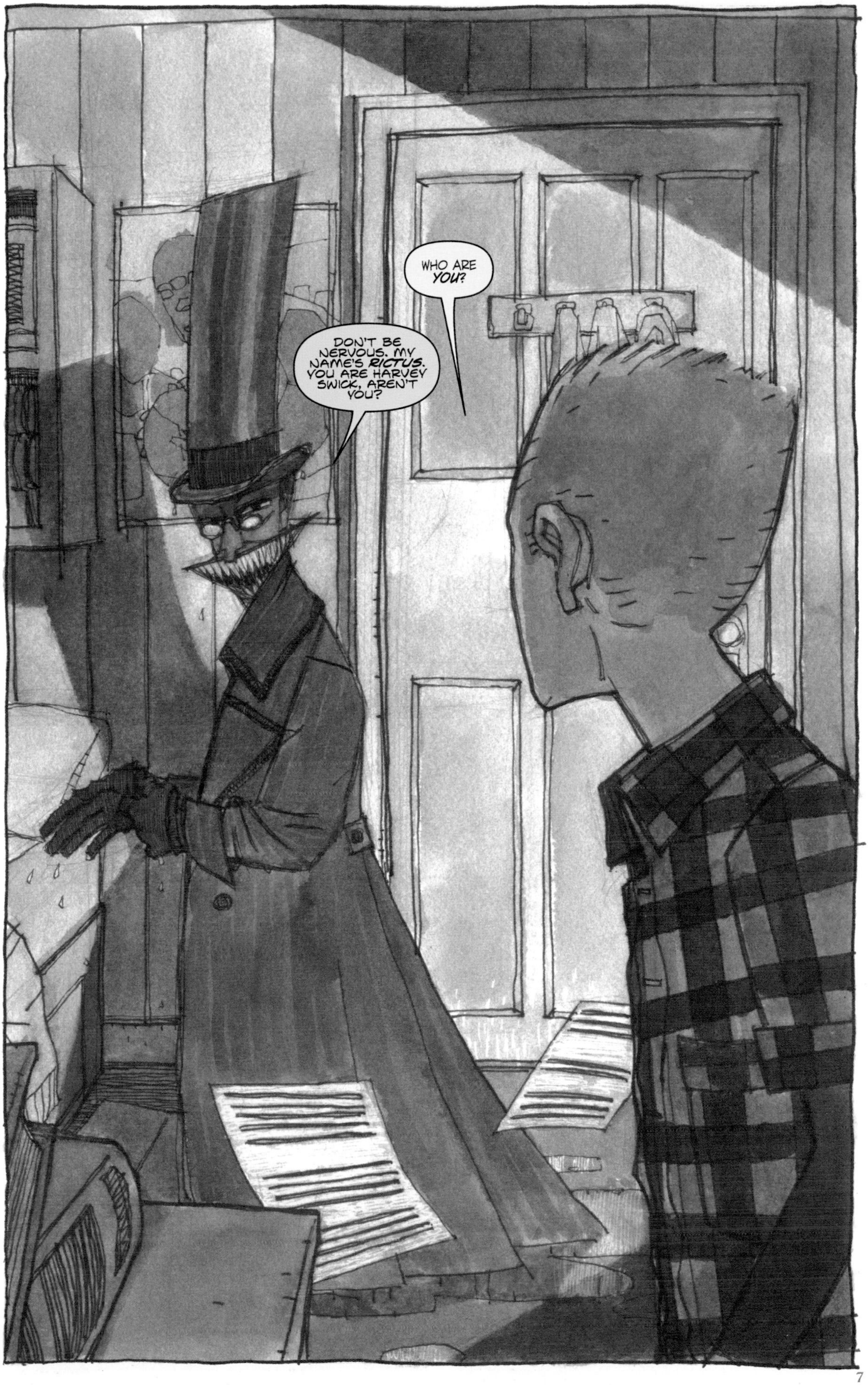
WHO ARE YOU?
DON'T BE NERVOUS. MY NAME'S RICTUS. YOU ARE HARVEY SWICK, AREN'T YOU?

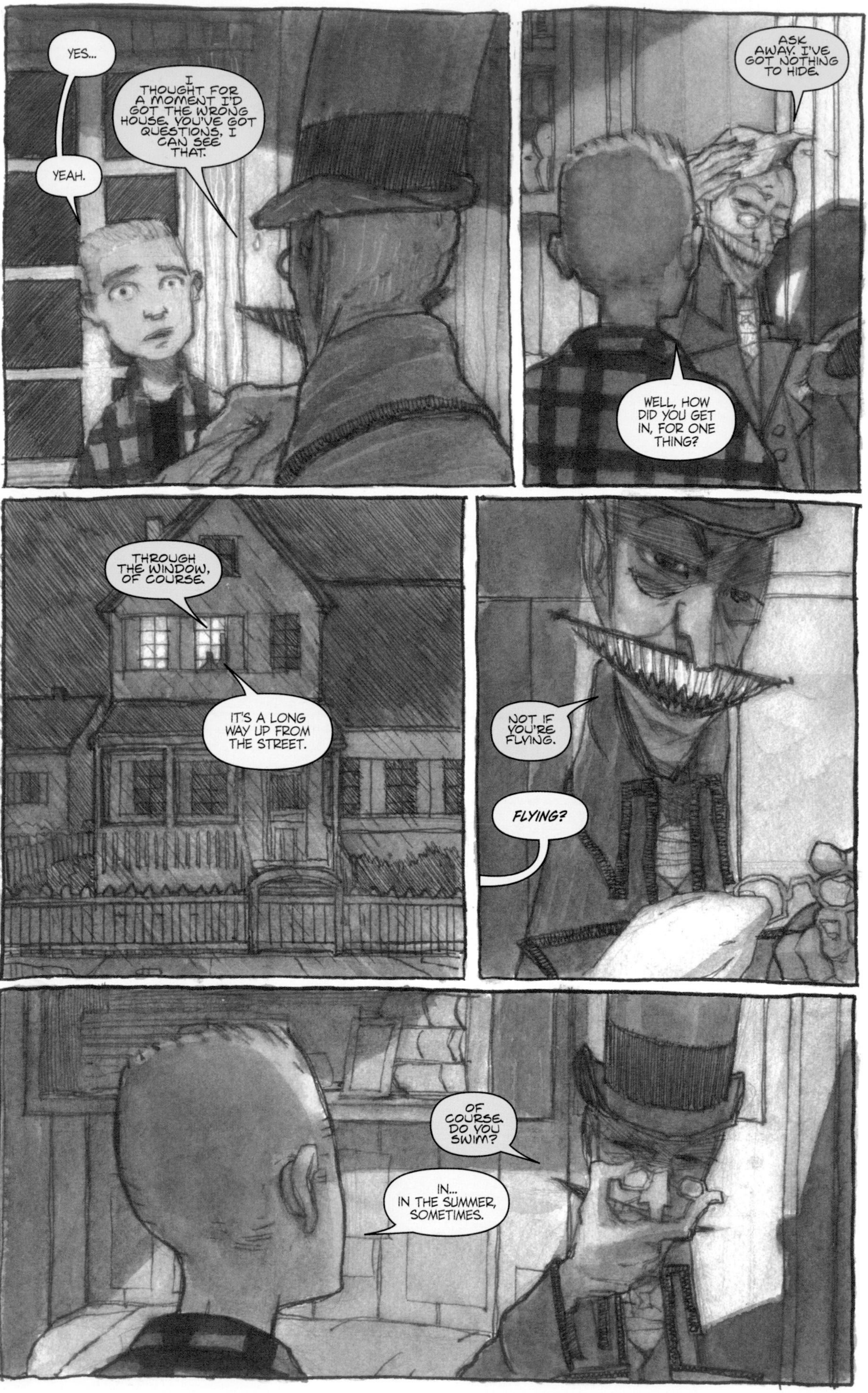
YES...
I THOUGHT FOR A MOMENT I'D GOT THE WRONG HOUSE. YOU'VE GOT QUESTIONS, I CAN SEE THAT.
YEAH.
ASK AWAY. I'VE GOT NOTHING TO HIDE.
WELL, HOW DID YOU GET IN, FOR ONE THING?
THROUGH THE WINDOW, OF COURSE.
IT'S A LONG WAY UP FROM THE STREET.
NOT IF YOU'RE FLYING.
FLYING?
OF COURSE. DO YOU SWIM?
IN... IN THE SUMMER, SOMETIMES.

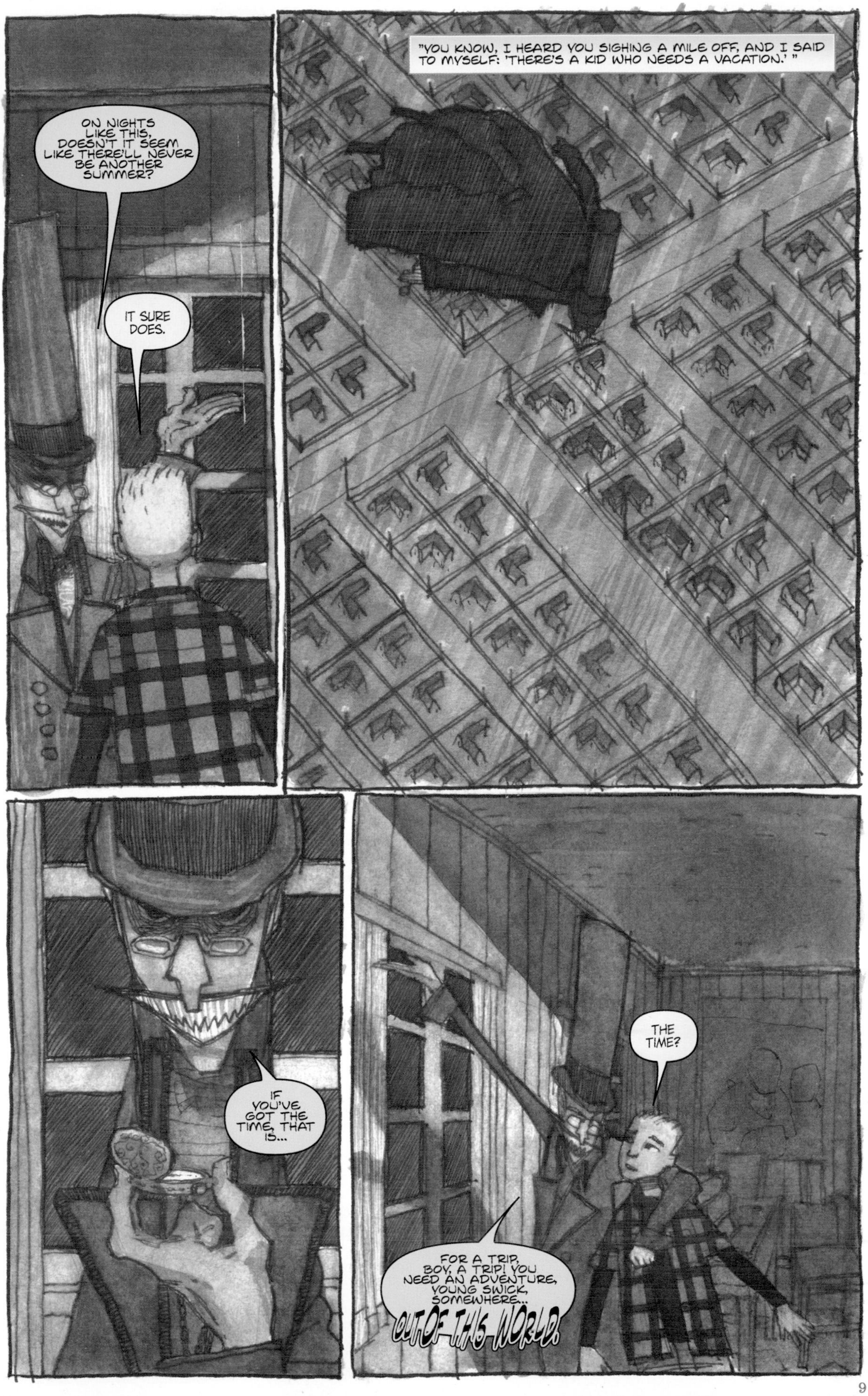
ON NIGHTS LIKE THIS, DOESN'T IT SEEM LIKE THERE'LL NEVER BE ANOTHER SUMMER?
IT SURE DOES.
"YOU KNOW, I HEARD YOU SIGHING A MILE OFF, AND I SAID TO MYSELF: 'THERE'S A KID WHO NEEDS A VACATION.' "
IF YOU'VE GOT THE TIME, THAT IS...
THE TIME?
FOR A TRIP, BOY, A TRIP! YOU NEED AN ADVENTURE, YOUNG SWICK, SOMEWHERE...
OUT OF THIS WORLD.

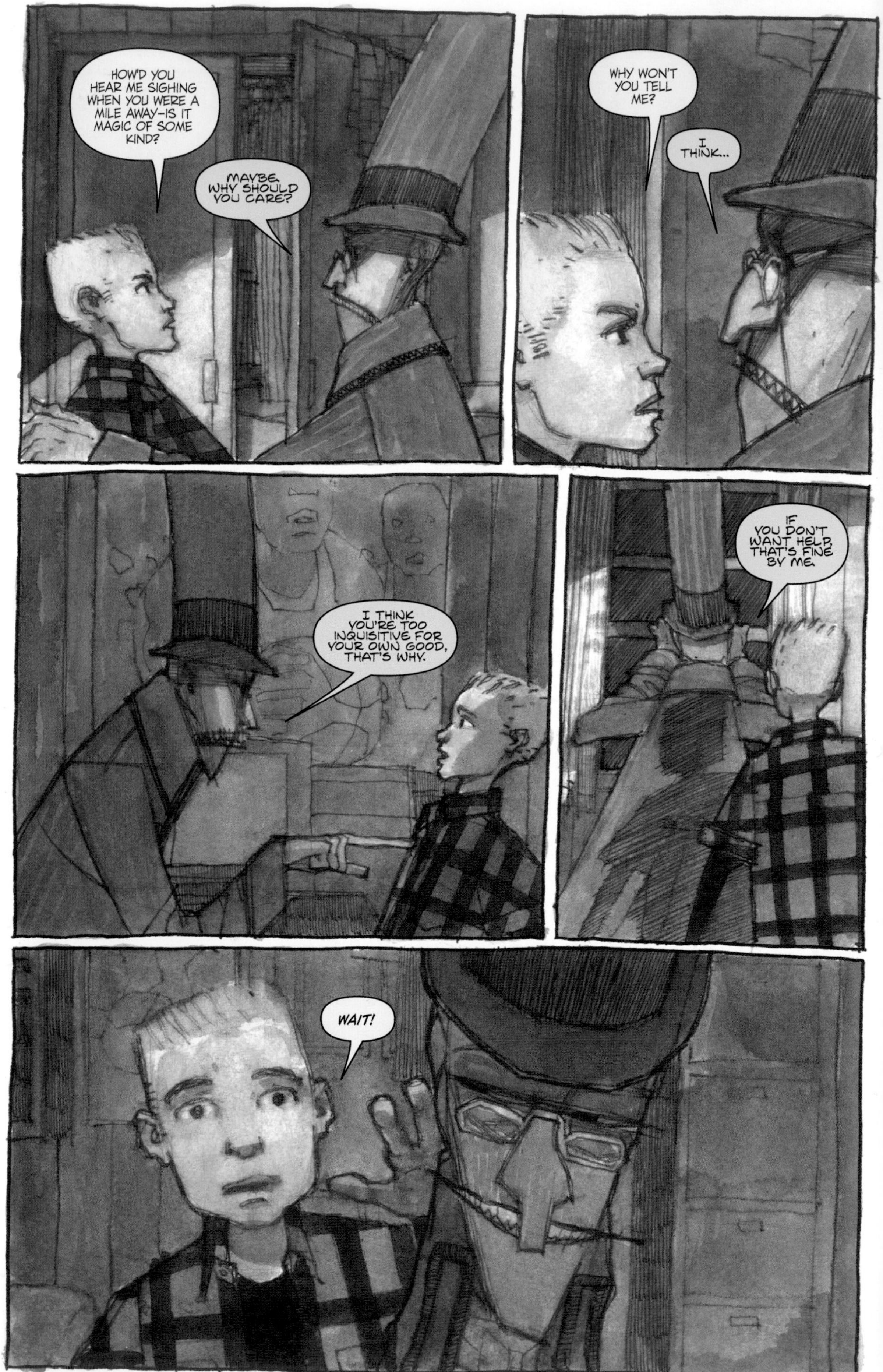
HOW'D YOU HEAR ME SIGHING WHEN YOU WERE A MILE AWAY–IS IT MAGIC OF SOME KIND?
MAYBE. WHY SHOULD YOU CARE?
WHY WON'T YOU TELL ME?
I THINK...
I THINK YOU'RE TOO INQUISITIVE FOR YOUR OWN GOOD, THAT'S WHY.
IF YOU DON'T WANT HELP, THAT'S FINE BY ME.
WAIT!

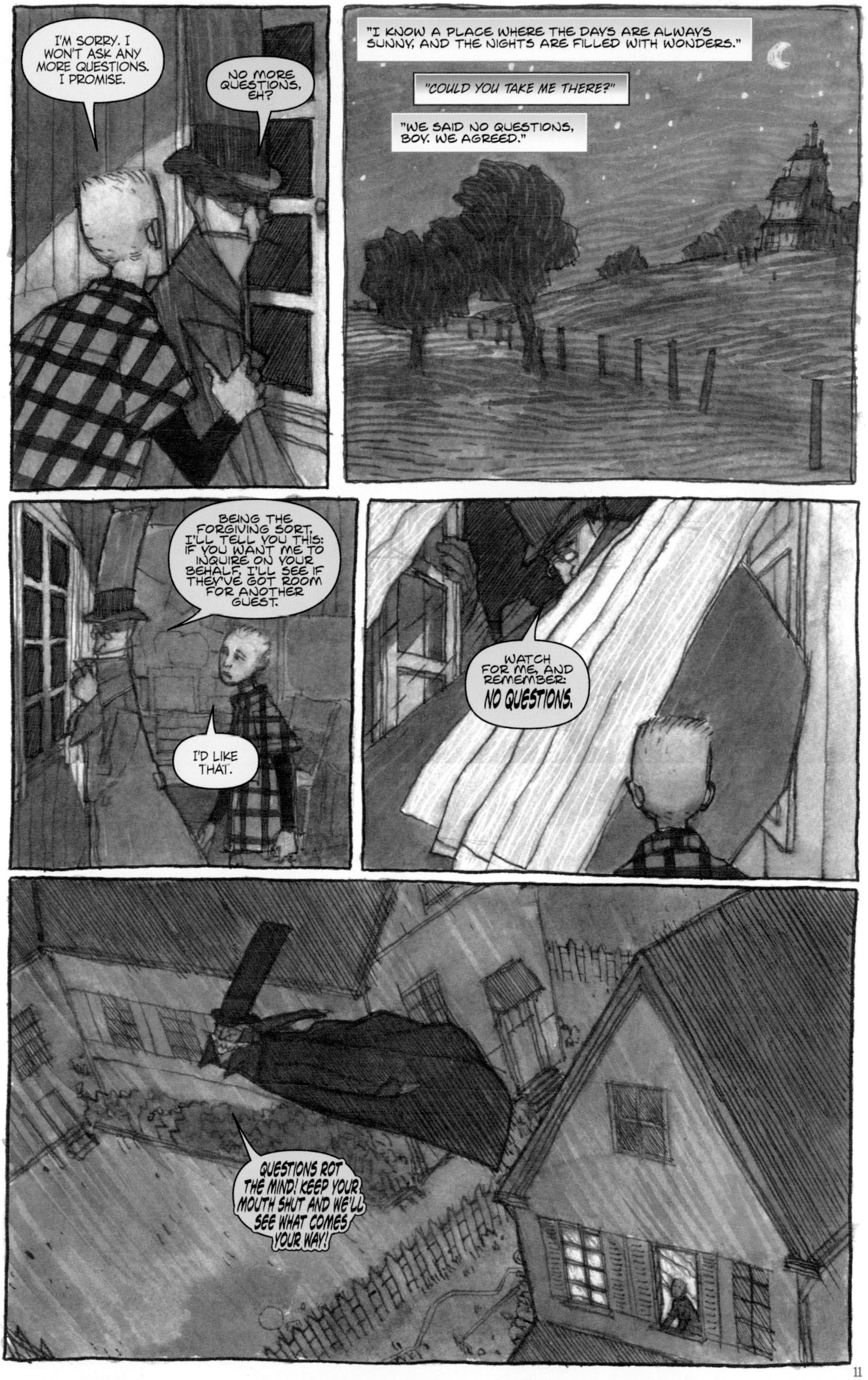
I'M SORRY. I WON'T ASK ANY MORE QUESTIONS. I PROMISE.
NO MORE QUESTIONS, EH?
"I KNOW A PLACE WHERE THE DAYS ARE ALWAYS SUNNY, AND THE NIGHTS ARE FILLED WITH WONDERS."
"COULD YOU TAKE ME THERE?"
"WE SAID NO QUESTIONS, BOY. WE AGREED."
BEING THE FORGIVING SORT, I'LL TELL YOU THIS: IF YOU WANT ME TO INQUIRE ON YOUR BEHALF, I'LL SEE IF THEY'VE GOT ROOM FOR ANOTHER GUEST.
I'D LIKE THAT.
WATCH FOR ME, AND REMEMBER: NO QUESTIONS.
QUESTIONS ROT THE MIND! KEEP YOUR MOUTH SHUT AND WE'LL SEE WHAT COMES YOUR WAY!

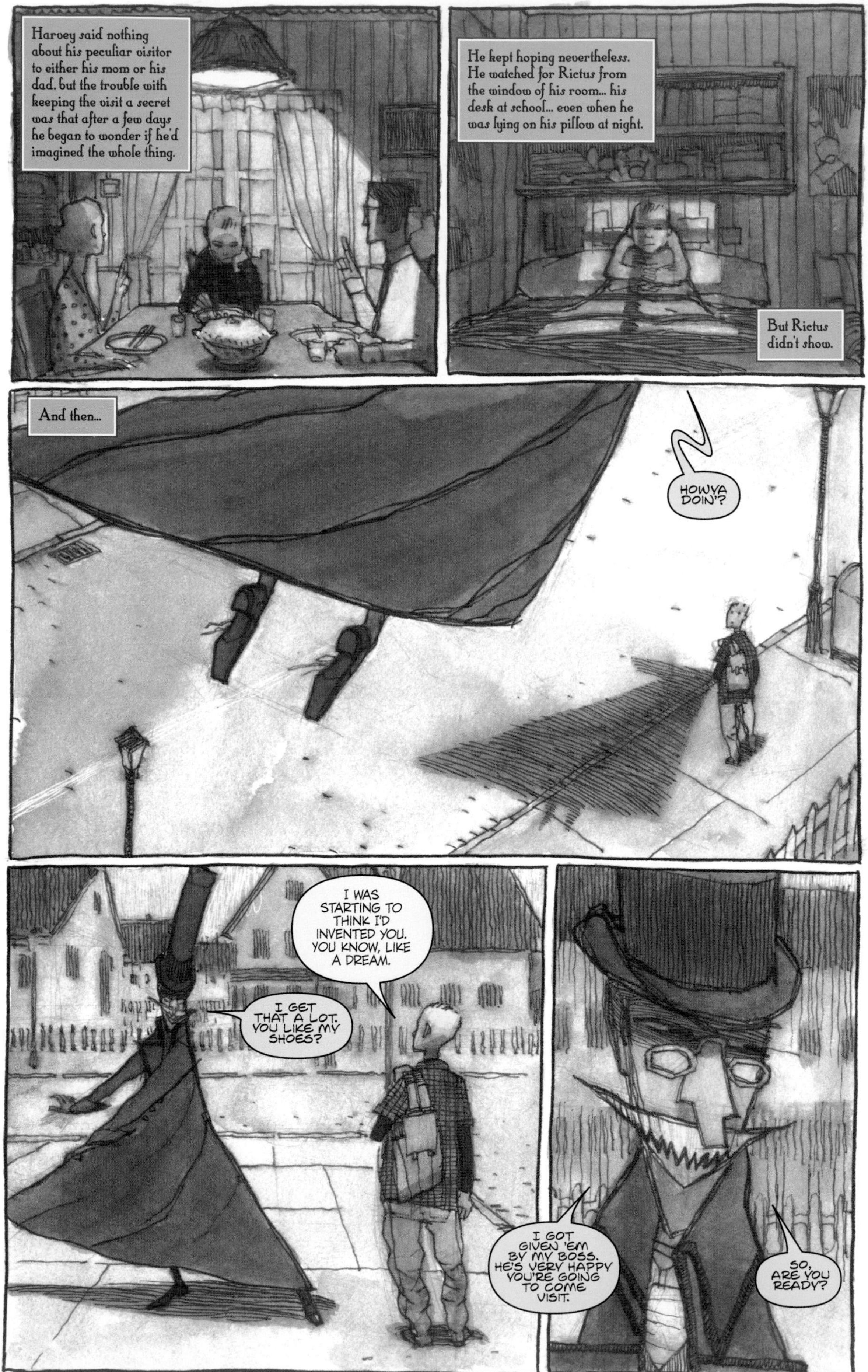

Harvey said nothing about his peculiar visitor to either his mom or his dad, but the trouble with keeping the visit a secret was that after a few days he began to wonder if he'd imagined the whole thing.
He kept hoping nevertheless. He watched for Rictus from the window of his room... his desk at school... even when he was lying on his pillow at night.
But Rictus didn't show.
And then...
HOWYA DOIN'?
I WAS STARTING TO THINK I'D INVENTED YOU. YOU KNOW, LIKE A DREAM.
I GET THAT A LOT. YOU LIKE MY SHOES?
I GOT GIVEN 'EM BY MY BOSS. HE'S VERY HAPPY YOU'RE GOING TO COME VISIT.
SO, ARE YOU READY?

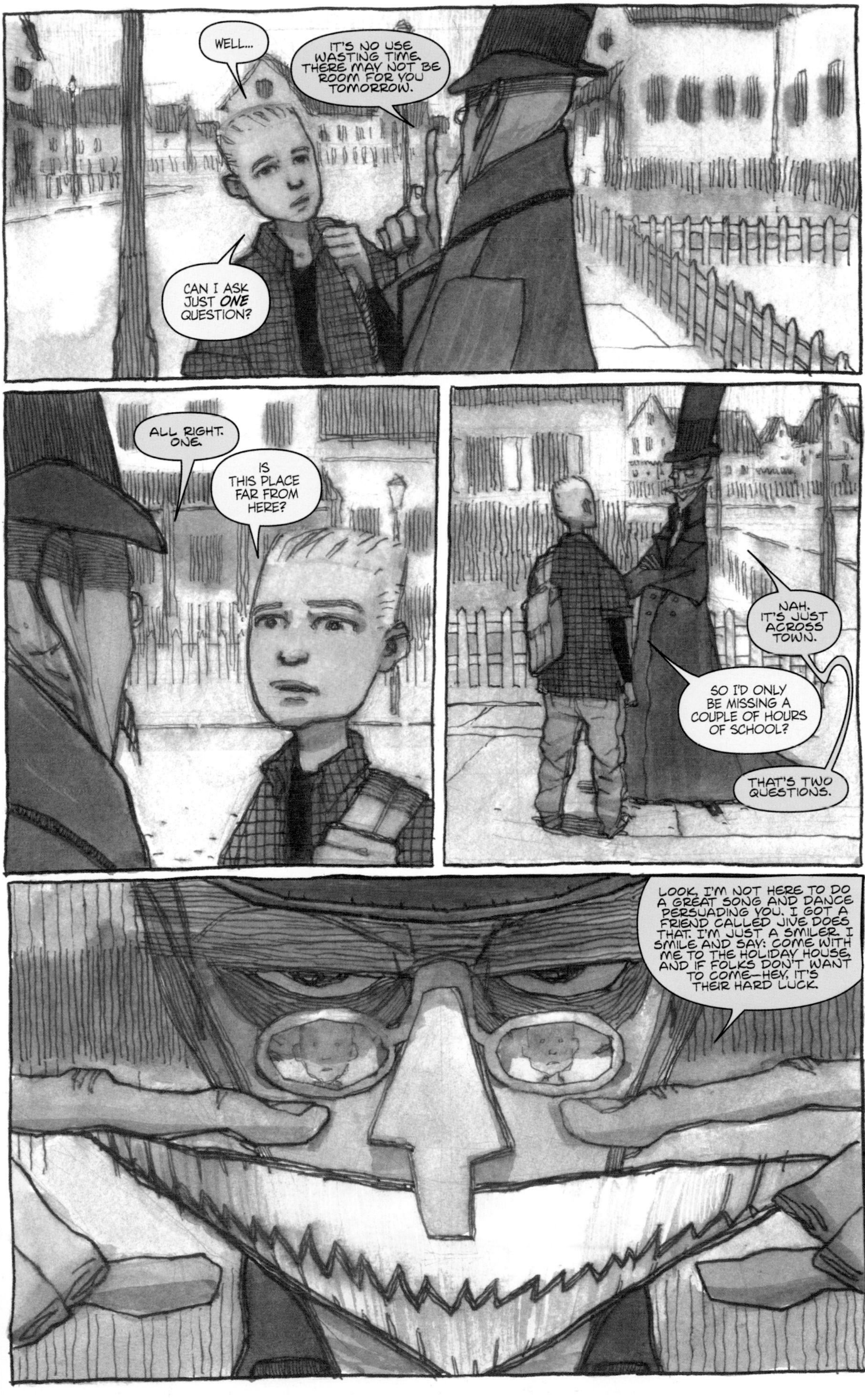
WELL...
IT'S NO USE WASTING TIME. THERE MAY NOT BE ROOM FOR YOU TOMORROW.
CAN I ASK JUST ***ONE*** QUESTION?
ALL RIGHT. ONE.
IS THIS PLACE FAR FROM HERE?
NAH. IT'S JUST ACROSS TOWN.
SO I'D ONLY BE MISSING A COUPLE OF HOURS OF SCHOOL?
THAT'S TWO QUESTIONS.
LOOK, I'M NOT HERE TO DO A GREAT SONG AND DANCE PERSUADING YOU. I GOT A FRIEND CALLED JIVE DOES THAT. I'M JUST A SMILER. I SMILE AND SAY: COME WITH ME TO THE HOLIDAY HOUSE, AND IF FOLKS DON'T WANT TO COME—HEY, IT'S THEIR HARD LUCK.

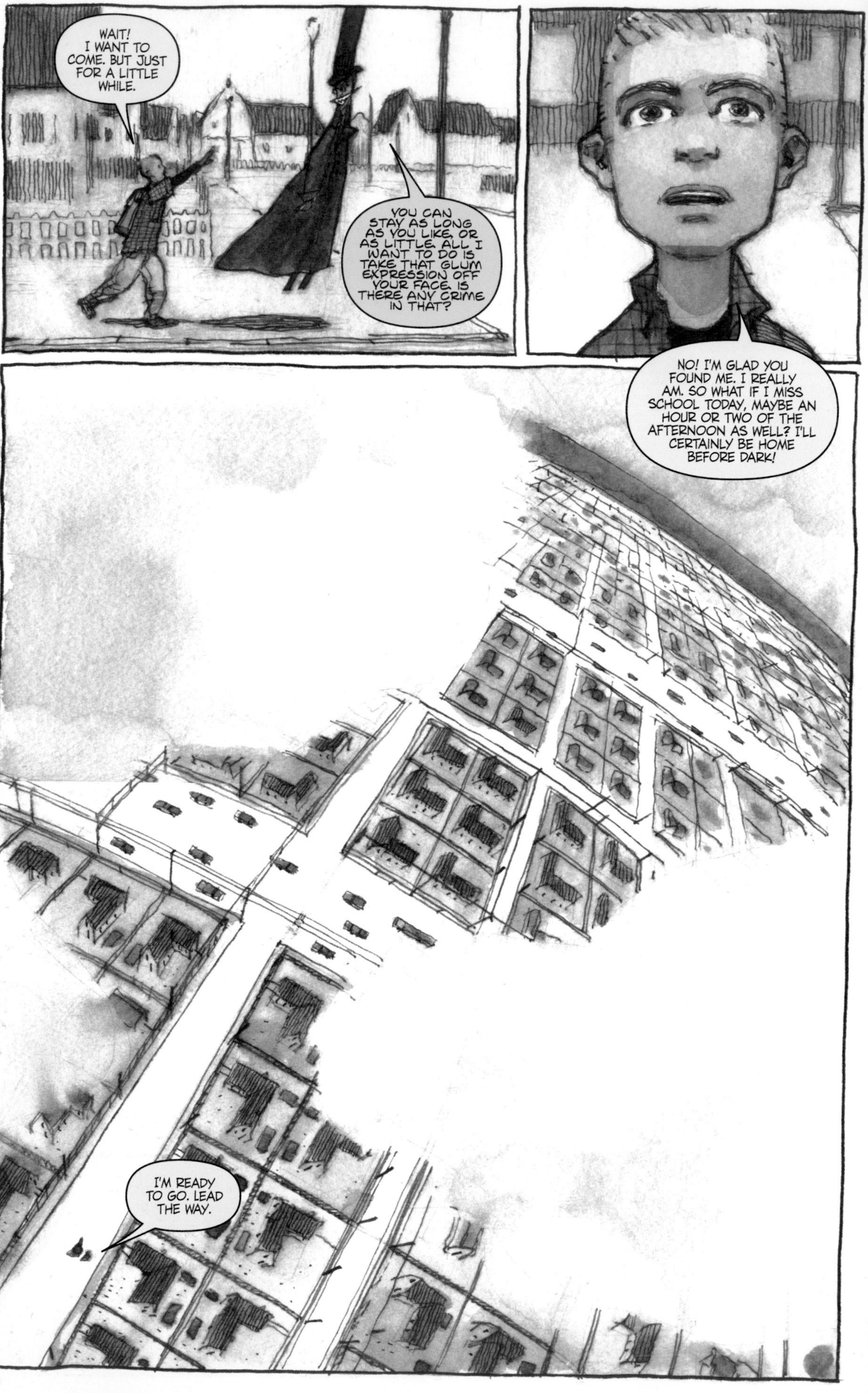
WAIT! I WANT TO COME. BUT JUST FOR A LITTLE WHILE.
YOU CAN STAY AS LONG AS YOU LIKE, OR AS LITTLE. ALL I WANT TO DO IS TAKE THAT GLUM EXPRESSION OFF YOUR FACE. IS THERE ANY CRIME IN THAT?
NO! I'M GLAD YOU FOUND ME. I REALLY AM. SO WHAT IF I MISS SCHOOL TODAY, MAYBE AN HOUR OR TWO OF THE AFTERNOON AS WELL? I'LL CERTAINLY BE HOME BEFORE DARK!
I'M READY TO GO. LEAD THE WAY.

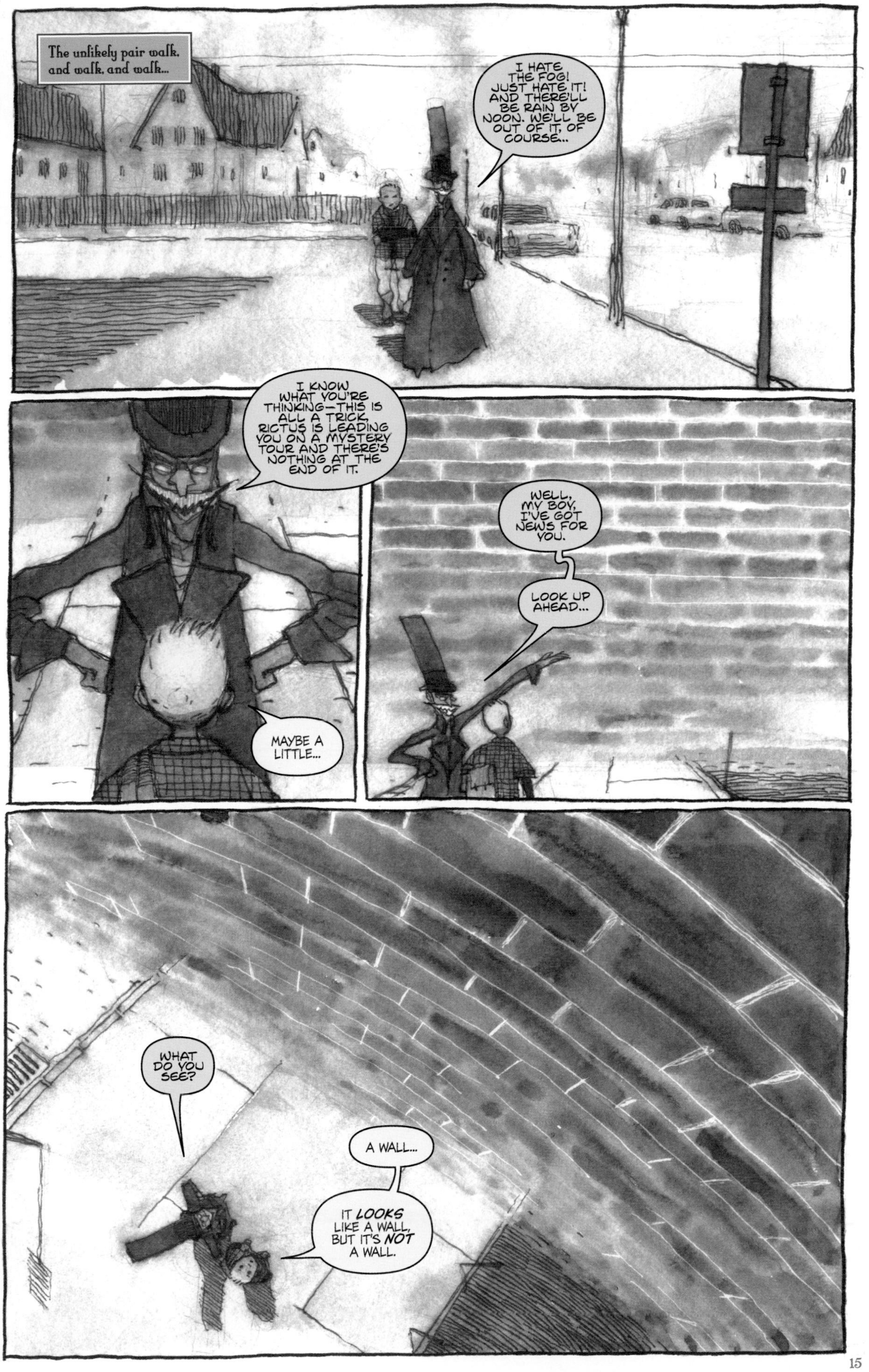

The unlikely pair walk, and walk, and walk...
I HATE THE FOG! JUST HATE IT! AND THERE'LL BE RAIN BY NOON. WE'LL BE OUT OF IT, OF COURSE...
I KNOW WHAT YOU'RE THINKING—THIS IS ALL A TRICK. RICTUS IS LEADING YOU ON A MYSTERY TOUR AND THERE'S NOTHING AT THE END OF IT.
MAYBE A LITTLE...
WELL, MY BOY, I'VE GOT NEWS FOR YOU.
LOOK UP AHEAD...
WHAT DO YOU SEE?
A WALL...
IT *LOOKS* LIKE A WALL, BUT IT'S *NOT* A WALL.

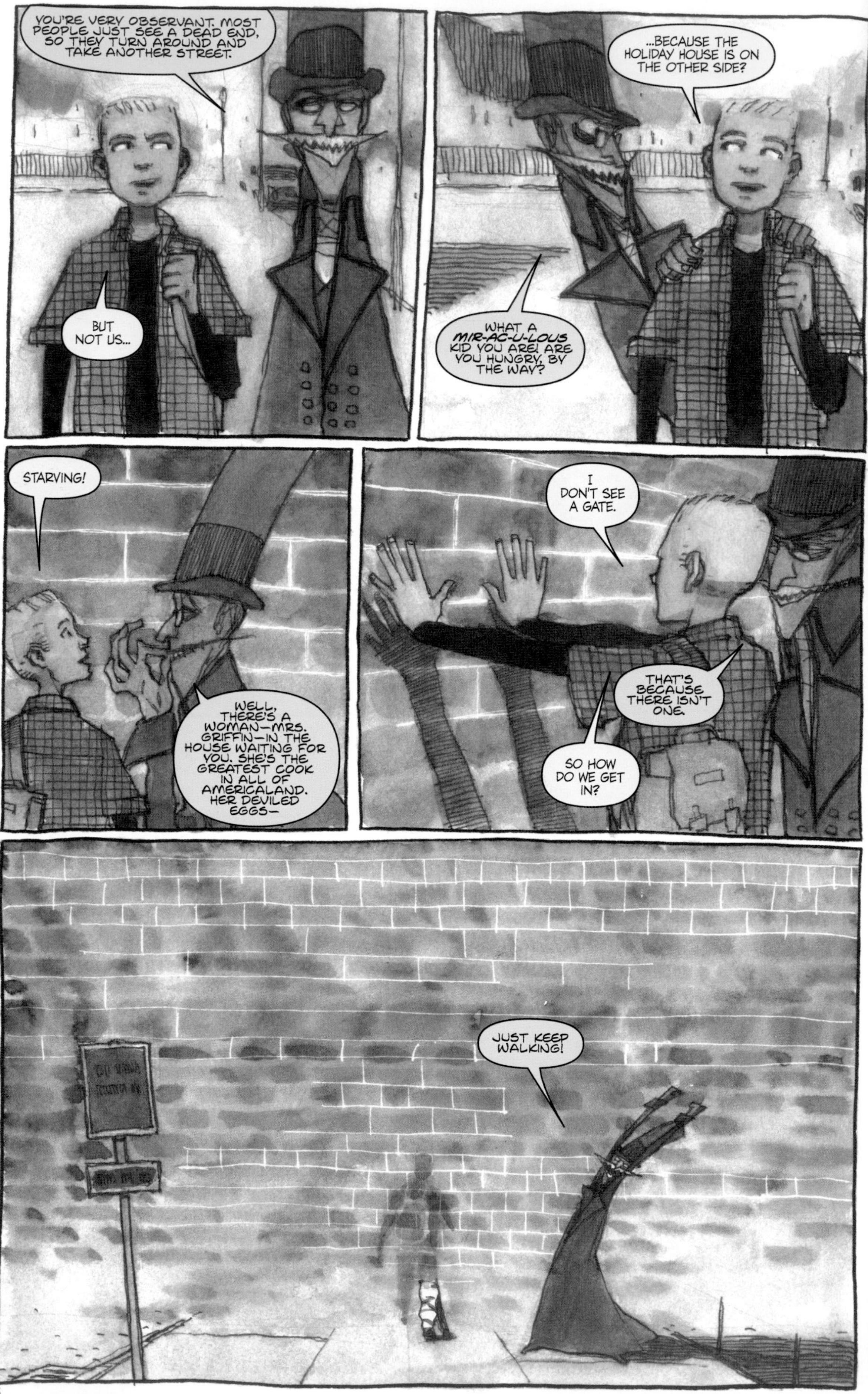
YOU'RE VERY OBSERVANT. MOST PEOPLE JUST SEE A DEAD END, SO THEY TURN AROUND AND TAKE ANOTHER STREET.
BUT NOT US...
...BECAUSE THE HOLIDAY HOUSE IS ON THE OTHER SIDE?
WHAT A *MIR-AC-U-LOUS* KID YOU ARE! ARE YOU HUNGRY, BY THE WAY?
STARVING!
WELL, THERE'S A WOMAN—MRS. GRIFFIN—IN THE HOUSE WAITING FOR YOU. SHE'S THE GREATEST COOK IN ALL OF AMERICALAND. HER DEVILED EGGS—
I DON'T SEE A GATE.
THAT'S BECAUSE THERE ISN'T ONE.
SO HOW DO WE GET IN?
JUST KEEP WALKING!

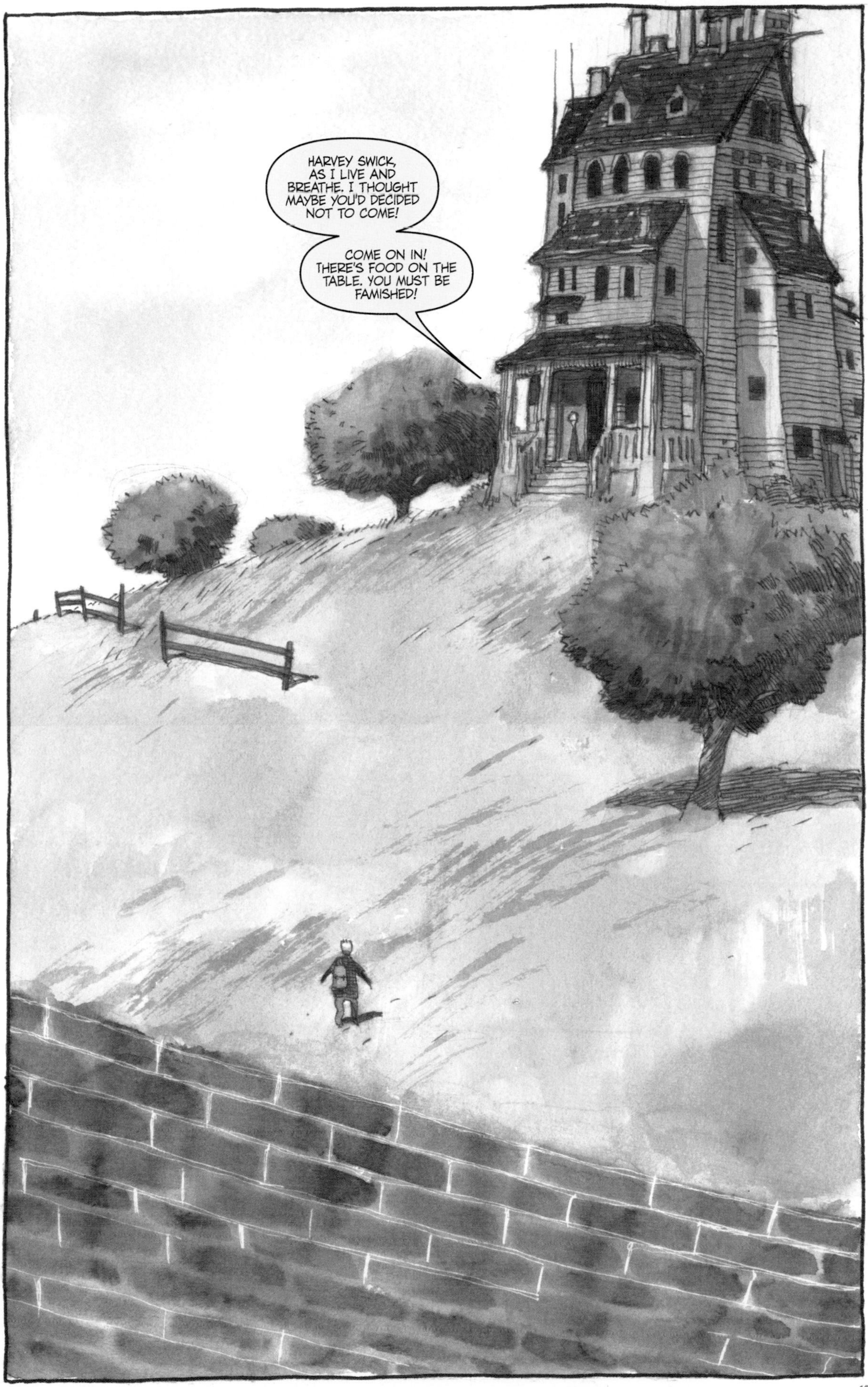
HARVEY SWICK, AS I LIVE AND BREATHE. I THOUGHT MAYBE YOU'D DECIDED NOT TO COME!
COME ON IN! THERE'S FOOD ON THE TABLE. YOU MUST BE FAMISHED!

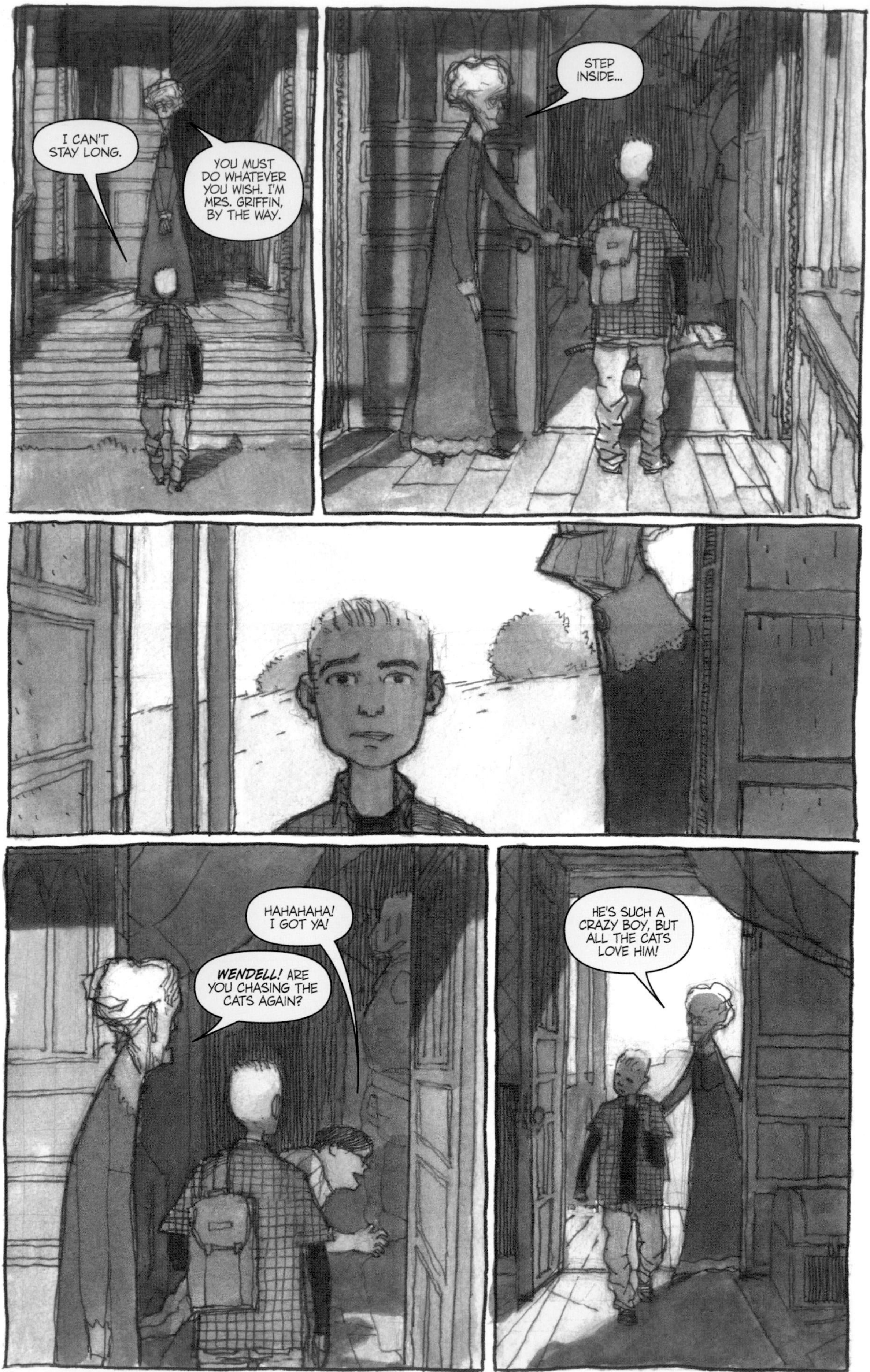
I CAN'T STAY LONG.
YOU MUST DO WHATEVER YOU WISH. I'M MRS. GRIFFIN, BY THE WAY.
STEP INSIDE...
HAHAHAHA! I GOT YA!
WENDELL! ARE YOU CHASING THE CATS AGAIN?
HE'S SUCH A CRAZY BOY, BUT ALL THE CATS LOVE HIM!

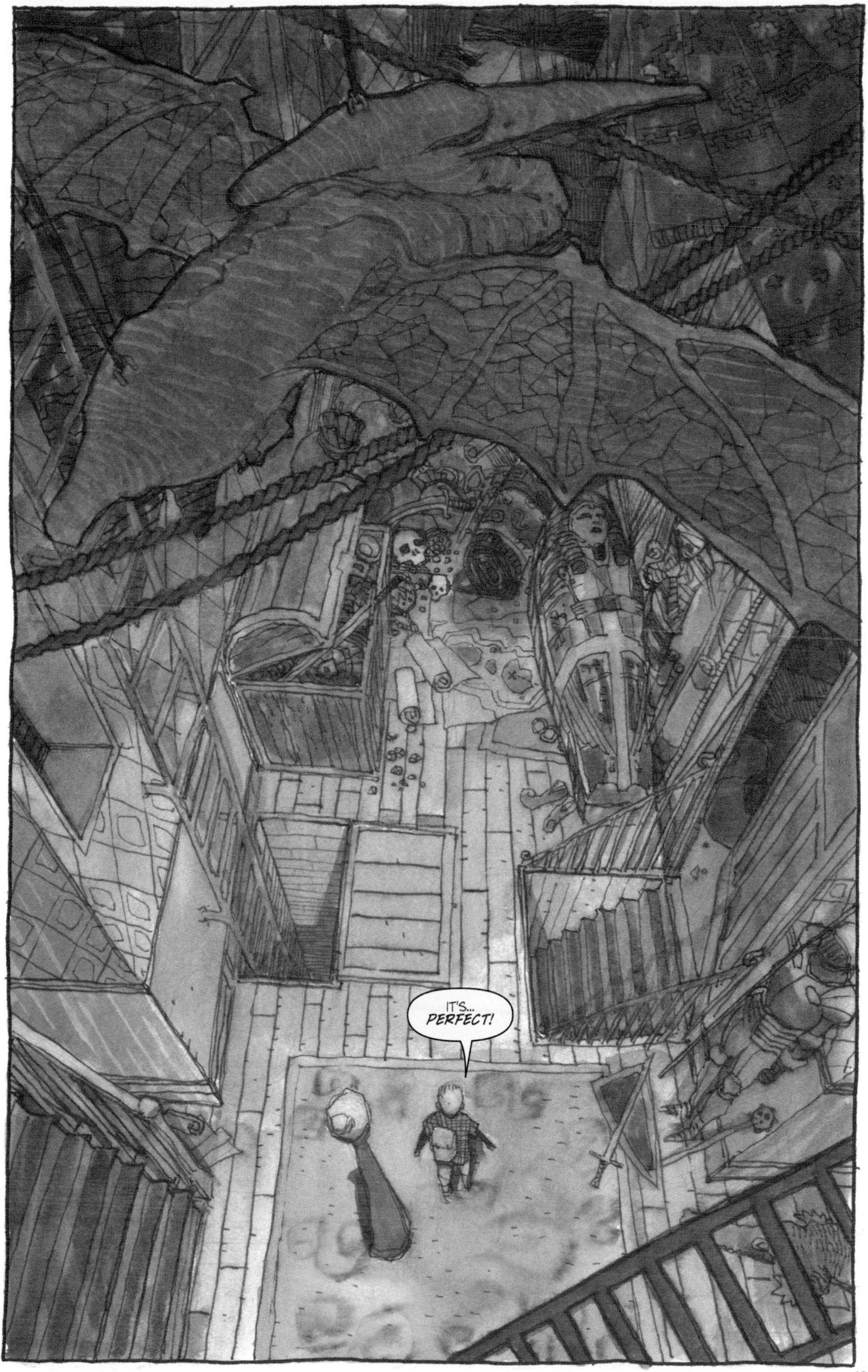
IT'S...
PERFECT!

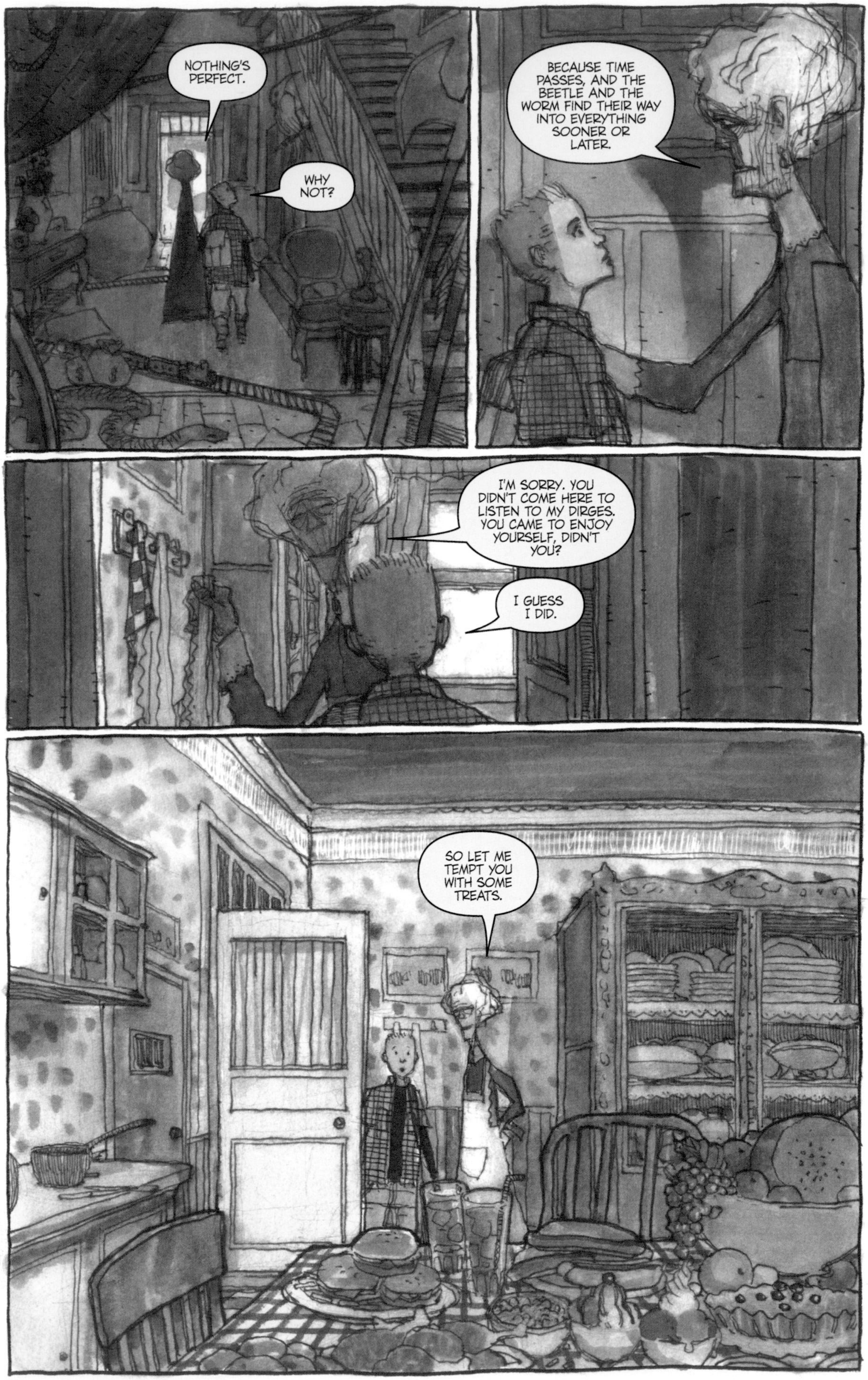
NOTHING'S PERFECT.
WHY NOT?
BECAUSE TIME PASSES, AND THE BEETLE AND THE WORM FIND THEIR WAY INTO EVERYTHING SOONER OR LATER.
I'M SORRY. YOU DIDN'T COME HERE TO LISTEN TO MY DIRGES. YOU CAME TO ENJOY YOURSELF, DIDN'T YOU?
I GUESS I DID.
SO LET ME TEMPT YOU WITH SOME TREATS.

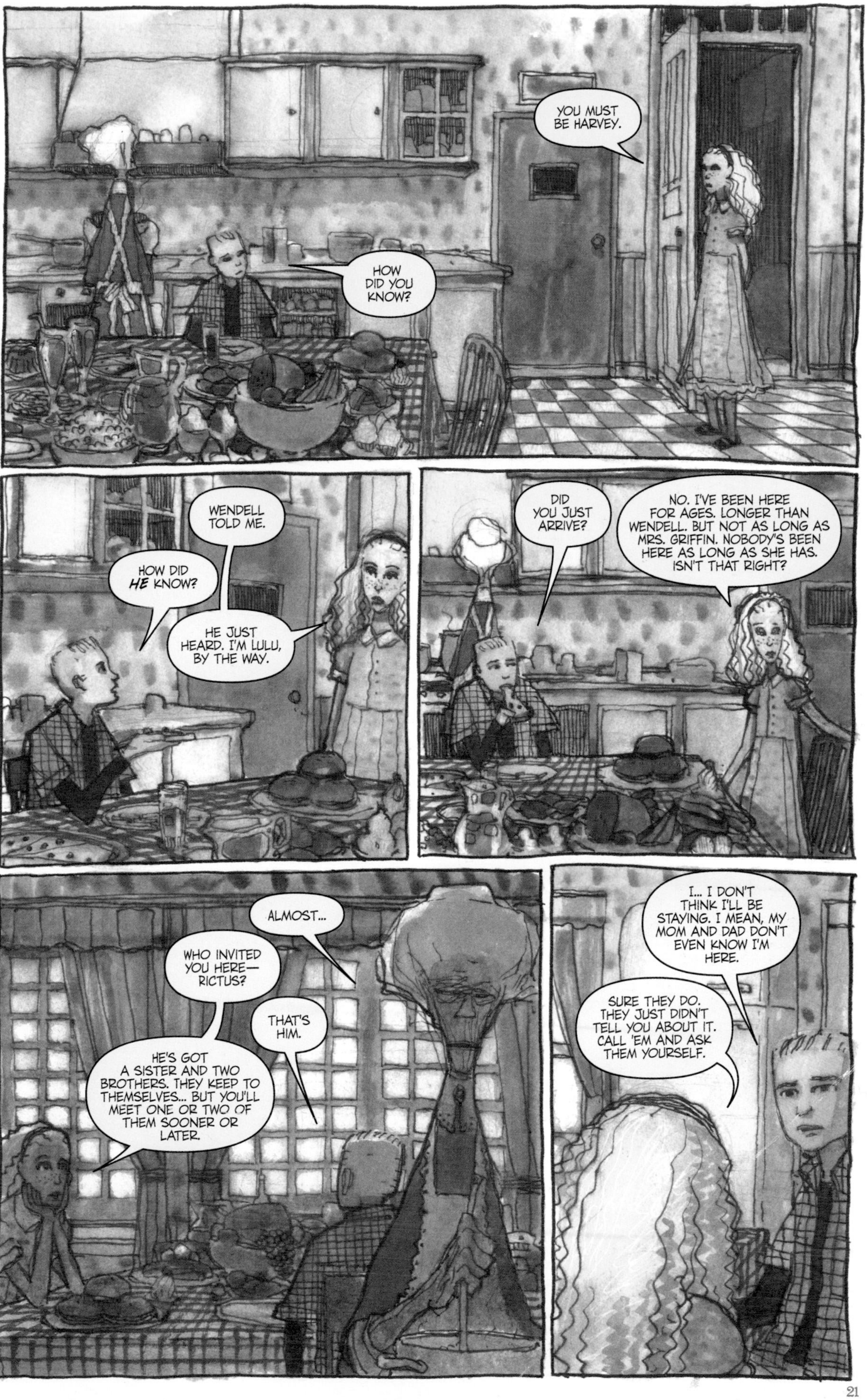
YOU MUST BE HARVEY.
HOW DID YOU KNOW?
WENDELL TOLD ME.
HOW DID *HE* KNOW?
HE JUST HEARD. I'M LULU, BY THE WAY.
DID YOU JUST ARRIVE?
NO. I'VE BEEN HERE FOR AGES. LONGER THAN WENDELL. BUT NOT AS LONG AS MRS. GRIFFIN. NOBODY'S BEEN HERE AS LONG AS SHE HAS. ISN'T THAT RIGHT?
ALMOST...
WHO INVITED YOU HERE—RICTUS?
THAT'S HIM.
HE'S GOT A SISTER AND TWO BROTHERS. THEY KEEP TO THEMSELVES... BUT YOU'LL MEET ONE OR TWO OF THEM SOONER OR LATER.
I... I DON'T THINK I'LL BE STAYING. I MEAN, MY MOM AND DAD DON'T EVEN KNOW I'M HERE.
SURE THEY DO. THEY JUST DIDN'T TELL YOU ABOUT IT. CALL 'EM AND ASK THEM YOURSELF.

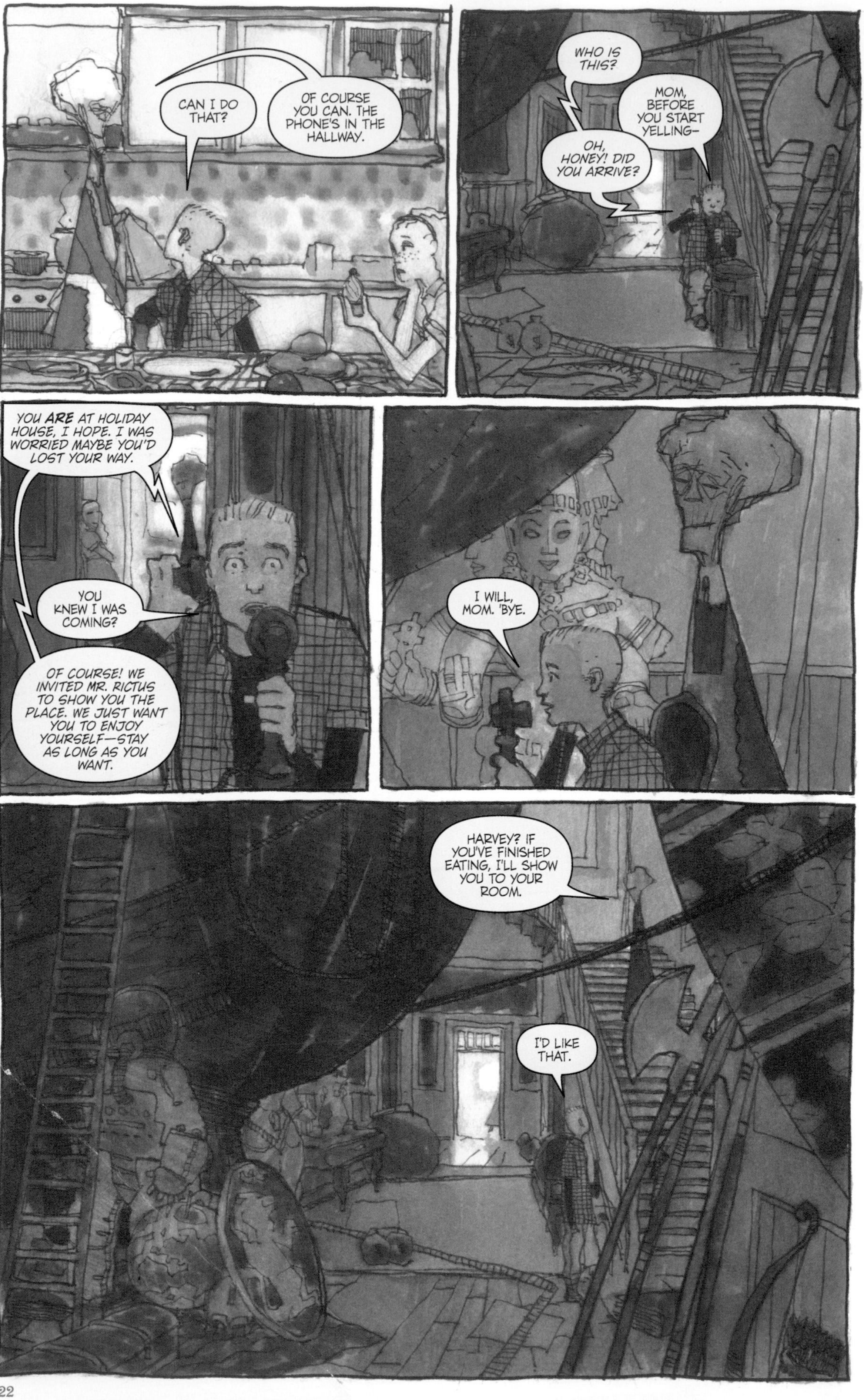

CAN I DO THAT?
OF COURSE YOU CAN. THE PHONE'S IN THE HALLWAY.
WHO IS THIS?
MOM, BEFORE YOU START YELLING—
OH, HONEY! DID YOU ARRIVE?
YOU **ARE** AT HOLIDAY HOUSE, I HOPE. I WAS WORRIED MAYBE YOU'D LOST YOUR WAY.
YOU KNEW I WAS COMING?
OF COURSE! WE INVITED MR. RICTUS TO SHOW YOU THE PLACE. WE JUST WANT YOU TO ENJOY YOURSELF—STAY AS LONG AS YOU WANT.
I WILL, MOM. 'BYE.
HARVEY? IF YOU'VE FINISHED EATING, I'LL SHOW YOU TO YOUR ROOM.
I'D LIKE THAT.

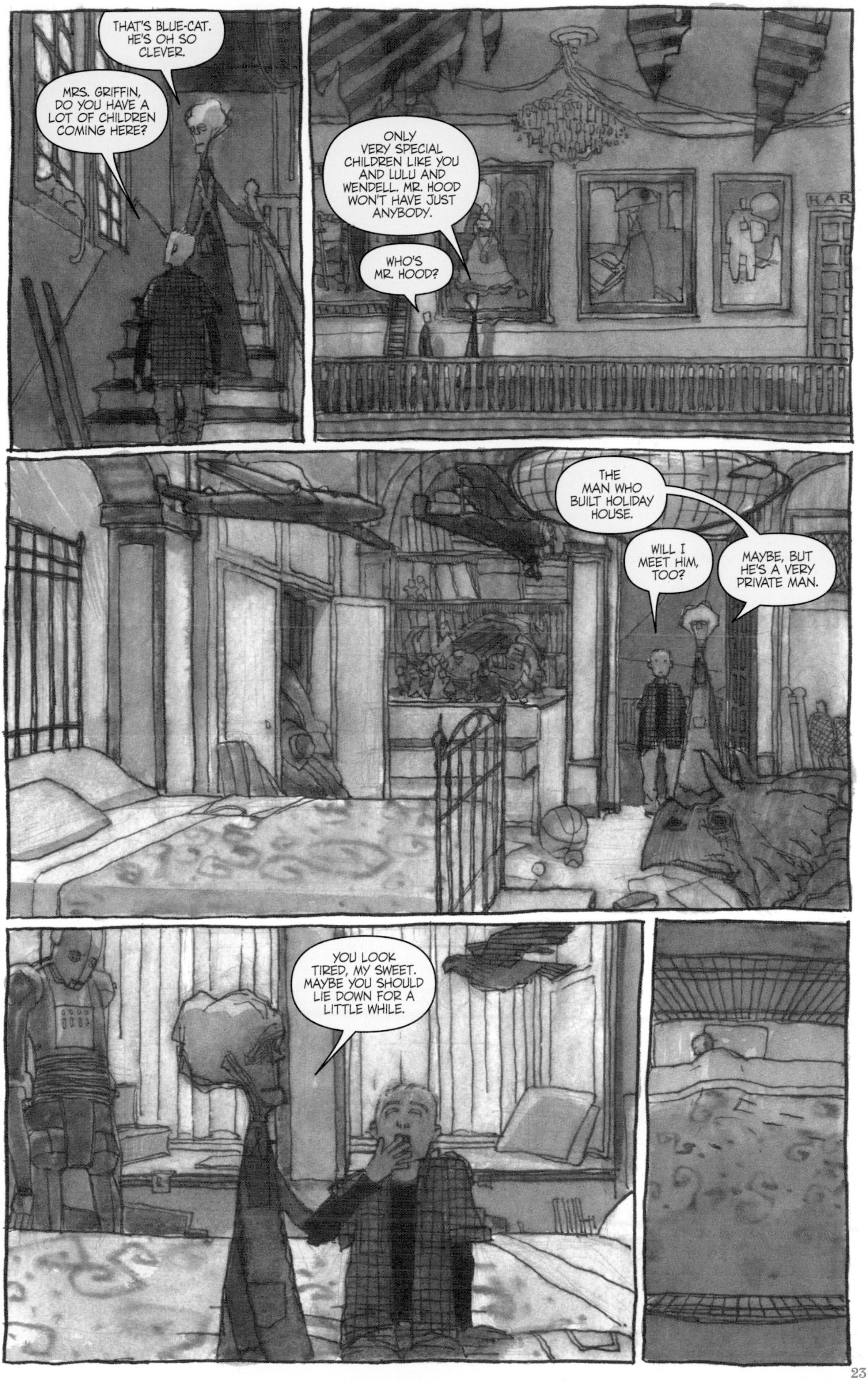
THAT'S BLUE-CAT. HE'S OH SO CLEVER.
MRS. GRIFFIN, DO YOU HAVE A LOT OF CHILDREN COMING HERE?
ONLY VERY SPECIAL CHILDREN LIKE YOU AND LULU AND WENDELL. MR. HOOD WON'T HAVE JUST ANYBODY.
WHO'S MR. HOOD?
THE MAN WHO BUILT HOLIDAY HOUSE.
WILL I MEET HIM, TOO?
MAYBE, BUT HE'S A VERY PRIVATE MAN.
YOU LOOK TIRED, MY SWEET. MAYBE YOU SHOULD LIE DOWN FOR A LITTLE WHILE.

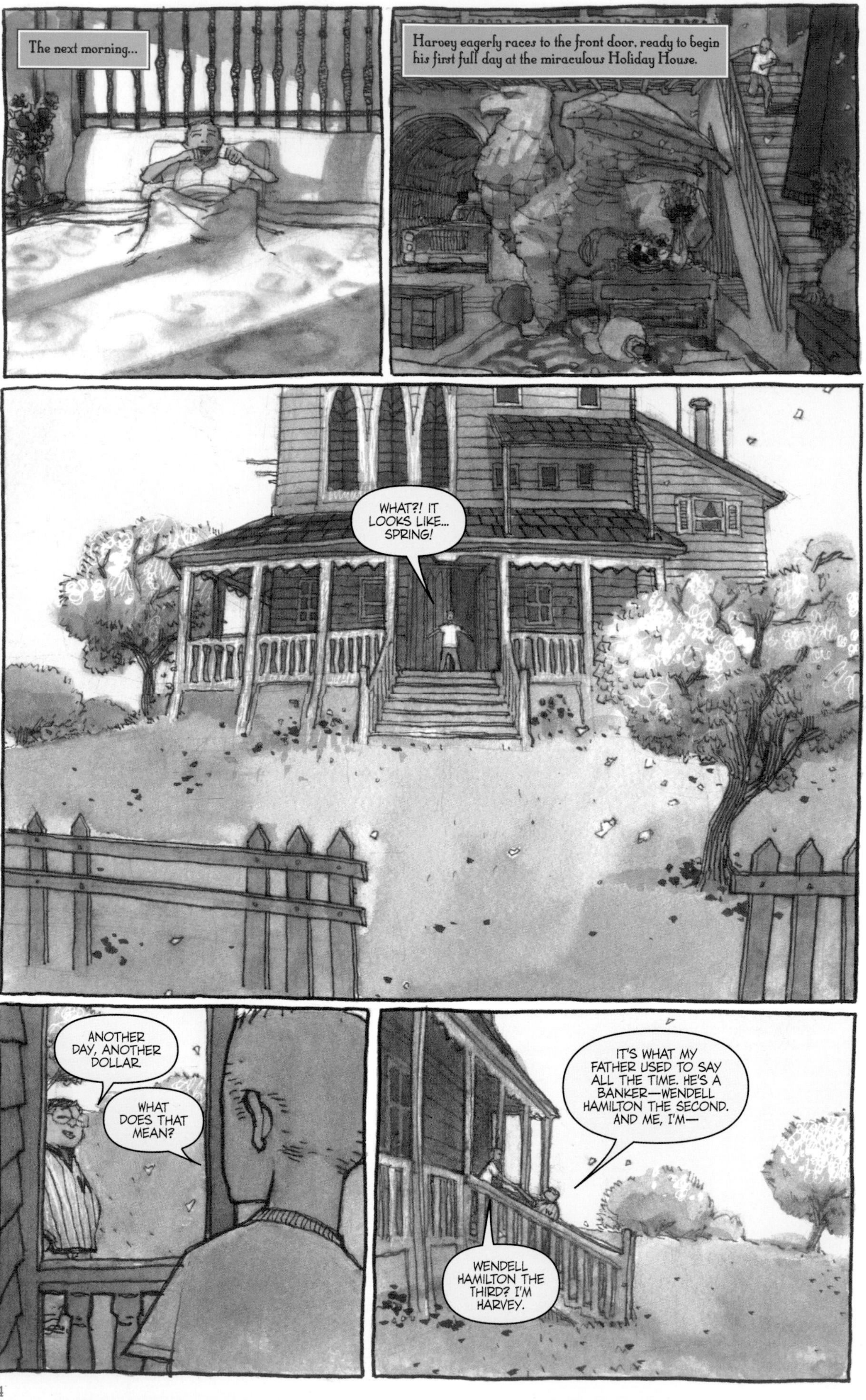
The next morning...
Harvey eagerly races to the front door, ready to begin his first full day at the miraculous Holiday House.
WHAT?! IT LOOKS LIKE... SPRING!
ANOTHER DAY, ANOTHER DOLLAR.
WHAT DOES THAT MEAN?
IT'S WHAT MY FATHER USED TO SAY ALL THE TIME. HE'S A BANKER—WENDELL HAMILTON THE SECOND. AND ME, I'M—
WENDELL HAMILTON THE THIRD? I'M HARVEY.

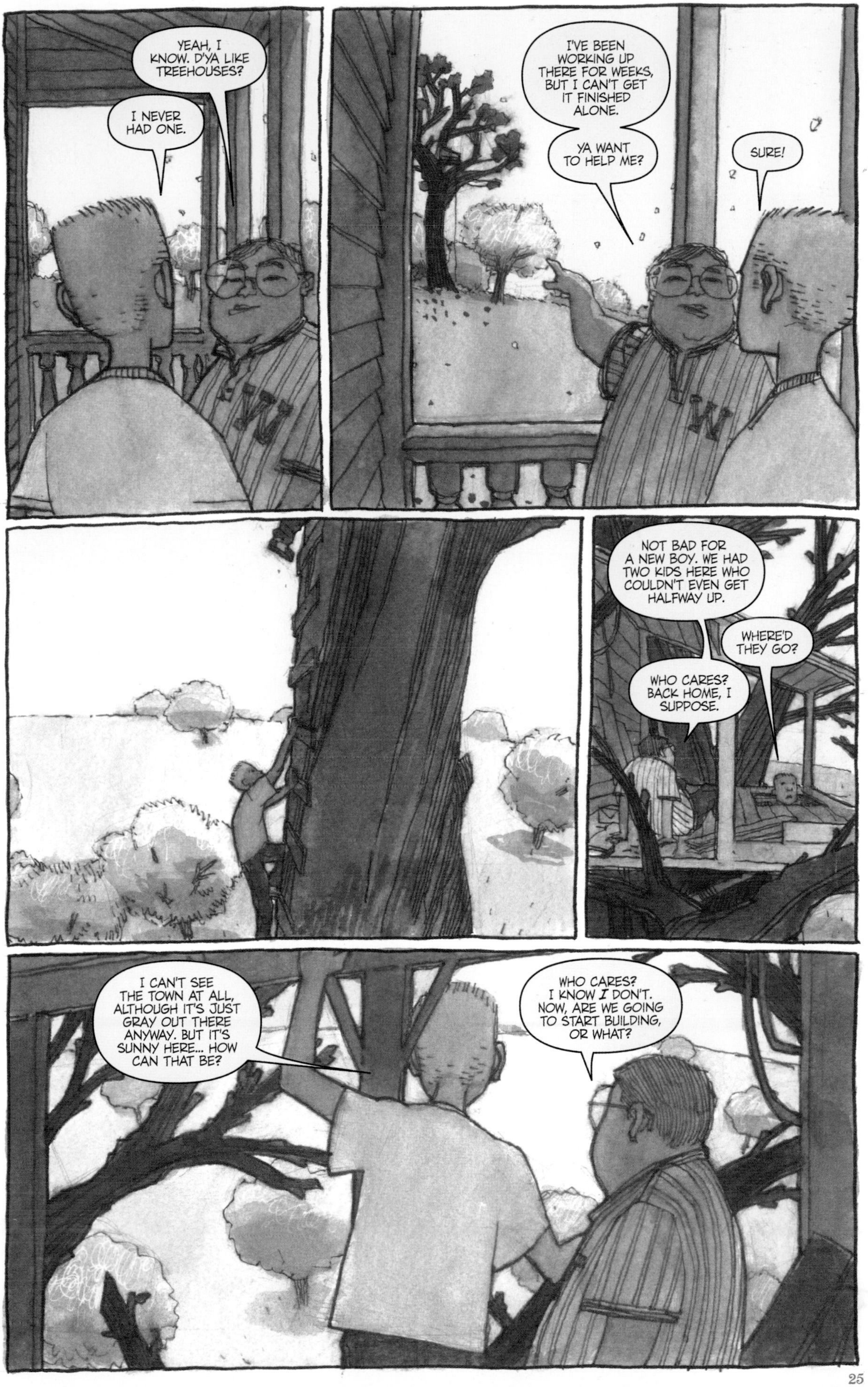
YEAH, I KNOW. D'YA LIKE TREEHOUSES?
I NEVER HAD ONE.
I'VE BEEN WORKING UP THERE FOR WEEKS, BUT I CAN'T GET IT FINISHED ALONE.
YA WANT TO HELP ME?
SURE!
NOT BAD FOR A NEW BOY. WE HAD TWO KIDS HERE WHO COULDN'T EVEN GET HALFWAY UP.
WHERE'D THEY GO?
WHO CARES? BACK HOME, I SUPPOSE.
I CAN'T SEE THE TOWN AT ALL, ALTHOUGH IT'S JUST GRAY OUT THERE ANYWAY. BUT IT'S SUNNY HERE... HOW CAN THAT BE?
WHO CARES? I KNOW *I* DON'T. NOW, ARE WE GOING TO START BUILDING, OR WHAT?

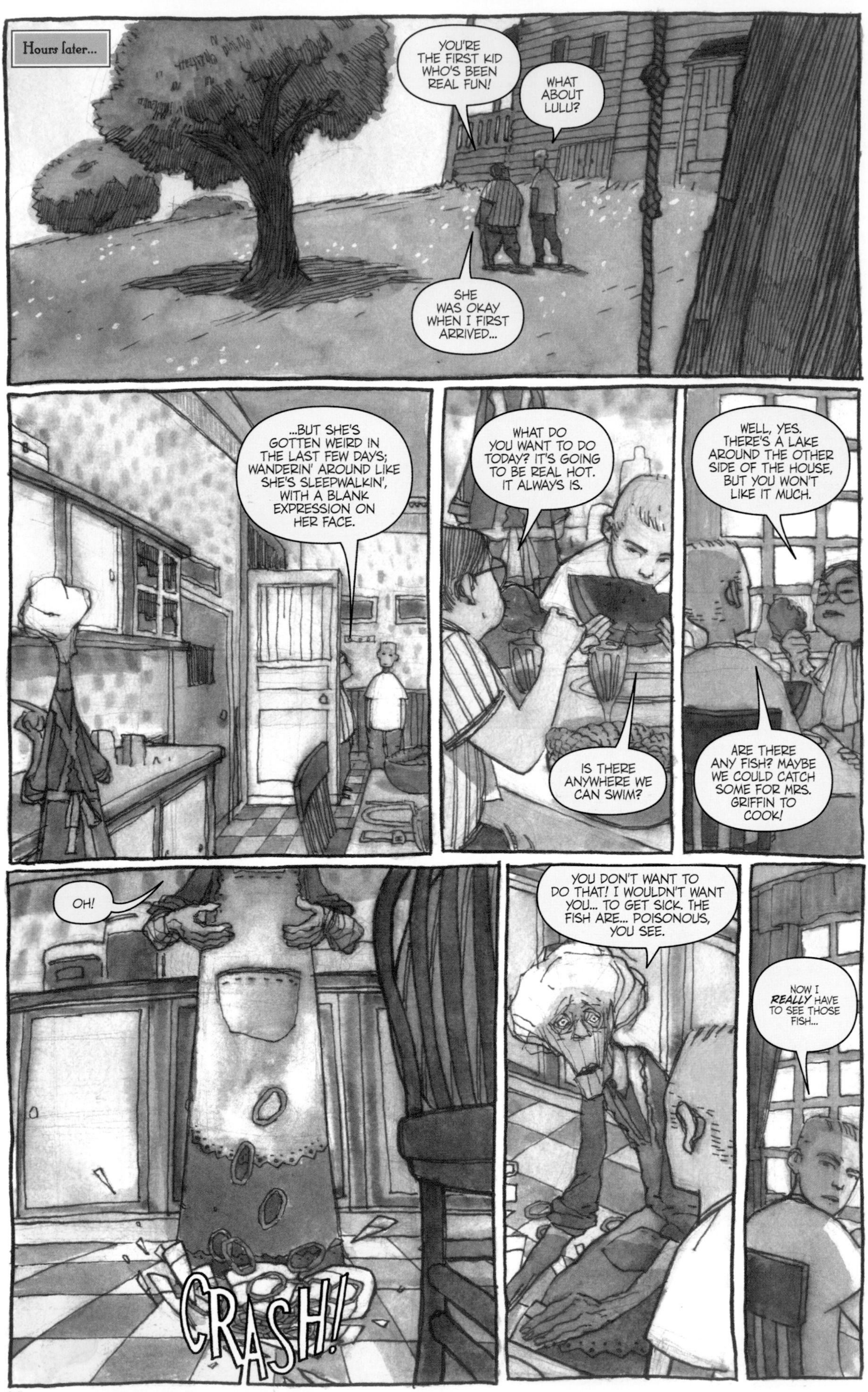
Hours later...
YOU'RE THE FIRST KID WHO'S BEEN REAL FUN!
WHAT ABOUT LULU?
SHE WAS OKAY WHEN I FIRST ARRIVED...
...BUT SHE'S GOTTEN WEIRD IN THE LAST FEW DAYS; WANDERIN' AROUND LIKE SHE'S SLEEPWALKIN', WITH A BLANK EXPRESSION ON HER FACE.
WHAT DO YOU WANT TO DO TODAY? IT'S GOING TO BE REAL HOT. IT ALWAYS IS.
IS THERE ANYWHERE WE CAN SWIM?
WELL, YES. THERE'S A LAKE AROUND THE OTHER SIDE OF THE HOUSE, BUT YOU WON'T LIKE IT MUCH.
ARE THERE ANY FISH? MAYBE WE COULD CATCH SOME FOR MRS. GRIFFIN TO COOK!
OH!
CRASH!
YOU DON'T WANT TO DO THAT! I WOULDN'T WANT YOU... TO GET SICK. THE FISH ARE... POISONOUS, YOU SEE.
NOW I REALLY HAVE TO SEE THOSE FISH...

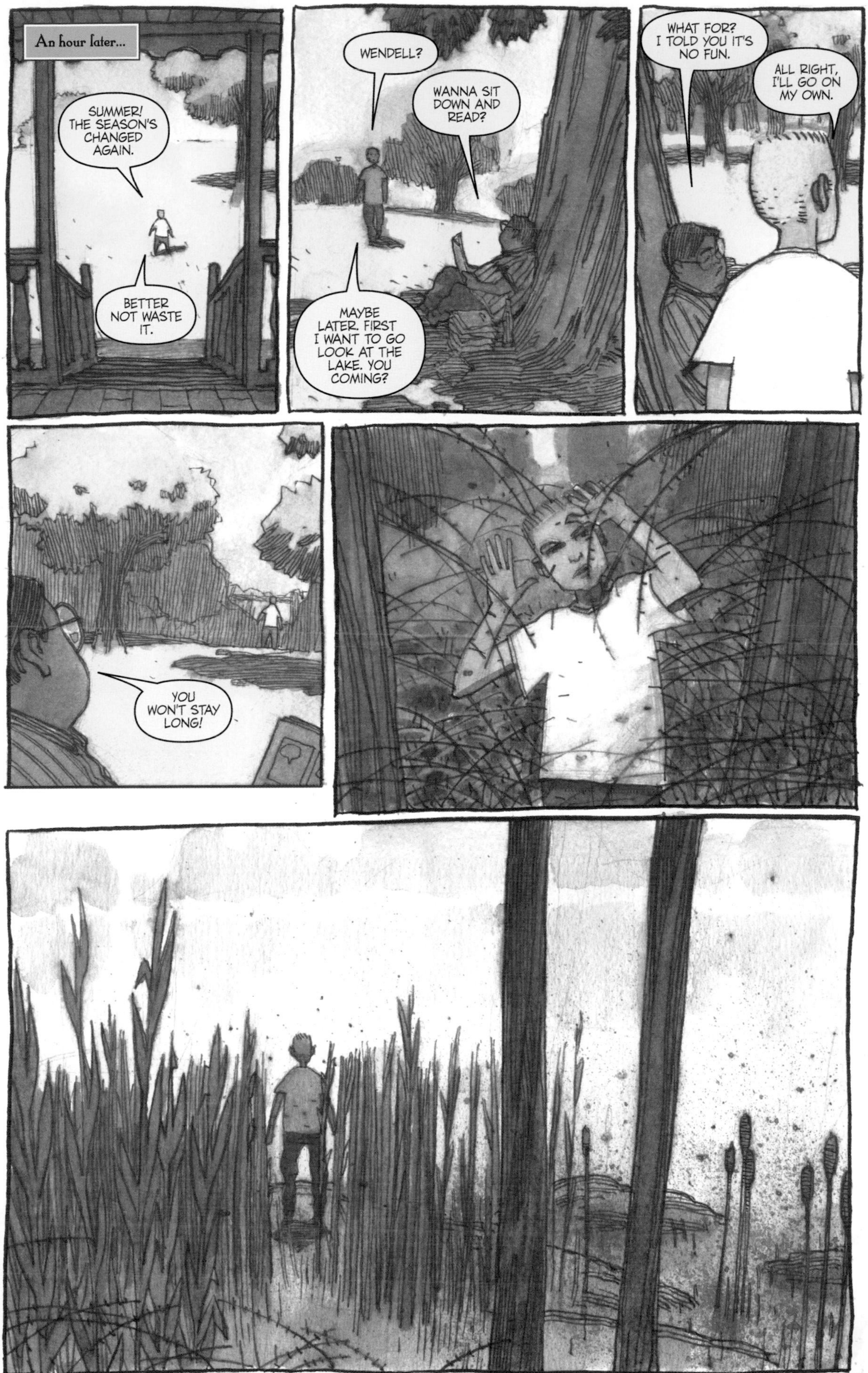
An hour later...
SUMMER! THE SEASON'S CHANGED AGAIN.
BETTER NOT WASTE IT.
WENDELL?
WANNA SIT DOWN AND READ?
MAYBE LATER. FIRST I WANT TO GO LOOK AT THE LAKE. YOU COMING?
WHAT FOR? I TOLD YOU IT'S NO FUN.
ALL RIGHT, I'LL GO ON MY OWN.
YOU WON'T STAY LONG!

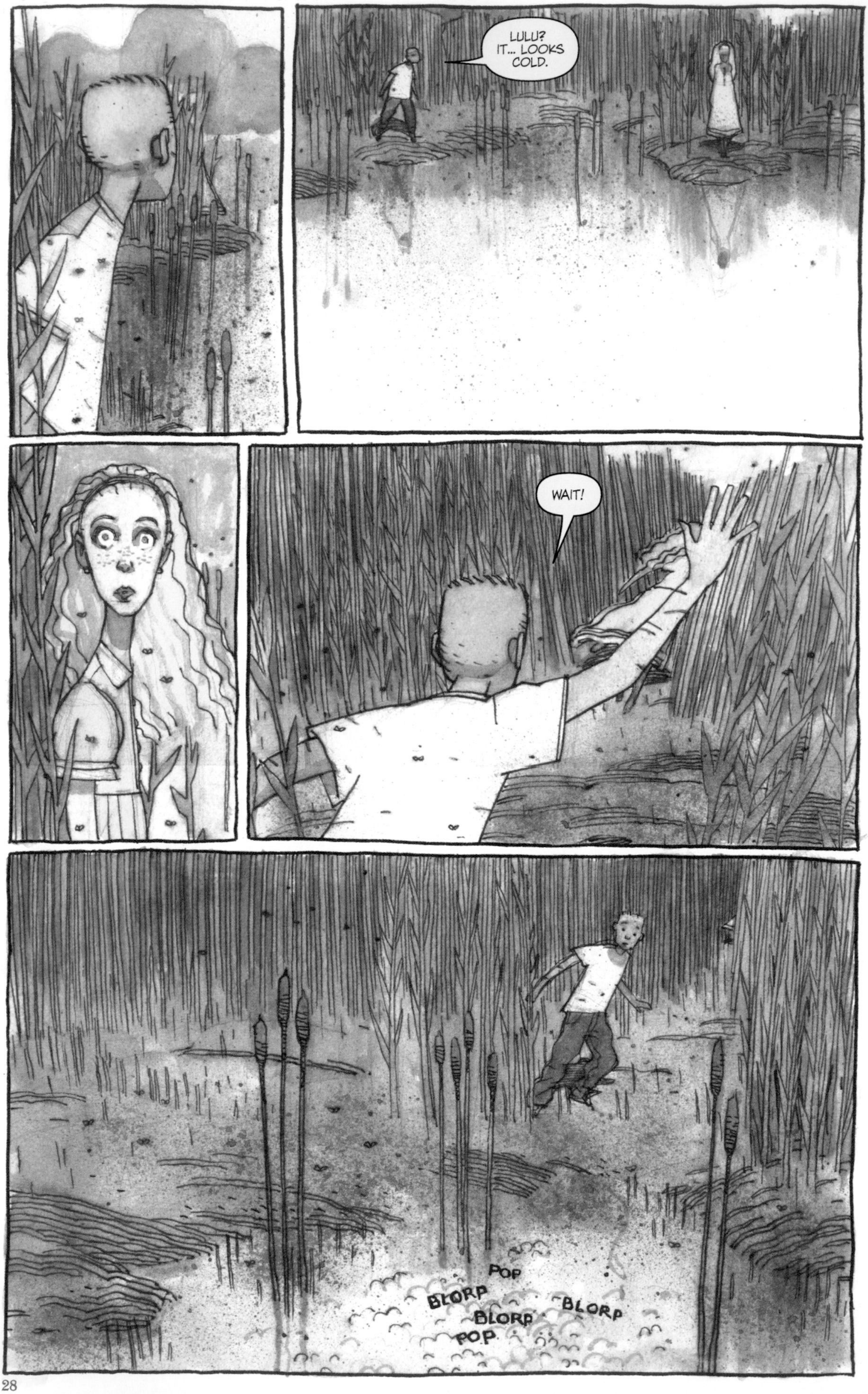
LULU? IT... LOOKS COLD.
WAIT!
POP
BLORP
BLORP
BLORP
POP

OH!

SPLASH

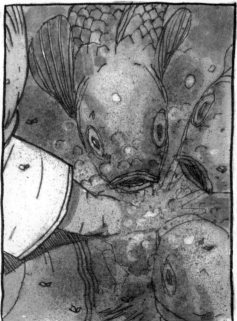

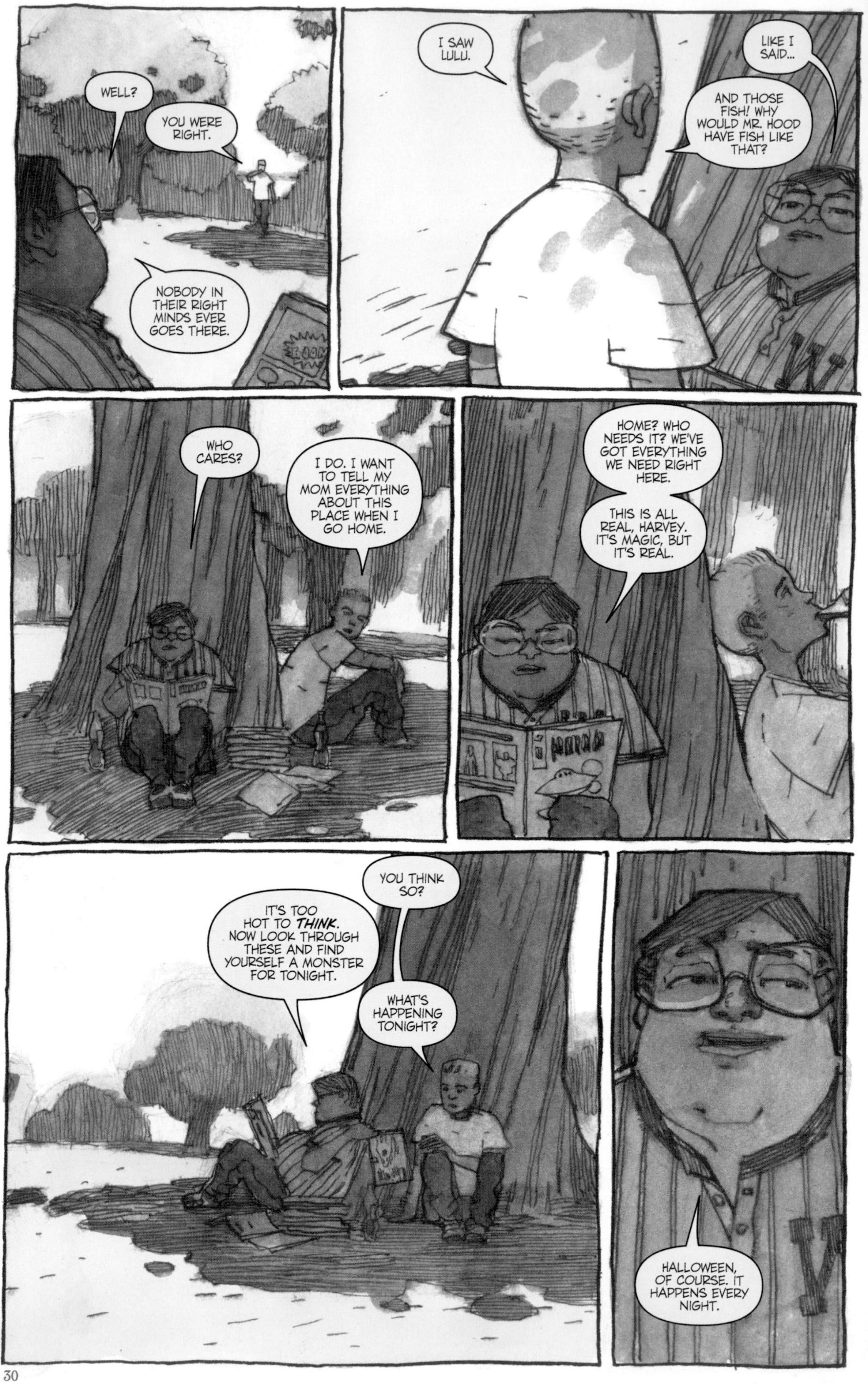
WELL?
YOU WERE RIGHT.
NOBODY IN THEIR RIGHT MINDS EVER GOES THERE.
I SAW LULU.
LIKE I SAID...
AND THOSE FISH! WHY WOULD MR. HOOD HAVE FISH LIKE THAT?
WHO CARES?
I DO. I WANT TO TELL MY MOM EVERYTHING ABOUT THIS PLACE WHEN I GO HOME.
HOME? WHO NEEDS IT? WE'VE GOT EVERYTHING WE NEED RIGHT HERE.
THIS IS ALL REAL, HARVEY. IT'S MAGIC, BUT IT'S REAL.
YOU THINK SO?
IT'S TOO HOT TO ***THINK***. NOW LOOK THROUGH THESE AND FIND YOURSELF A MONSTER FOR TONIGHT.
WHAT'S HAPPENING TONIGHT?
HALLOWEEN, OF COURSE. IT HAPPENS EVERY NIGHT.

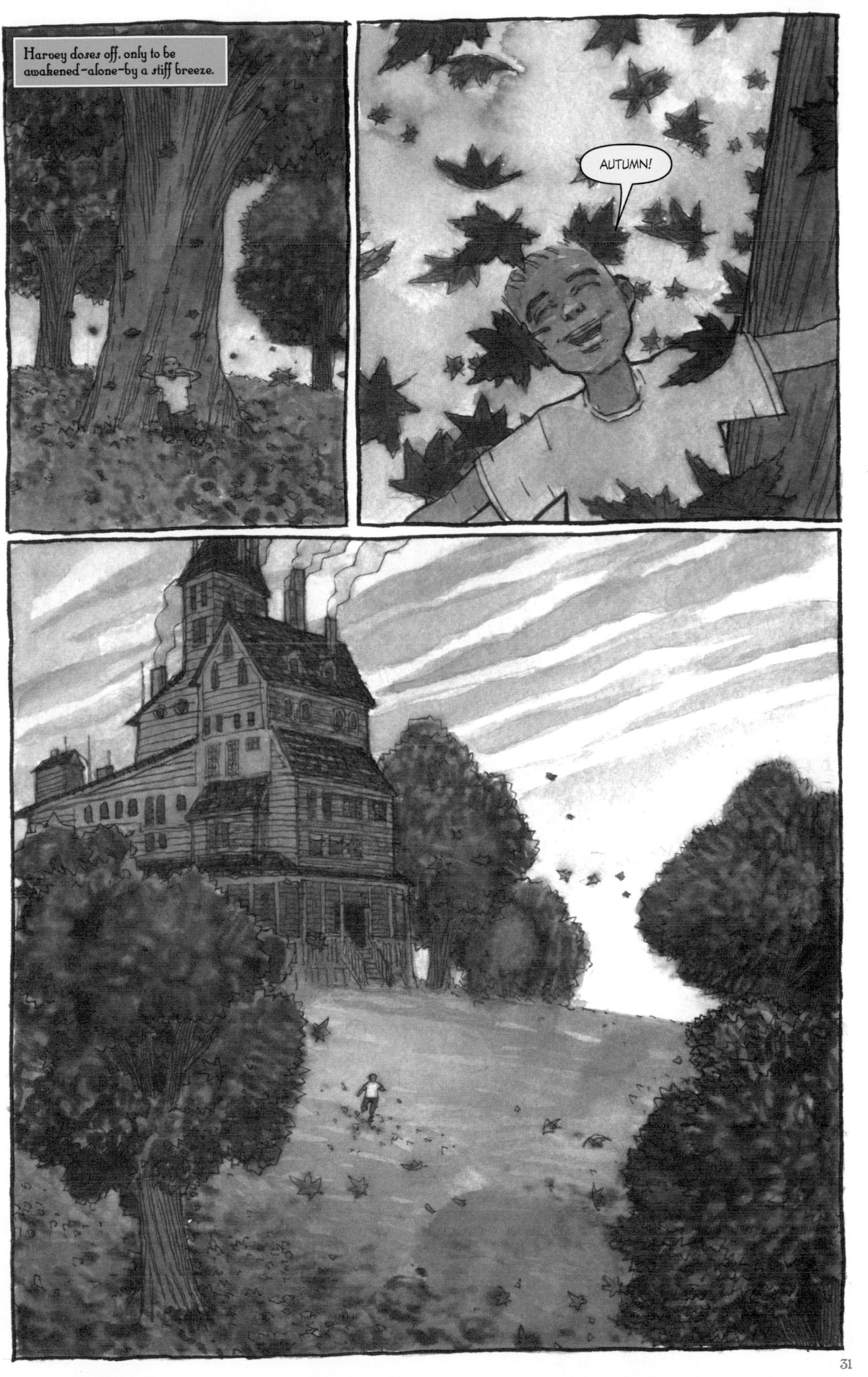

Harvey doses off, only to be awakened–alone–by a stiff breeze.
AUTUMN!

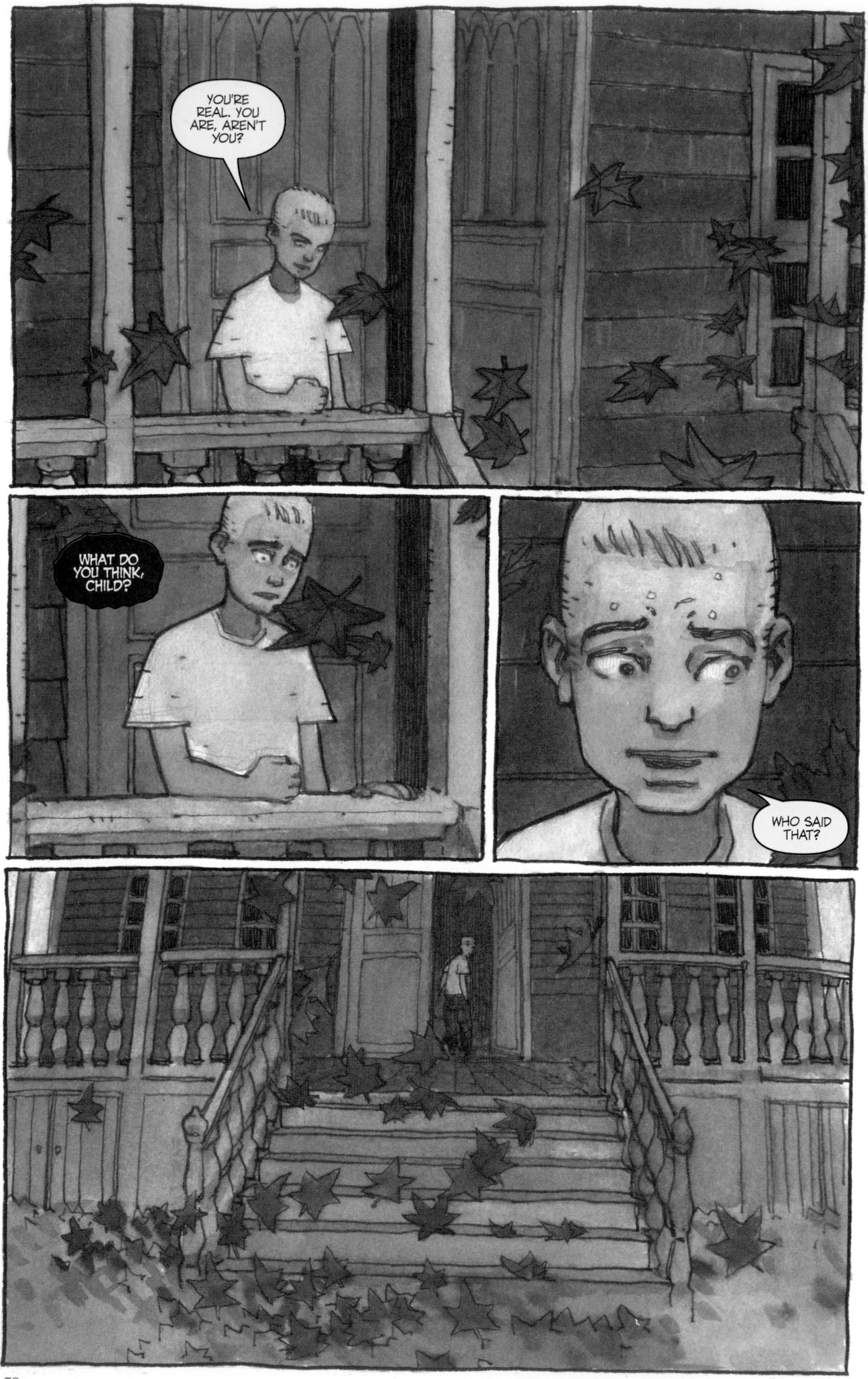
YOU'RE REAL. YOU ARE, AREN'T YOU?
WHAT DO YOU THINK, CHILD?
WHO SAID THAT?

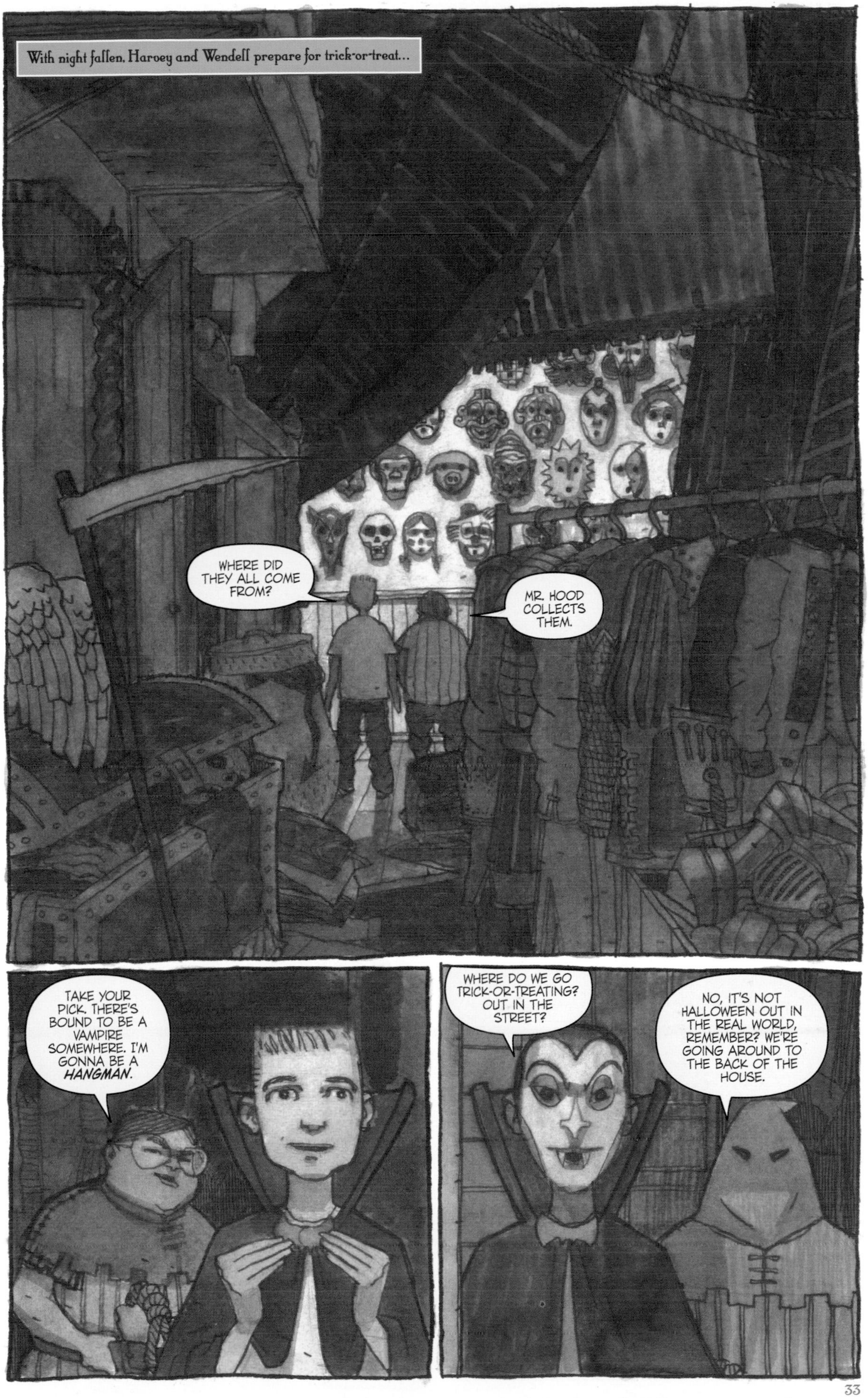
With night fallen, Harvey and Wendell prepare for trick-or-treat...
WHERE DID THEY ALL COME FROM?
MR. HOOD COLLECTS THEM.
TAKE YOUR PICK. THERE'S BOUND TO BE A VAMPIRE SOMEWHERE. I'M GONNA BE A *HANGMAN*.
WHERE DO WE GO TRICK-OR-TREATING? OUT IN THE STREET?
NO, IT'S NOT HALLOWEEN OUT IN THE REAL WORLD, REMEMBER? WE'RE GOING AROUND TO THE BACK OF THE HOUSE.

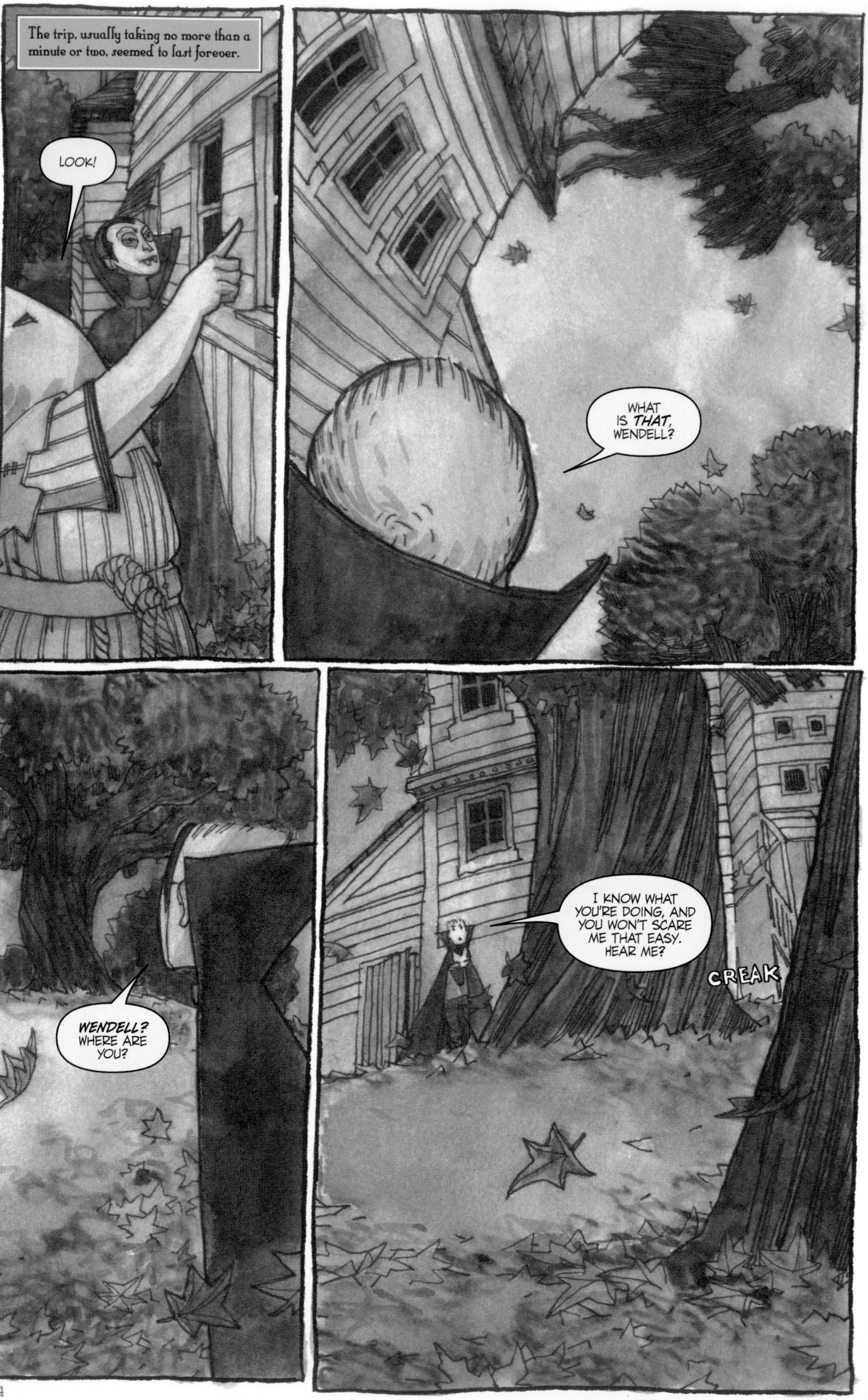

The trip, usually taking no more than a minute or two, seemed to last forever.
LOOK!
WHAT IS *THAT*, WENDELL?
WENDELL? WHERE ARE YOU?
I KNOW WHAT YOU'RE DOING, AND YOU WON'T SCARE ME THAT EASY. HEAR ME?
CREAK

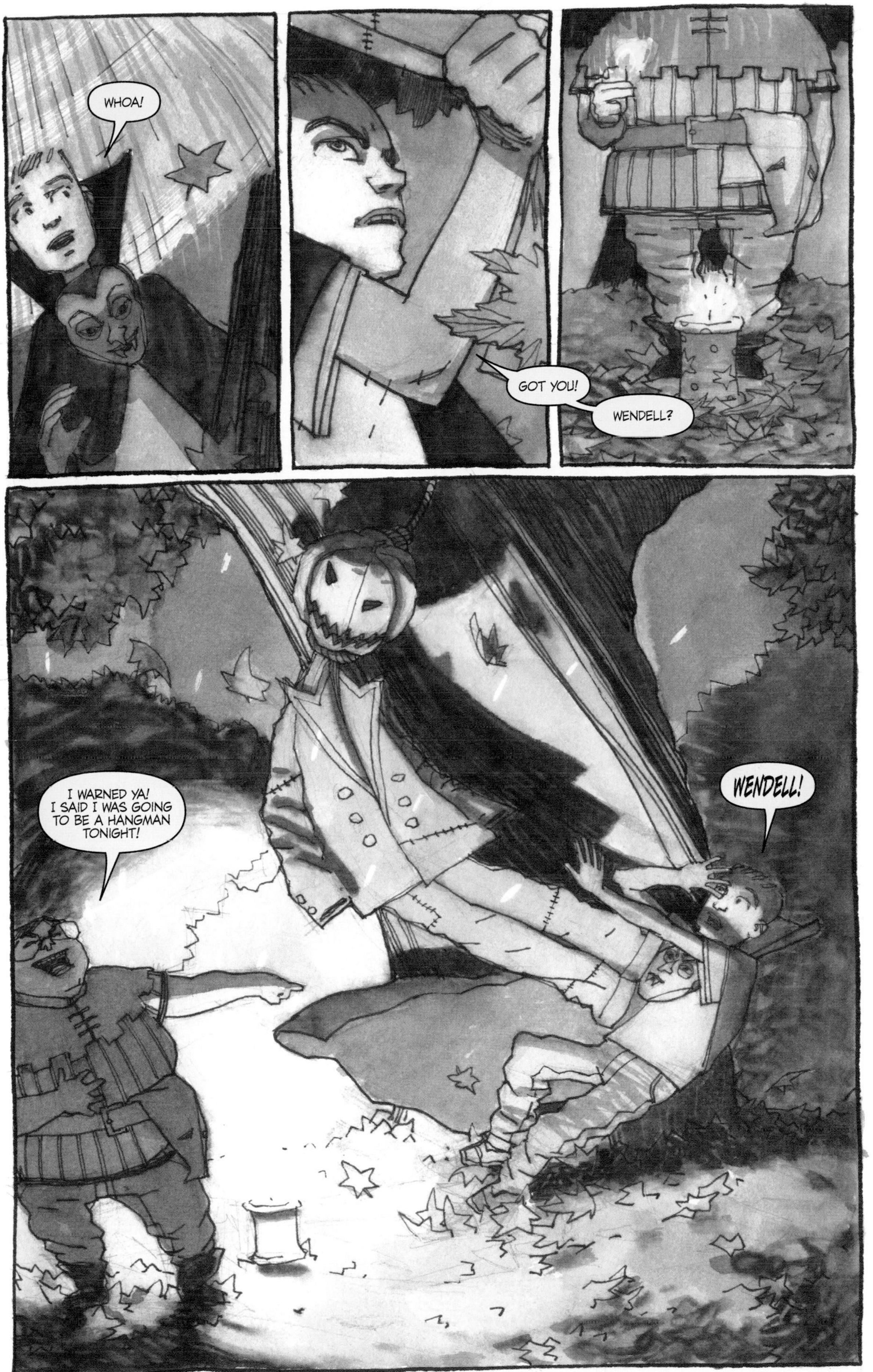
WHOA!
GOT YOU!
WENDELL?
I WARNED YA! I SAID I WAS GOING TO BE A HANGMAN TONIGHT!
WENDELL!

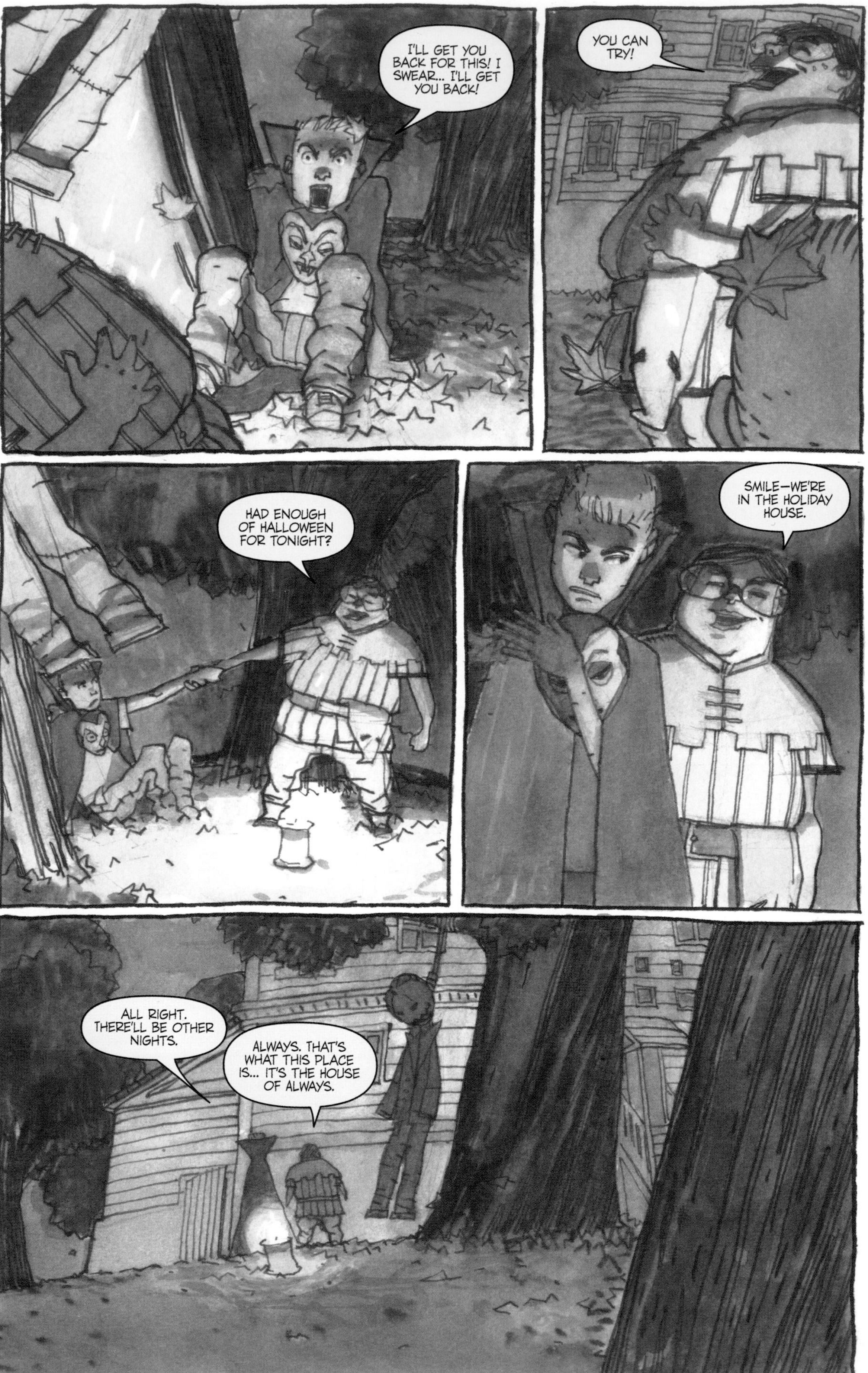
I'LL GET YOU BACK FOR THIS! I SWEAR... I'LL GET YOU BACK!
YOU CAN TRY!
HAD ENOUGH OF HALLOWEEN FOR TONIGHT?
SMILE—WE'RE IN THE HOLIDAY HOUSE.
ALL RIGHT. THERE'LL BE OTHER NIGHTS.
ALWAYS. THAT'S WHAT THIS PLACE IS... IT'S THE HOUSE OF ALWAYS.

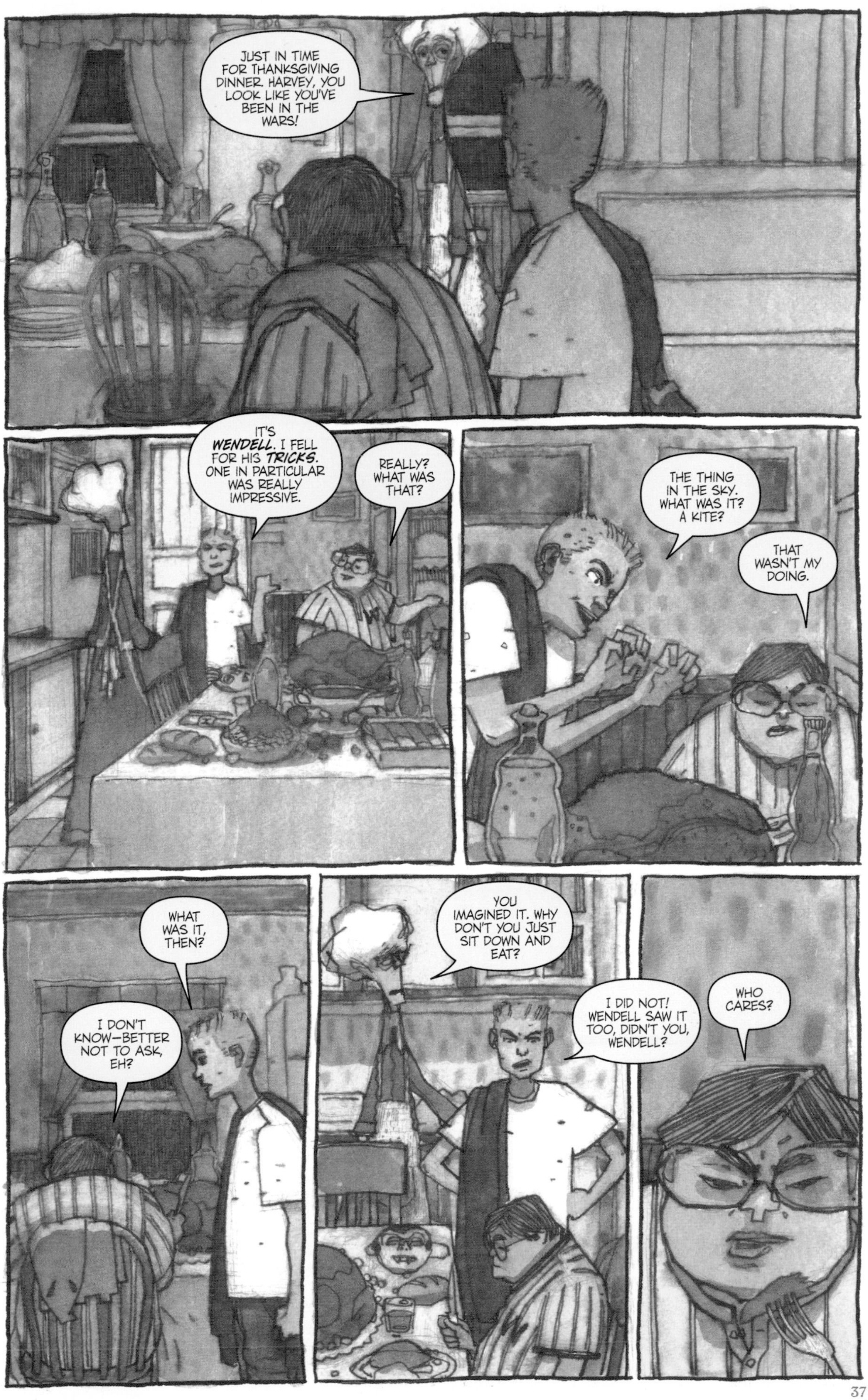
JUST IN TIME FOR THANKSGIVING DINNER. HARVEY, YOU LOOK LIKE YOU'VE BEEN IN THE WARS!
IT'S WENDELL. I FELL FOR HIS TRICKS. ONE IN PARTICULAR WAS REALLY IMPRESSIVE.
REALLY? WHAT WAS THAT?
THE THING IN THE SKY. WHAT WAS IT? A KITE?
THAT WASN'T MY DOING.
WHAT WAS IT, THEN?
I DON'T KNOW—BETTER NOT TO ASK, EH?
YOU IMAGINED IT. WHY DON'T YOU JUST SIT DOWN AND EAT?
I DID NOT! WENDELL SAW IT TOO, DIDN'T YOU, WENDELL?
WHO CARES?

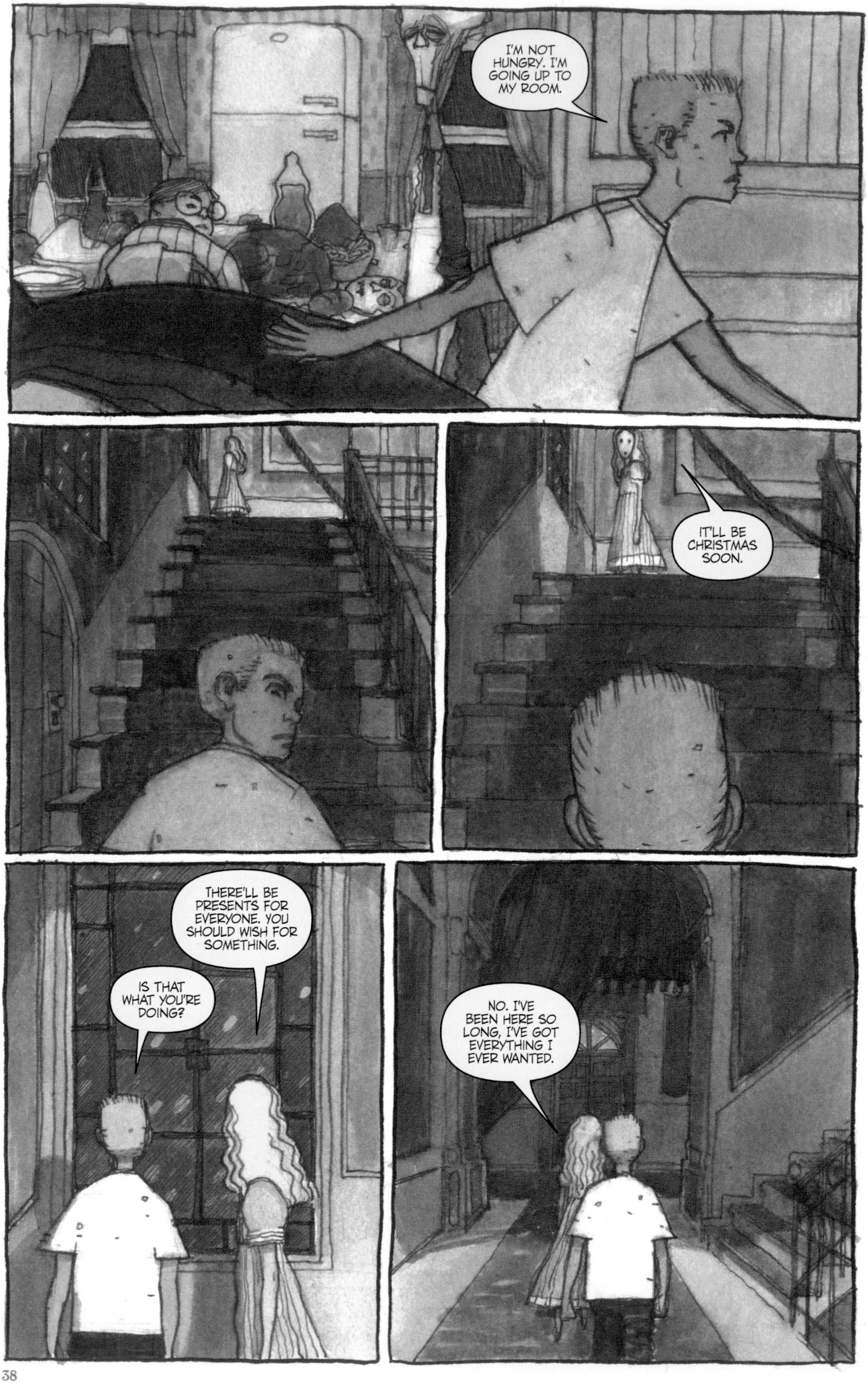
I'M NOT HUNGRY. I'M GOING UP TO MY ROOM.
IT'LL BE CHRISTMAS SOON.
THERE'LL BE PRESENTS FOR EVERYONE. YOU SHOULD WISH FOR SOMETHING.
IS THAT WHAT YOU'RE DOING?
NO. I'VE BEEN HERE SO LONG, I'VE GOT EVERYTHING I EVER WANTED.

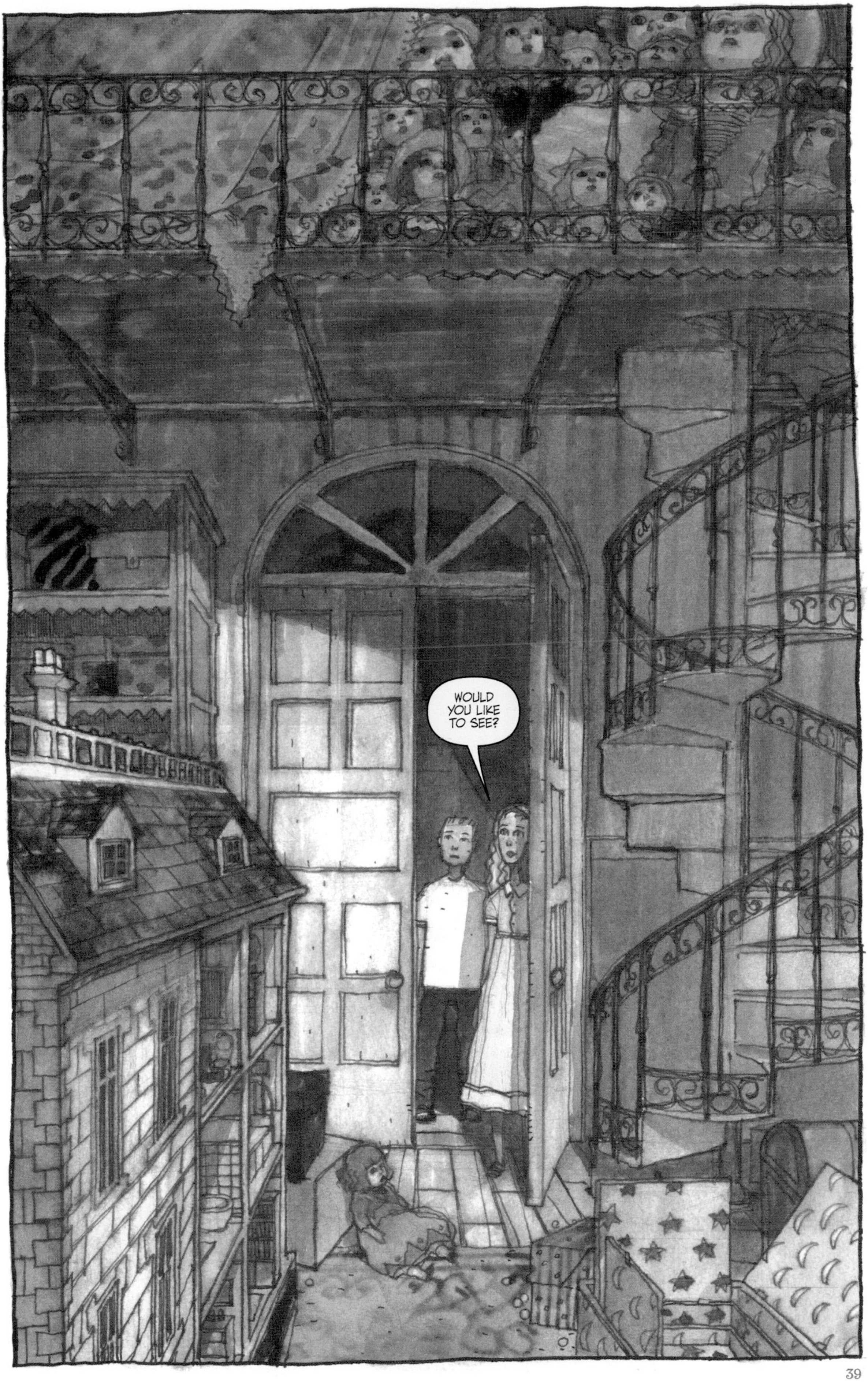
WOULD YOU LIKE TO SEE?

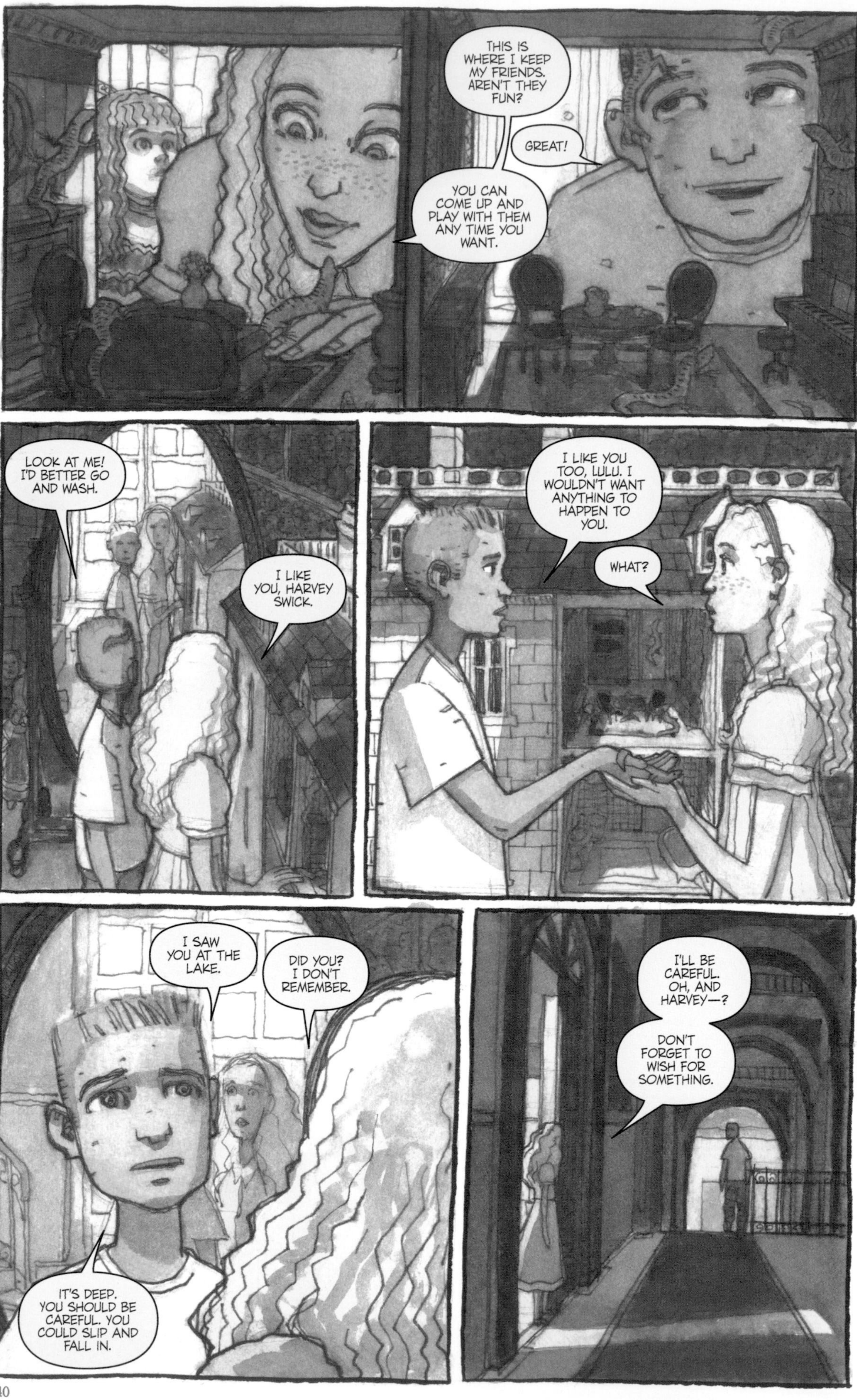
THIS IS WHERE I KEEP MY FRIENDS. AREN'T THEY FUN?
GREAT!
YOU CAN COME UP AND PLAY WITH THEM ANY TIME YOU WANT.
LOOK AT ME! I'D BETTER GO AND WASH.
I LIKE YOU, HARVEY SWICK.
I LIKE YOU TOO, LULU. I WOULDN'T WANT ANYTHING TO HAPPEN TO YOU.
WHAT?
I SAW YOU AT THE LAKE.
DID YOU? I DON'T REMEMBER.
IT'S DEEP. YOU SHOULD BE CAREFUL. YOU COULD SLIP AND FALL IN.
I'LL BE CAREFUL. OH, AND HARVEY—?
DON'T FORGET TO WISH FOR SOMETHING.

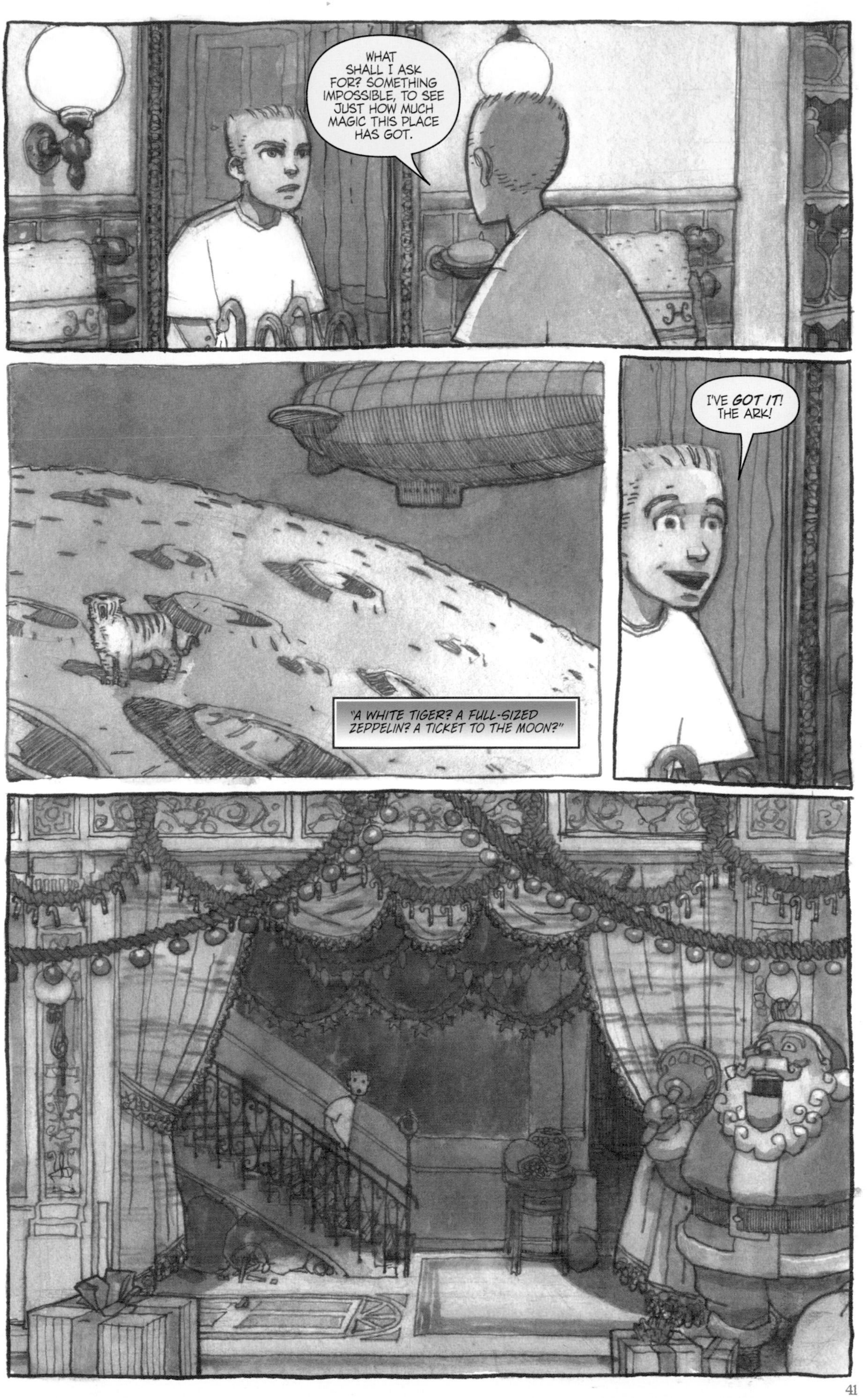
WHAT SHALL I ASK FOR? SOMETHING IMPOSSIBLE, TO SEE JUST HOW MUCH MAGIC THIS PLACE HAS GOT.
"A WHITE TIGER? A FULL-SIZED ZEPPELIN? A TICKET TO THE MOON?"
I'VE GOT IT! THE ARK!

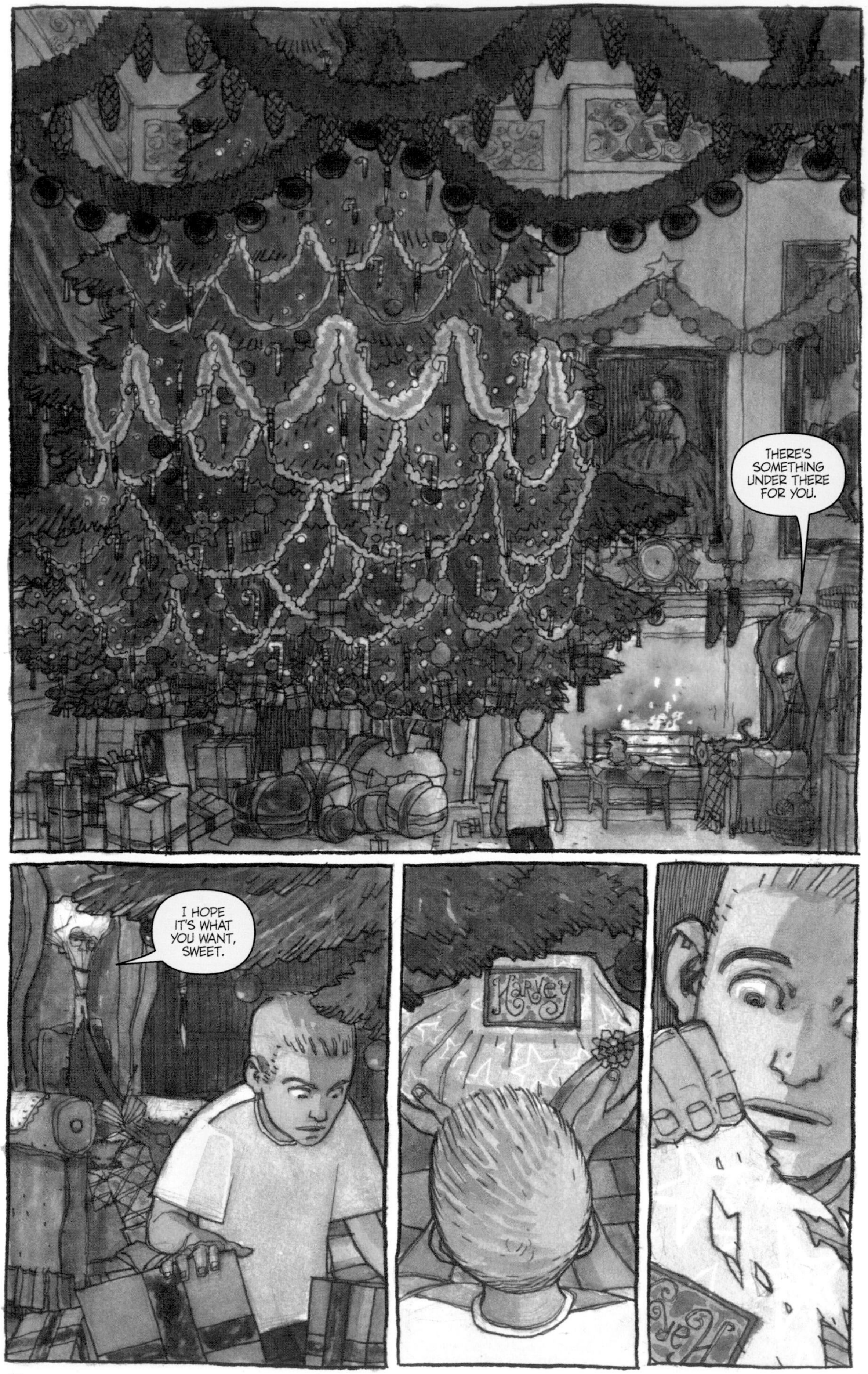
THERE'S SOMETHING UNDER THERE FOR YOU.
I HOPE IT'S WHAT YOU WANT, SWEET.
Harvey

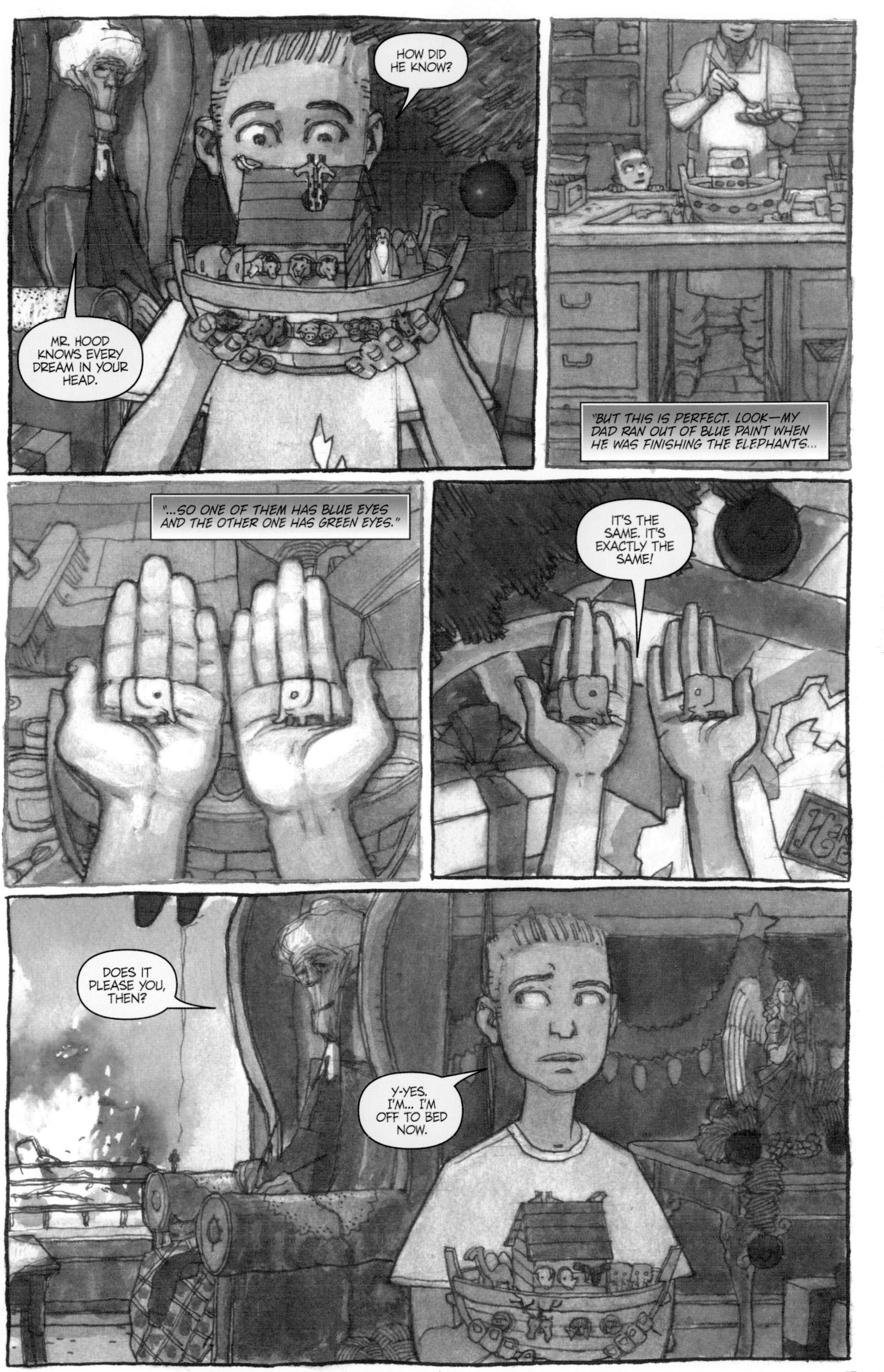
HOW DID HE KNOW?
MR. HOOD KNOWS EVERY DREAM IN YOUR HEAD.
"BUT THIS IS PERFECT. LOOK—MY DAD RAN OUT OF BLUE PAINT WHEN HE WAS FINISHING THE ELEPHANTS...
"...SO ONE OF THEM HAS BLUE EYES AND THE OTHER ONE HAS GREEN EYES."
IT'S THE SAME. IT'S EXACTLY THE SAME!
DOES IT PLEASE YOU, THEN?
Y-YES. I'M... I'M OFF TO BED NOW.

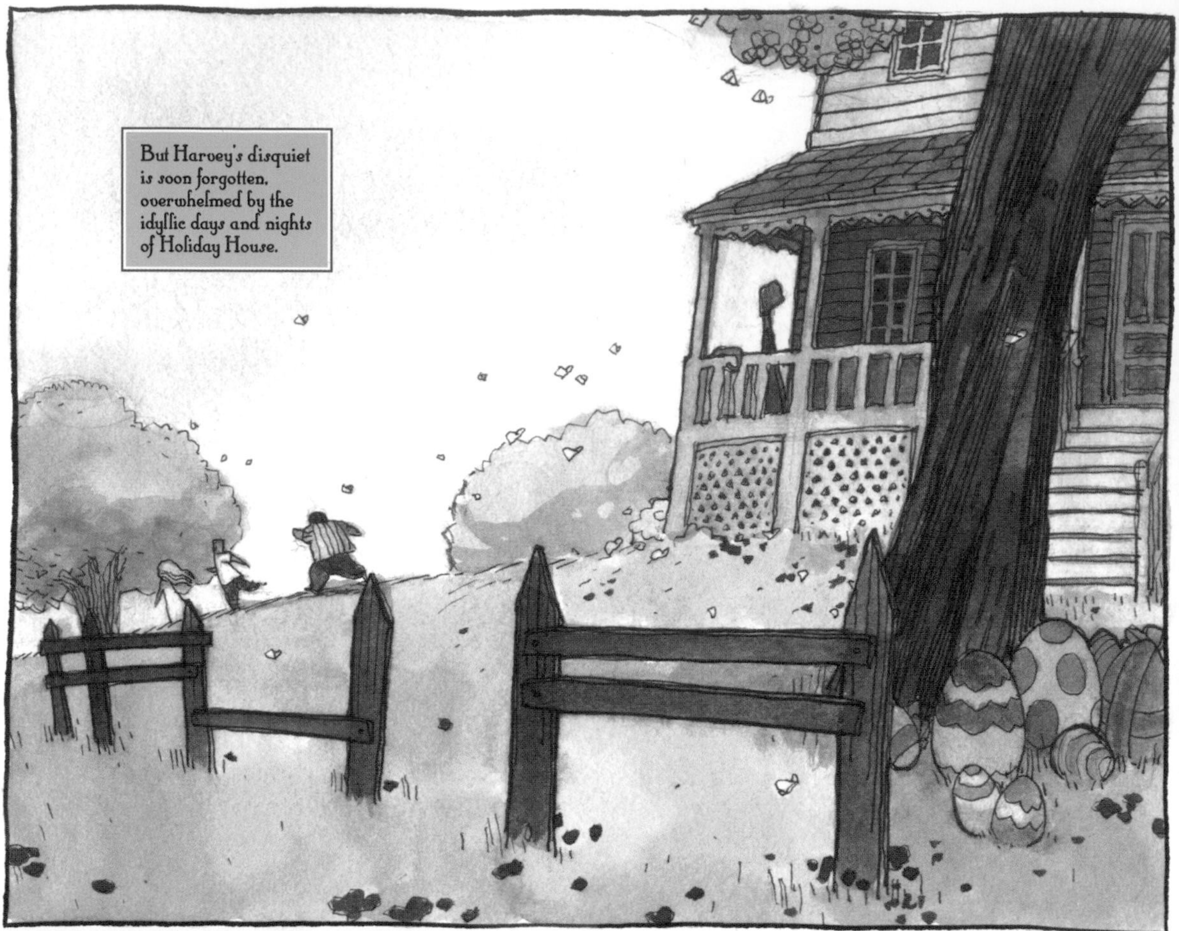
But Harvey's disquiet is soon forgotten, overwhelmed by the idyllic days and nights of Holiday House.

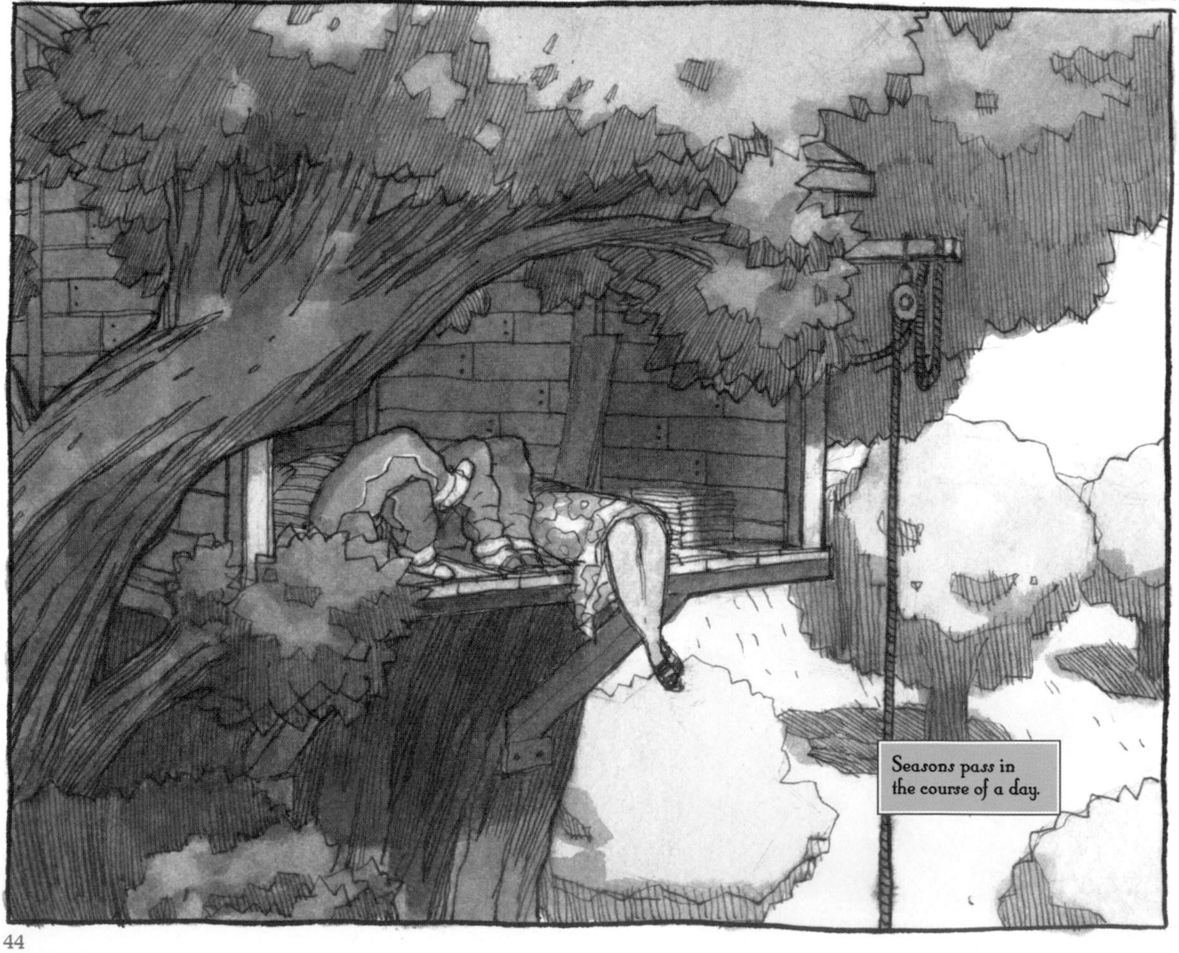
Seasons pass in the course of a day.

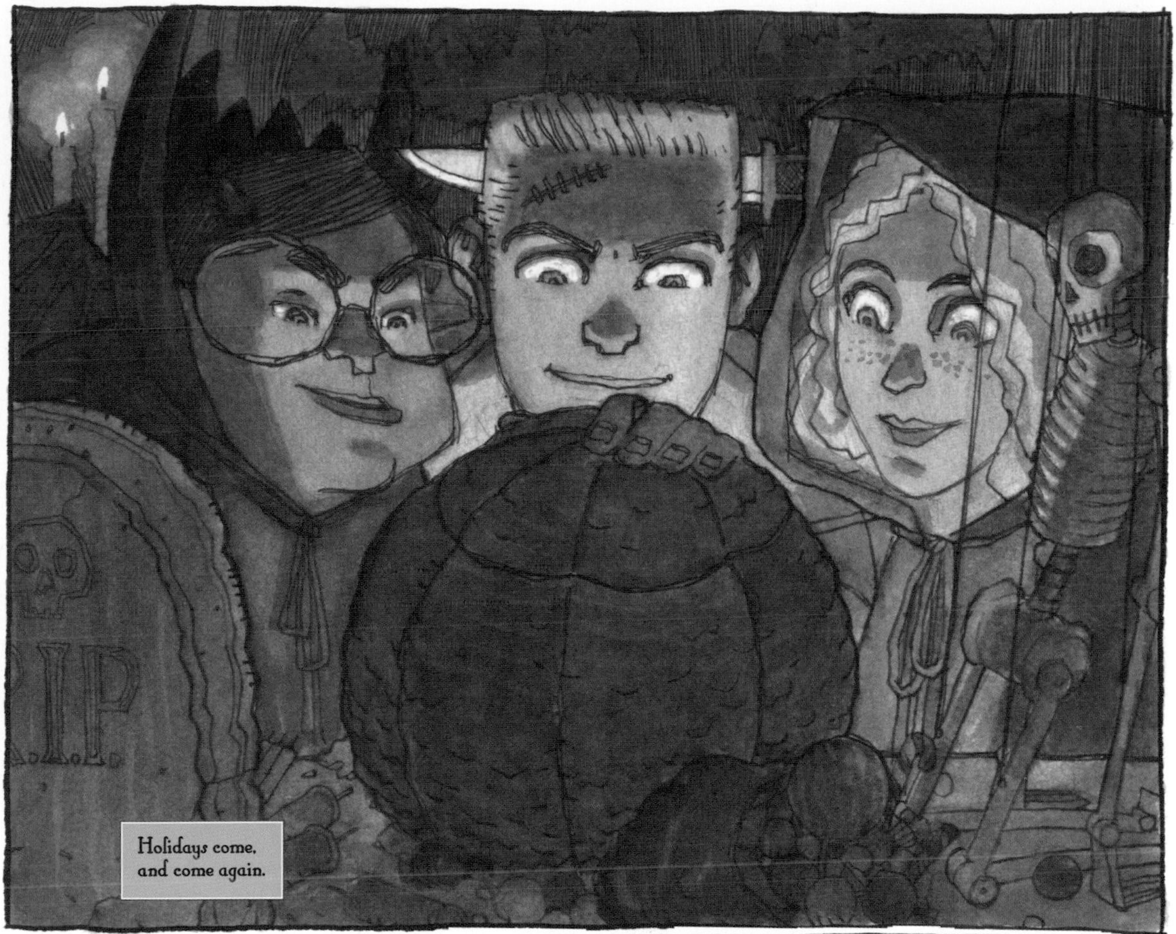
Holidays come, and come again.
R.I.P.

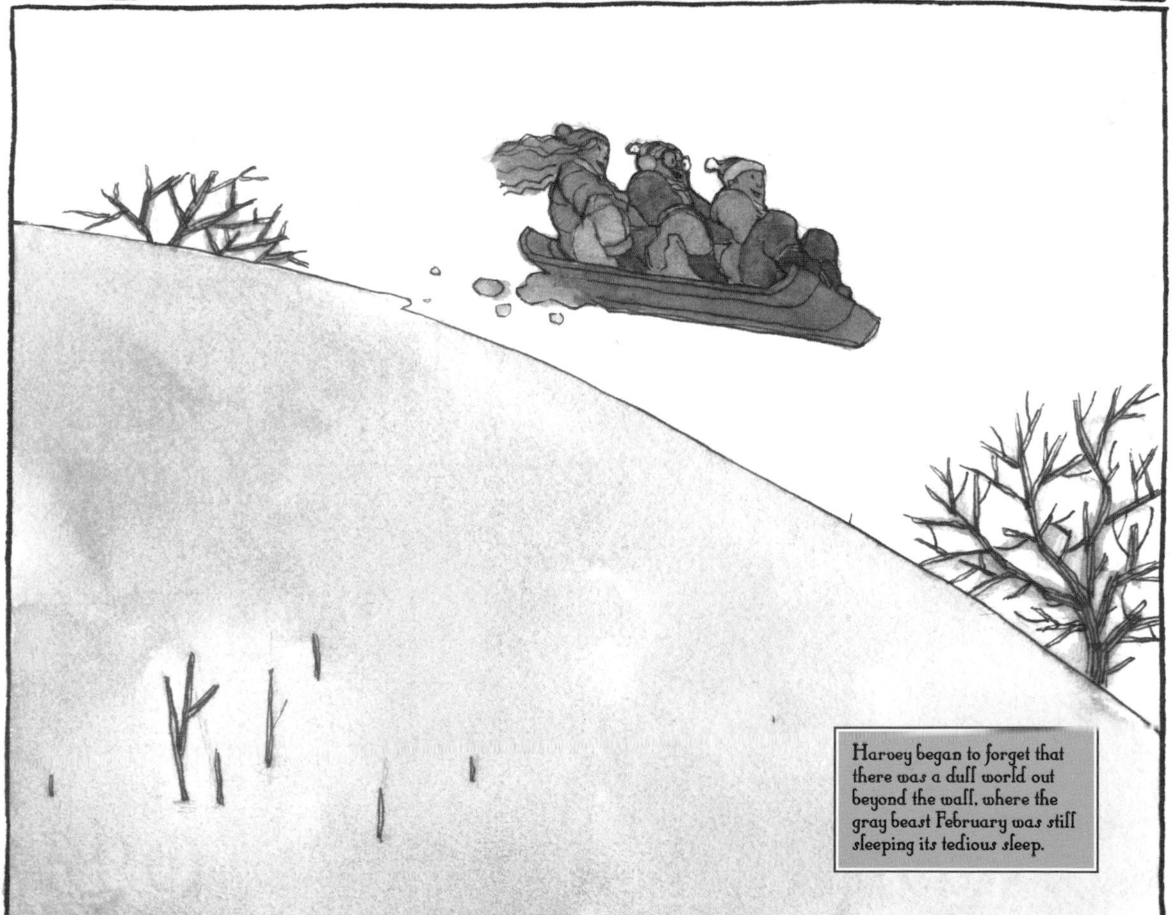
Harvey began to forget that there was a dull world out beyond the wall, where the gray beast February was still sleeping its tedious sleep.

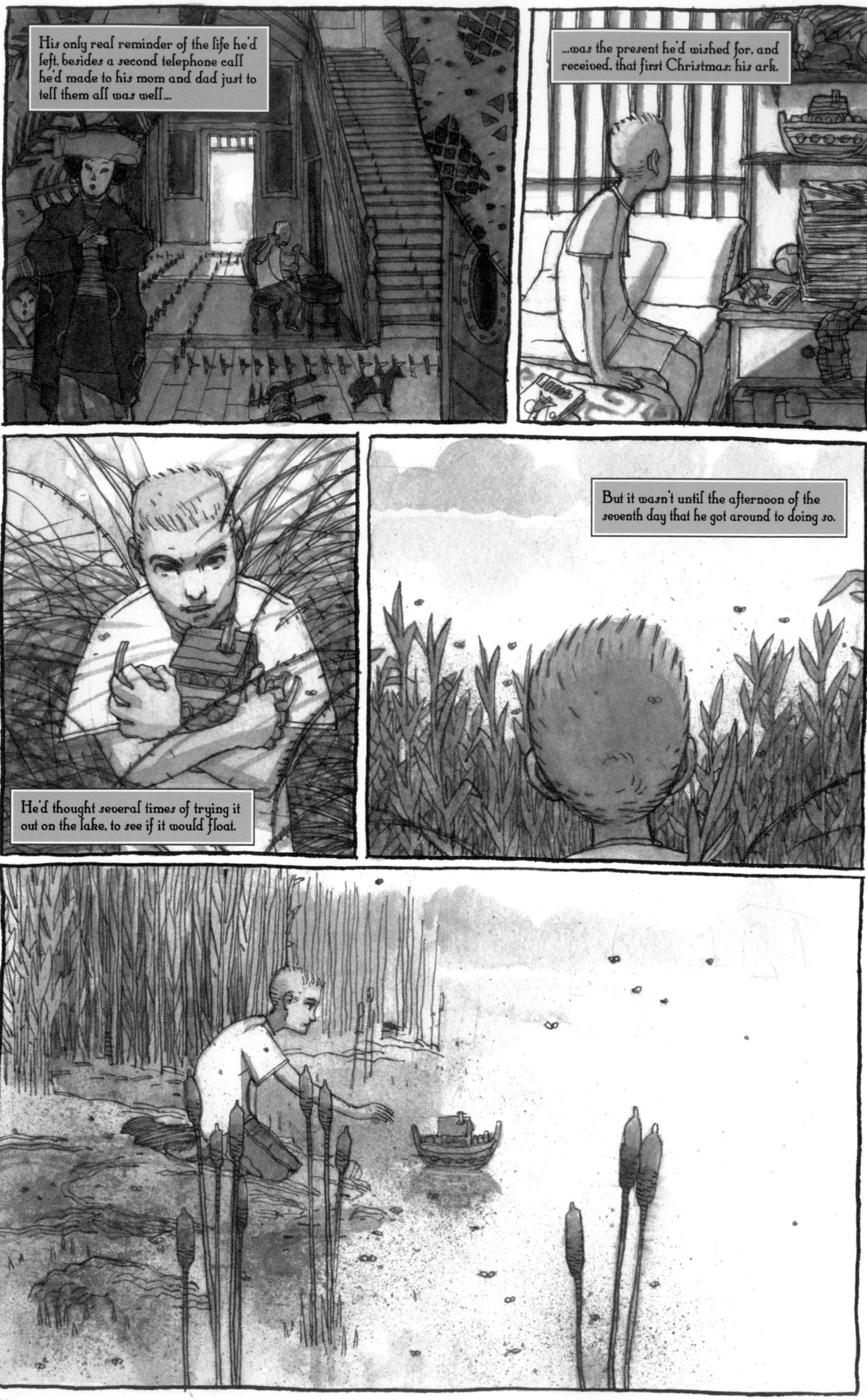
His only real reminder of the life he'd left, besides a second telephone call he'd made to his mom and dad just to tell them all was well...
...was the present he'd wished for, and received, that first Christmas: his ark.
He'd thought several times of trying it out on the lake, to see if it would float.
But it wasn't until the afternoon of the seventh day that he got around to doing so.

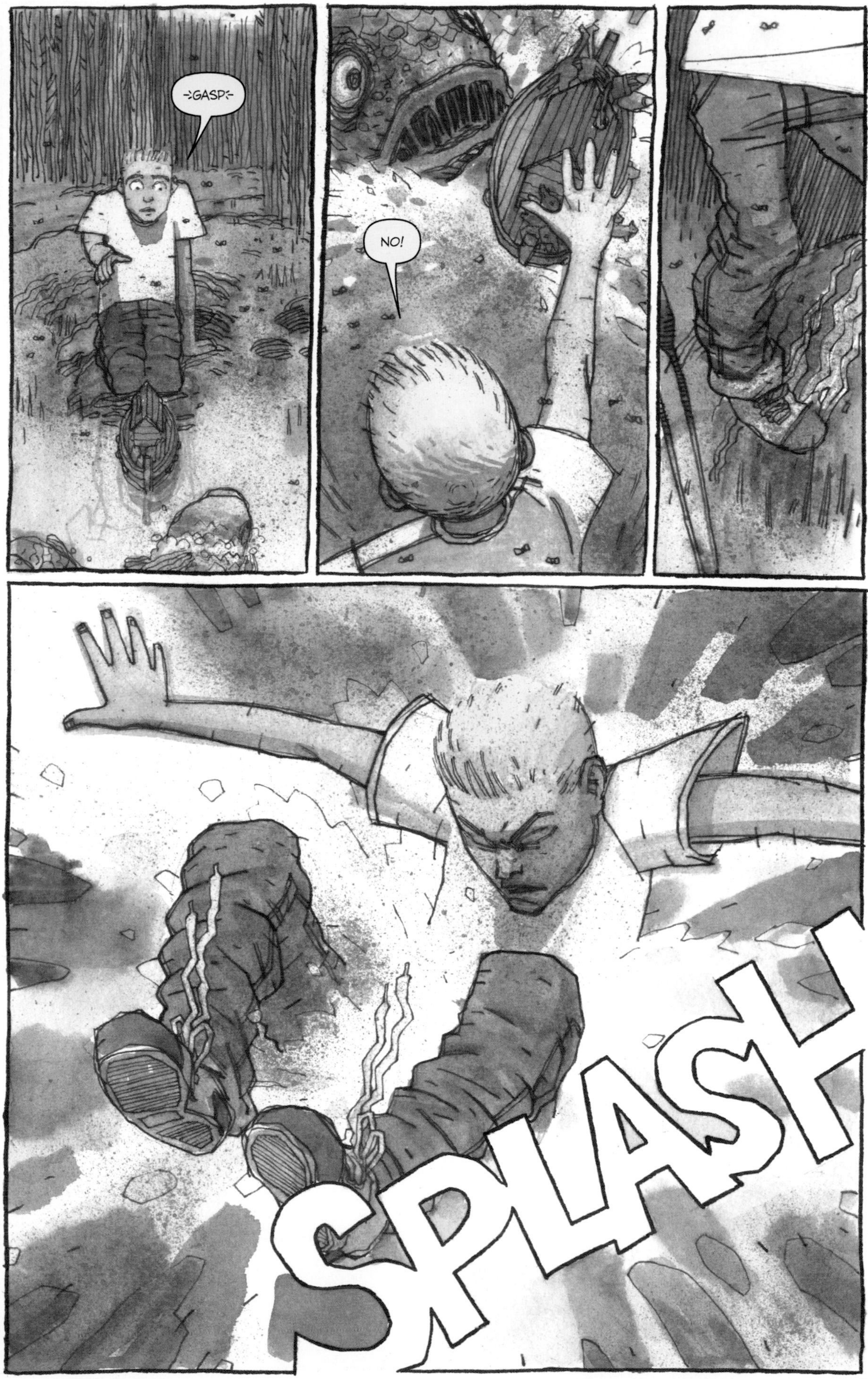
GASP
NO!
SPLASH

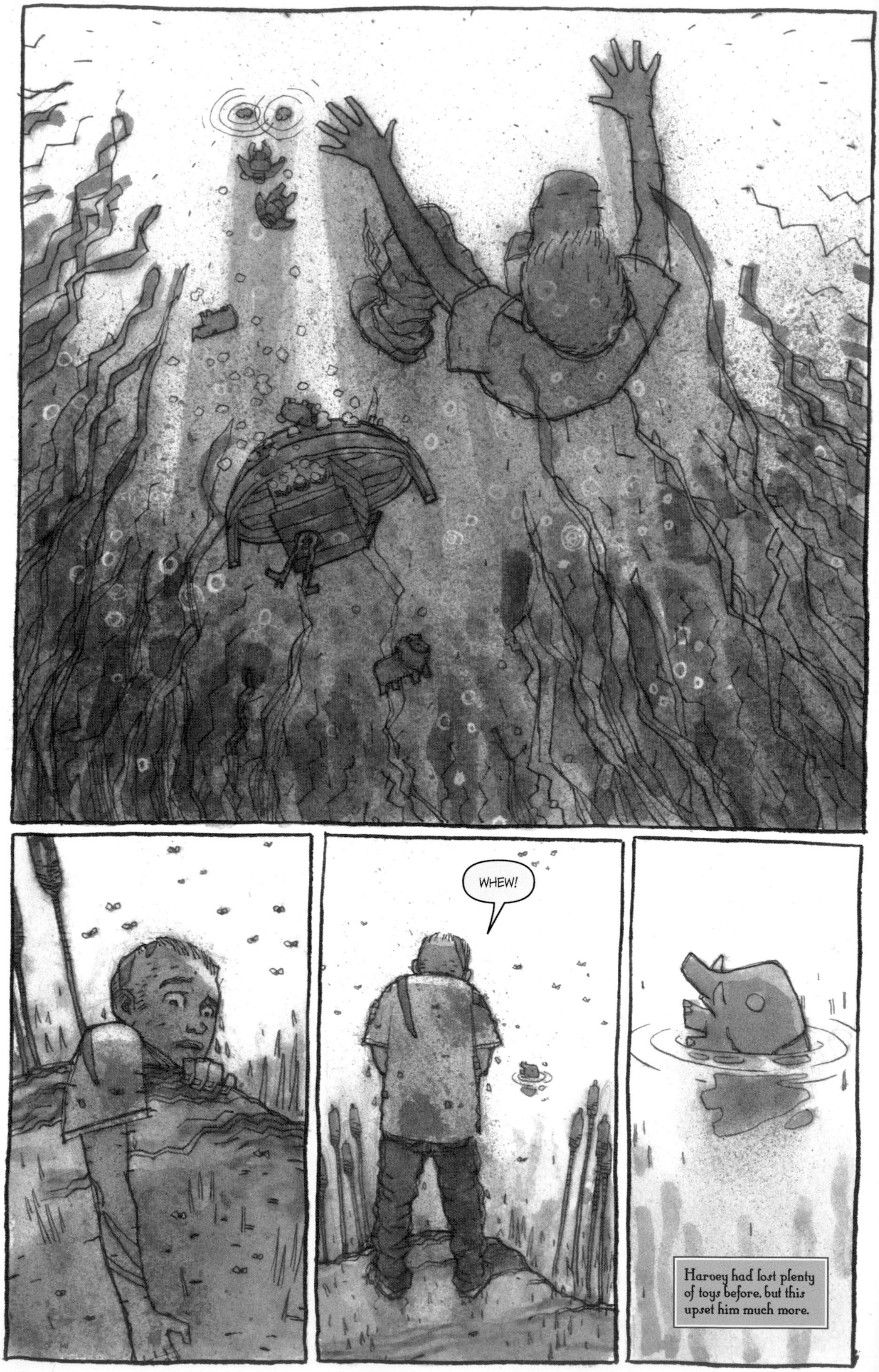
WHEW!
Harvey had lost plenty of toys before, but this upset him much more.

The lake now had something that he'd owned.

His possessions had gone into a nightmare place, full of monstrous things, and he felt as though a little part of himself had gone down with it, down into the dark.

Despite all entertainments that the Holiday House supplied so eagerly, it was a haunted place.

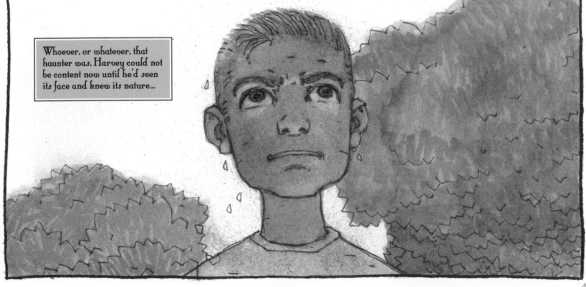

Whoever, or whatever, that haunter was, Harvey could not be content now until he'd seen its face and knew its nature...

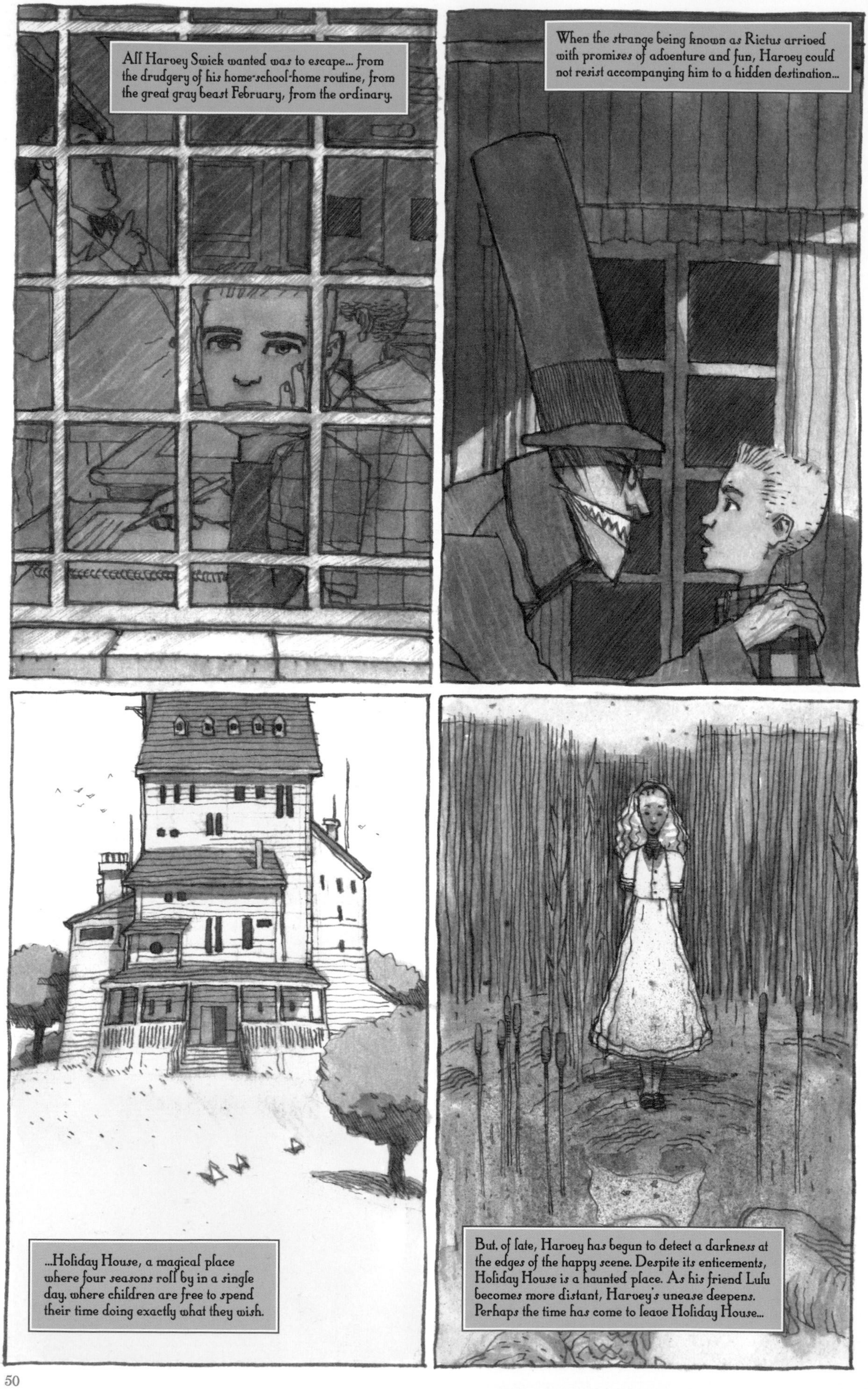
All Harvey Swick wanted was to escape... from the drudgery of his home-school-home routine, from the great gray beast February, from the ordinary.
When the strange being known as Rictus arrived with promises of adventure and fun, Harvey could not resist accompanying him to a hidden destination...
...Holiday House, a magical place where four seasons roll by in a single day, where children are free to spend their time doing exactly what they wish.
But, of late, Harvey has begun to detect a darkness at the edges of the happy scene. Despite its enticements, Holiday House is a haunted place. As his friend Lulu becomes more distant, Harvey's unease deepens. Perhaps the time has come to leave Holiday House...

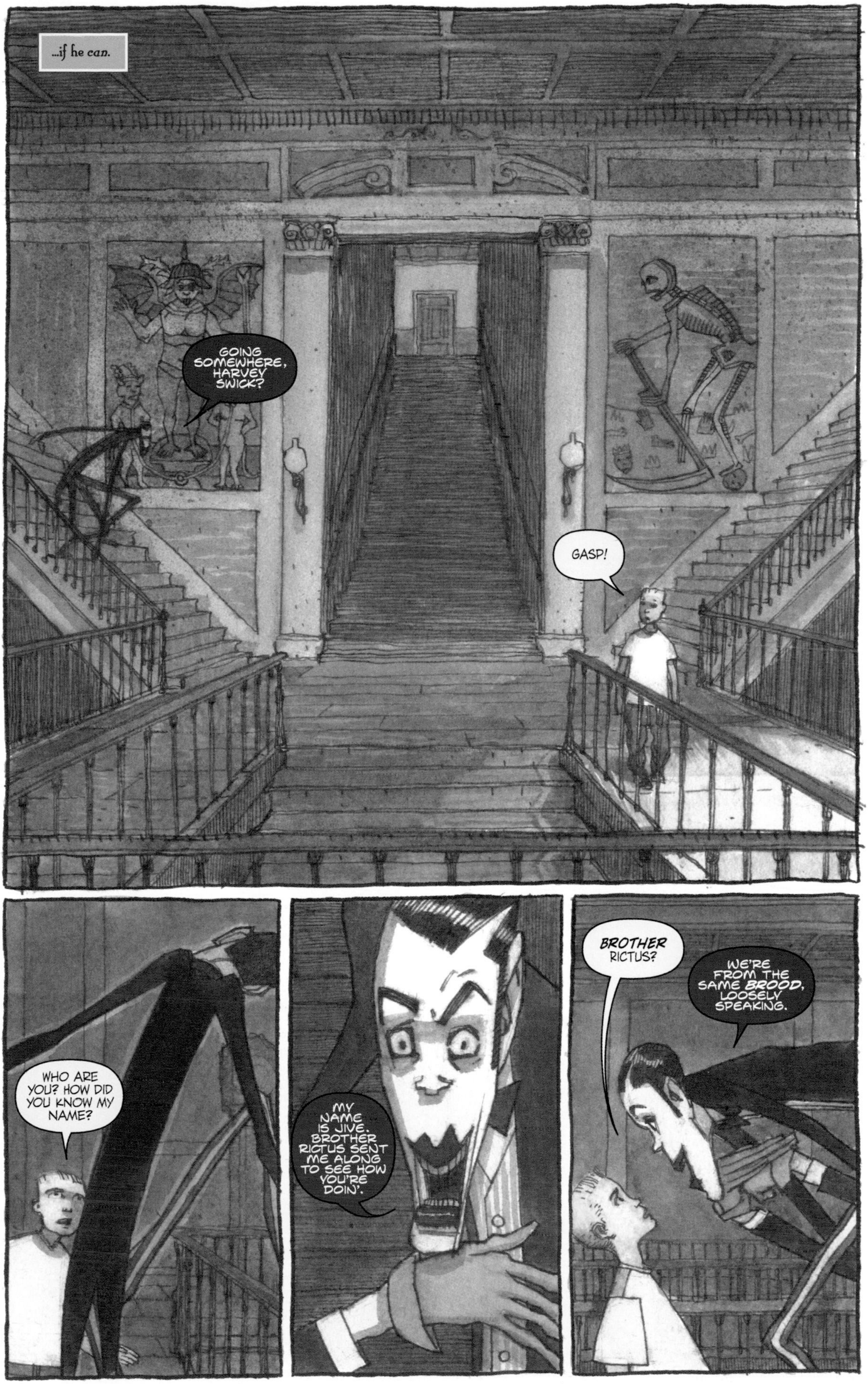
...if he can.
GOING SOMEWHERE, HARVEY SWICK?
GASP!
WHO ARE YOU? HOW DID YOU KNOW MY NAME?
MY NAME IS JIVE. BROTHER RICTUS SENT ME ALONG TO SEE HOW YOU'RE DOIN'.
BROTHER RICTUS?
WE'RE FROM THE SAME BROOD, LOOSELY SPEAKING.

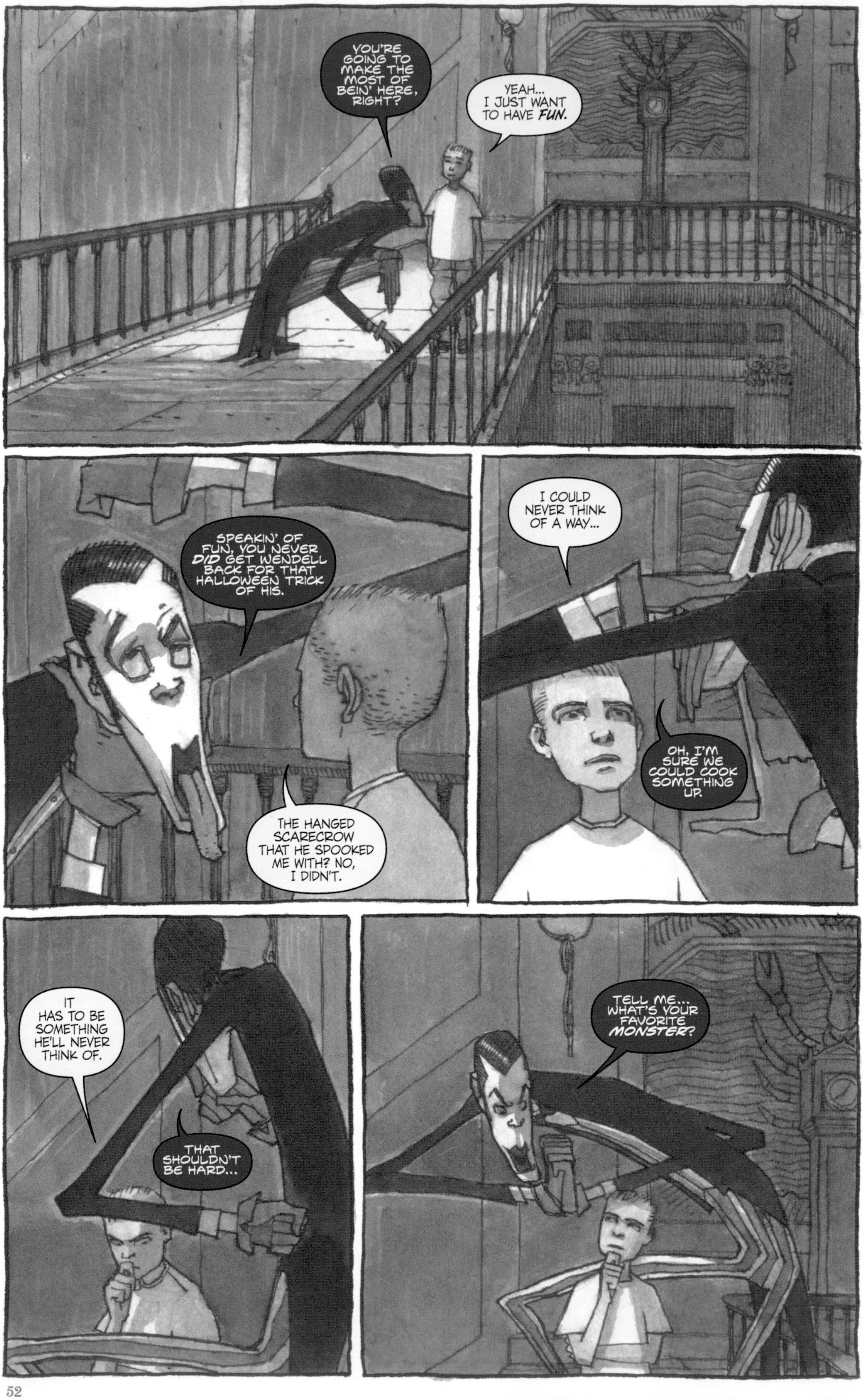

YOU'RE GOING TO MAKE THE MOST OF BEIN' HERE, RIGHT?
YEAH... I JUST WANT TO HAVE FUN.
SPEAKIN' OF FUN, YOU NEVER DID GET WENDELL BACK FOR THAT HALLOWEEN TRICK OF HIS.
THE HANGED SCARECROW THAT HE SPOOKED ME WITH? NO, I DIDN'T.
I COULD NEVER THINK OF A WAY...
OH, I'M SURE WE COULD COOK SOMETHING UP.
IT HAS TO BE SOMETHING HE'LL NEVER THINK OF.
THAT SHOULDN'T BE HARD...
TELL ME... WHAT'S YOUR FAVORITE MONSTER?

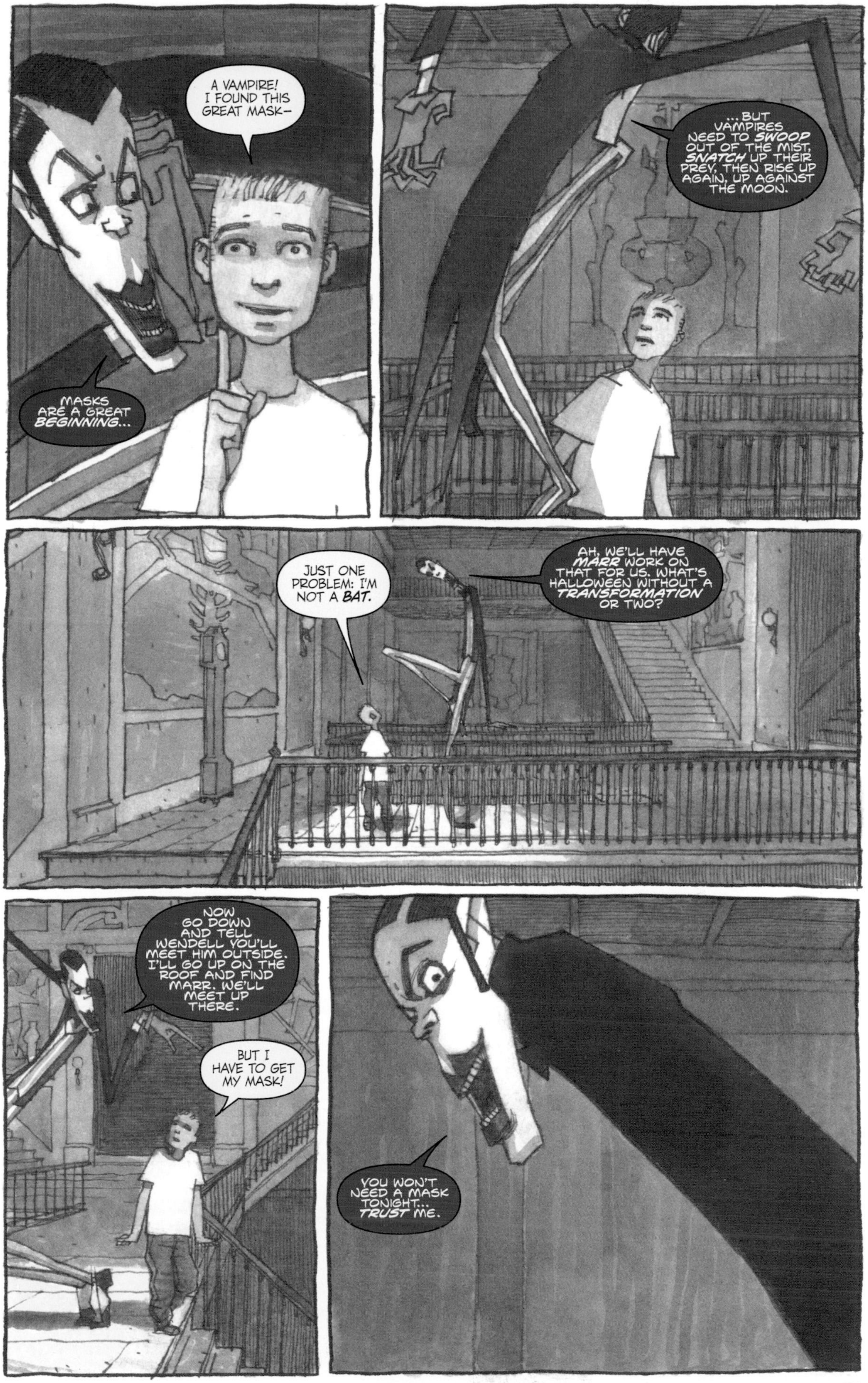
A VAMPIRE! I FOUND THIS GREAT MASK–
MASKS ARE A GREAT *BEGINNING*...
...BUT VAMPIRES NEED TO *SWOOP* OUT OF THE MIST, *SNATCH* UP THEIR PREY, THEN RISE UP AGAIN, UP AGAINST THE MOON.
JUST ONE PROBLEM: I'M NOT A *BAT.*
AH, WE'LL HAVE *MARR* WORK ON THAT FOR US. WHAT'S HALLOWEEN WITHOUT A *TRANSFORMATION* OR TWO?
NOW GO DOWN AND TELL WENDELL YOU'LL MEET HIM OUTSIDE. I'LL GO UP ON THE ROOF AND FIND MARR. WE'LL MEET UP THERE.
BUT I HAVE TO GET MY MASK!
YOU WON'T NEED A MASK TONIGHT... *TRUST* ME.

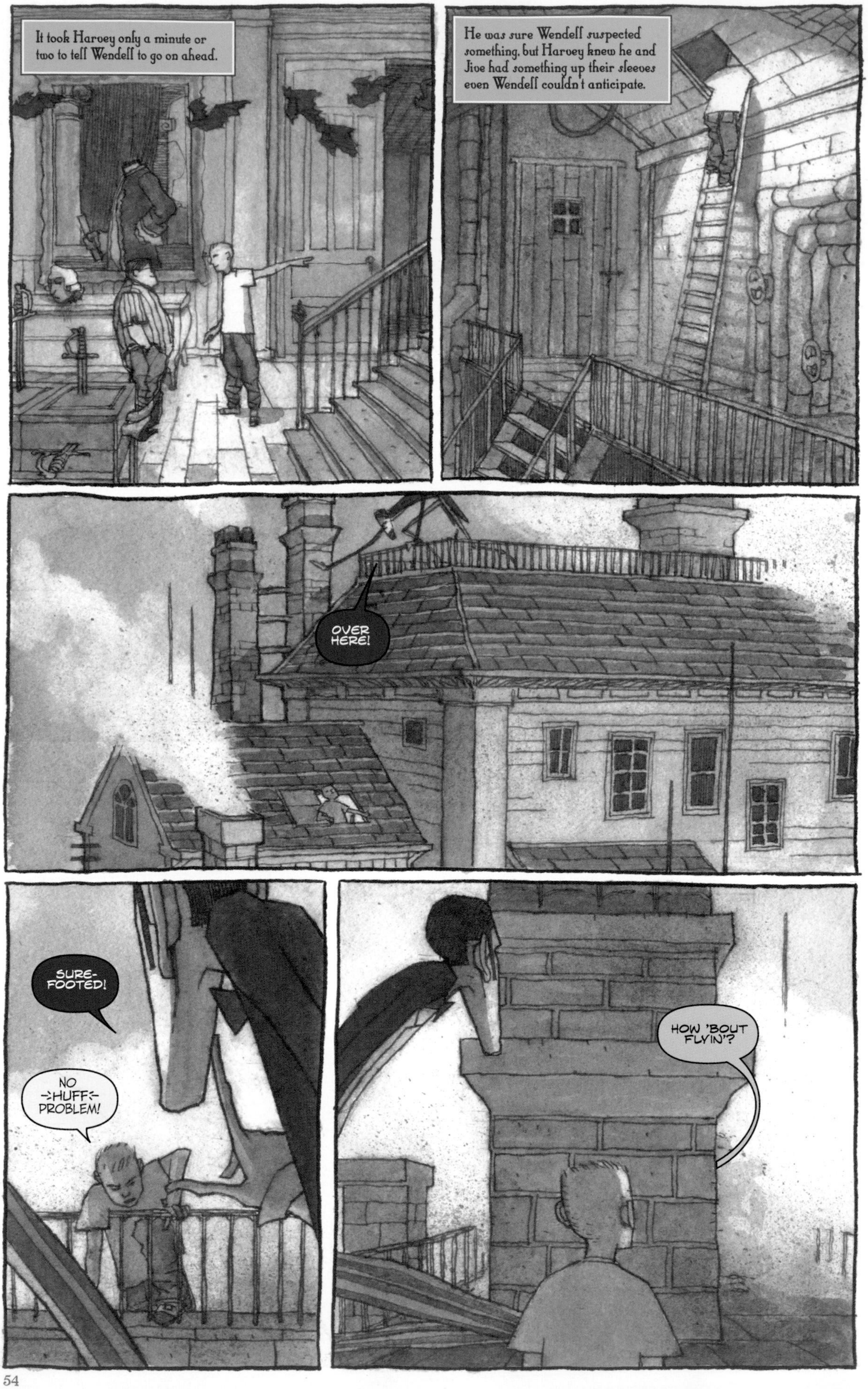
It took Harvey only a minute or two to tell Wendell to go on ahead.
He was sure Wendell suspected something, but Harvey knew he and Jive had something up their sleeves even Wendell couldn't anticipate.
OVER HERE!
SURE-FOOTED!
NO -HUFF- PROBLEM!
HOW 'BOUT FLYIN'?

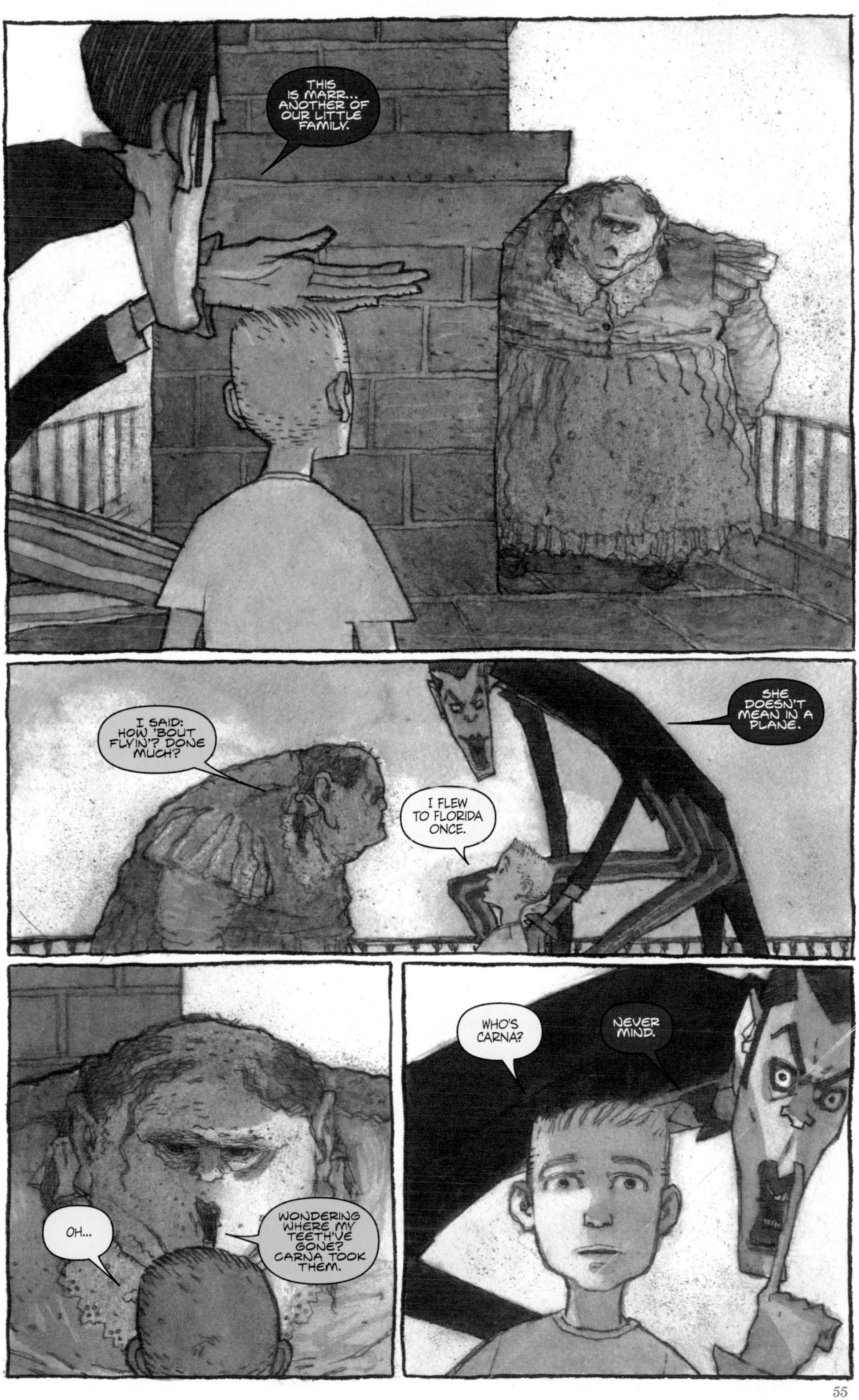
THIS IS MARR... ANOTHER OF OUR LITTLE FAMILY.
I SAID: HOW 'BOUT FLYIN'? DONE MUCH?
I FLEW TO FLORIDA ONCE.
SHE DOESN'T MEAN IN A PLANE.
OH...
WONDERING WHERE MY TEETH'VE GONE? CARNA TOOK THEM.
WHO'S CARNA?
NEVER MIND.

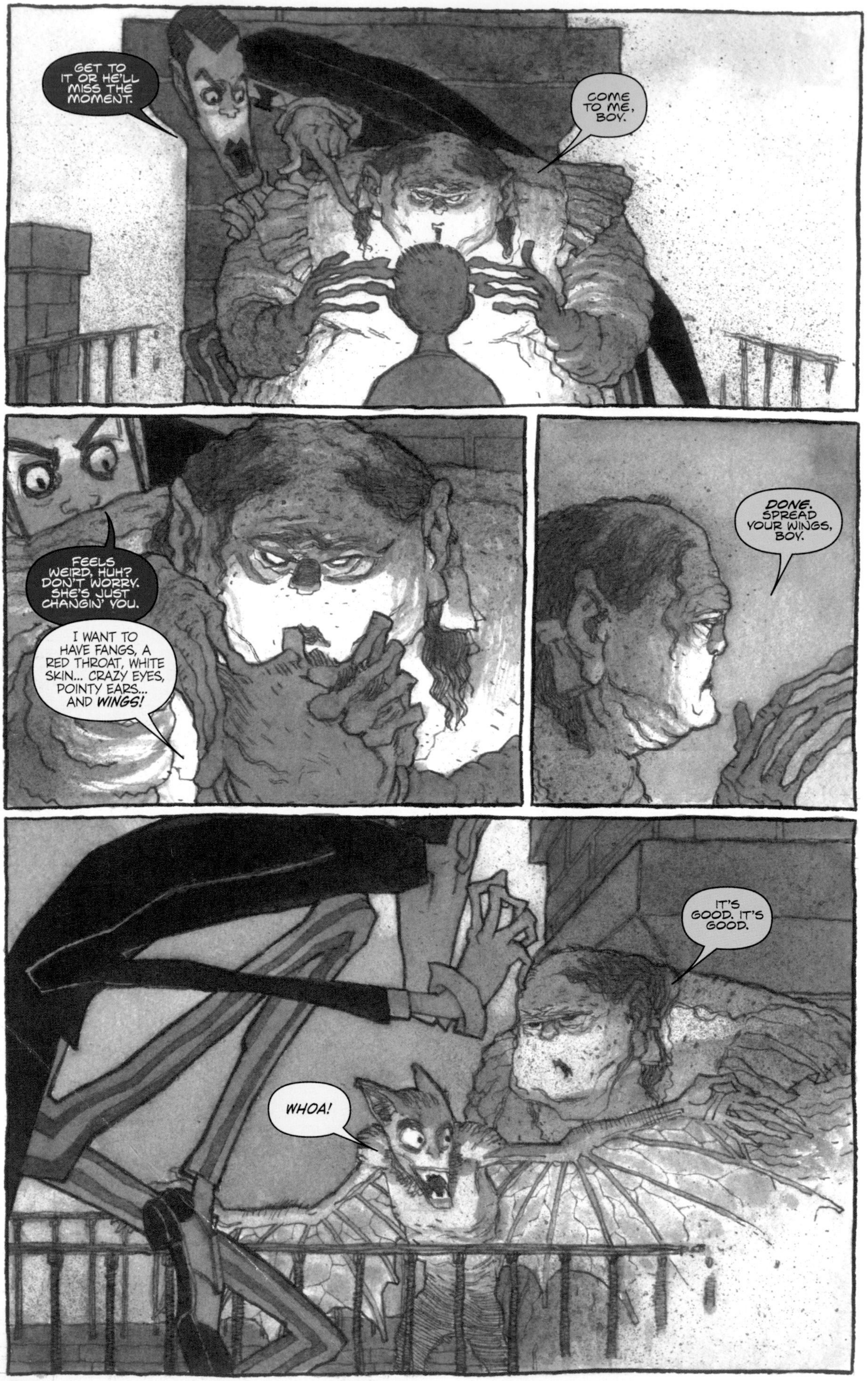
GET TO IT OR HE'LL MISS THE MOMENT.
COME TO ME, BOY.
FEELS WEIRD, HUH? DON'T WORRY. SHE'S JUST CHANGIN' YOU.
I WANT TO HAVE FANGS, A RED THROAT, WHITE SKIN... CRAZY EYES, POINTY EARS... AND WINGS!
DONE. SPREAD YOUR WINGS, BOY.
IT'S GOOD. IT'S GOOD.
WHOA!

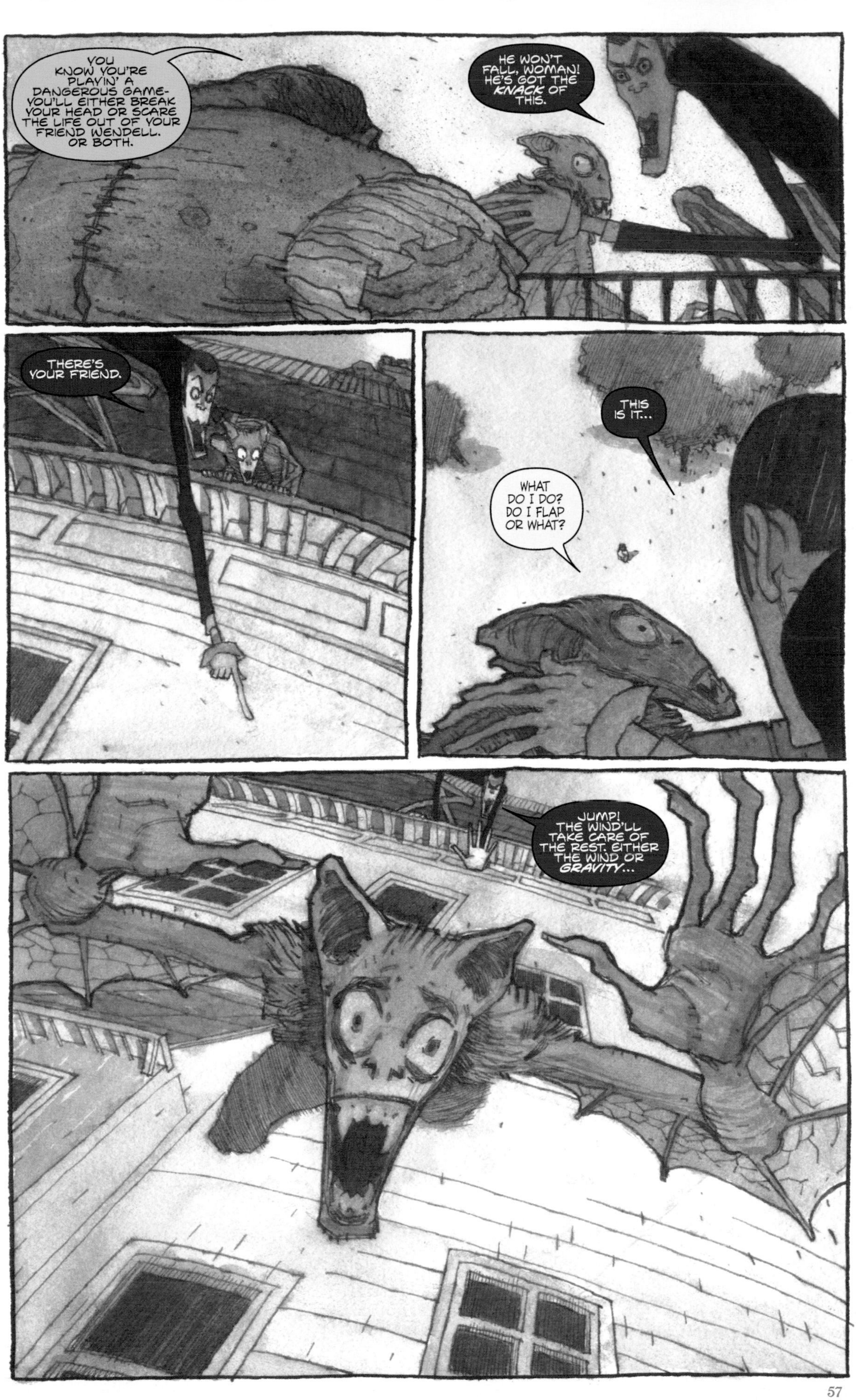
YOU KNOW YOU'RE PLAYIN' A DANGEROUS GAME- YOU'LL EITHER BREAK YOUR HEAD OR SCARE THE LIFE OUT OF YOUR FRIEND WENDELL. OR BOTH.
HE WON'T FALL, WOMAN! HE'S GOT THE KNACK OF THIS.
THERE'S YOUR FRIEND.
THIS IS IT...
WHAT DO I DO? DO I FLAP OR WHAT?
JUMP! THE WIND'LL TAKE CARE OF THE REST. EITHER THE WIND OR GRAVITY...

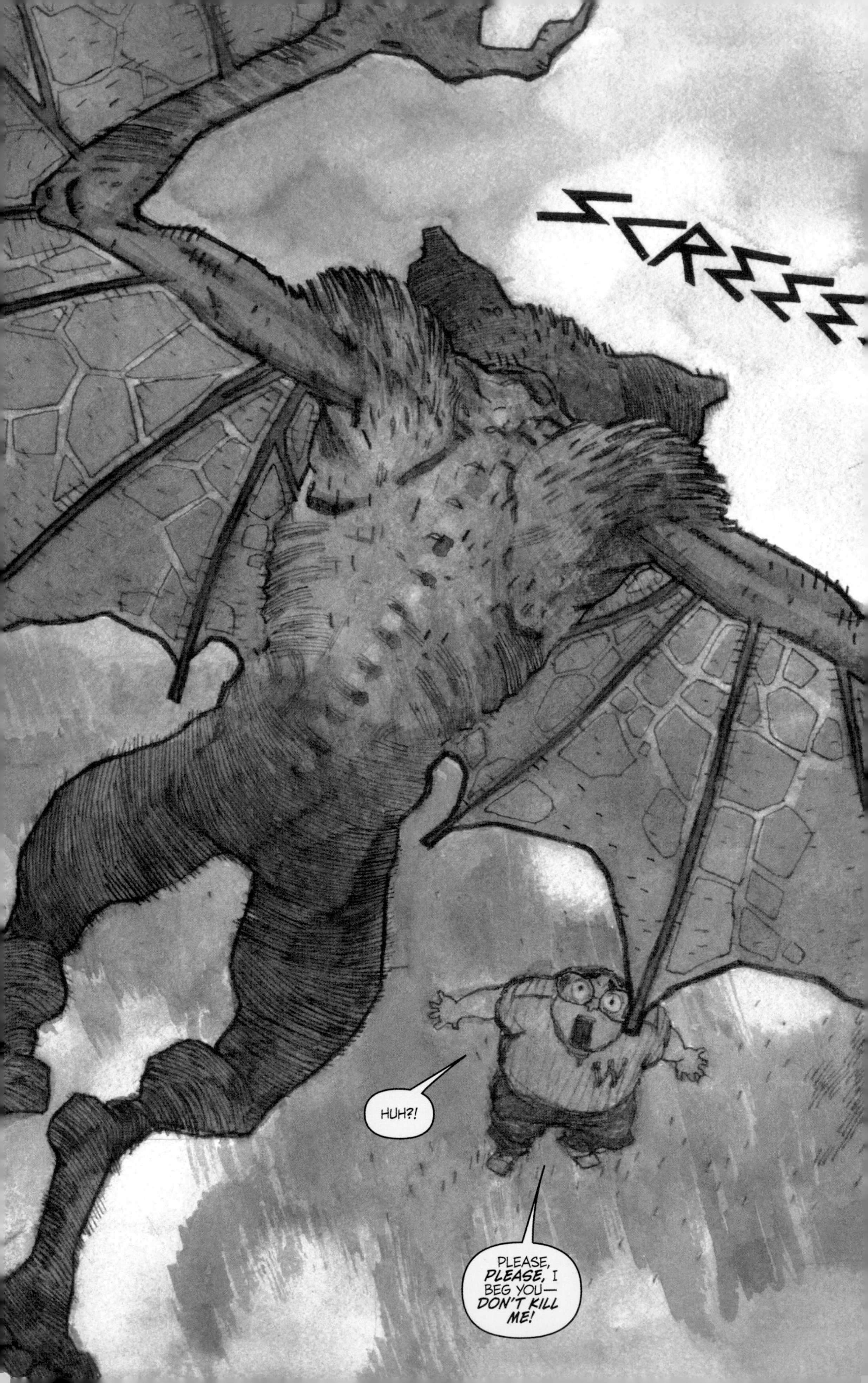
SCREEE...
HUH?!
PLEASE, PLEASE, I BEG YOU— DON'T KILL ME!

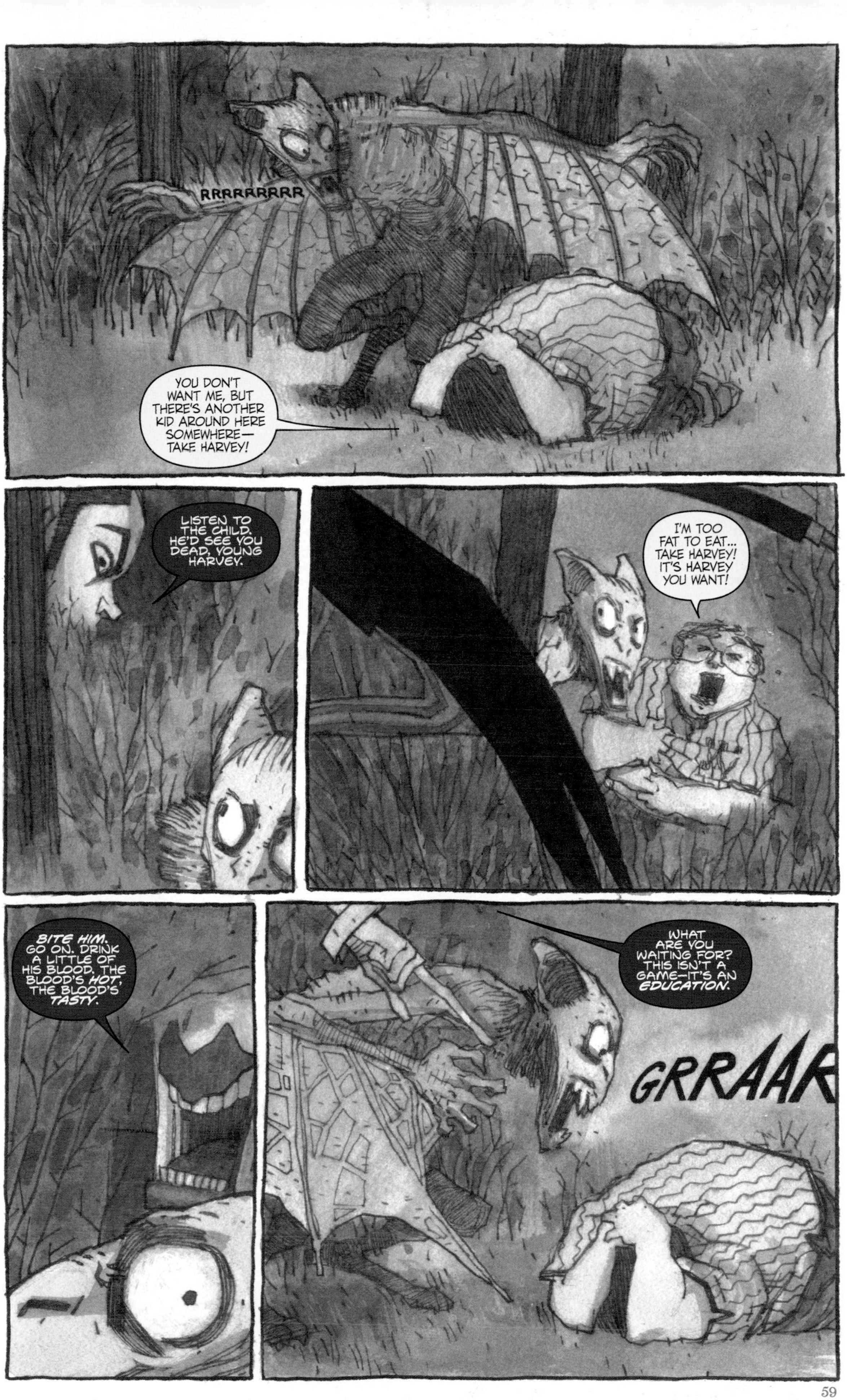
RRRRRRRRR
YOU DON'T WANT ME, BUT THERE'S ANOTHER KID AROUND HERE SOMEWHERE— TAKE HARVEY!
LISTEN TO THE CHILD. HE'D SEE YOU DEAD, YOUNG HARVEY.
I'M TOO FAT TO EAT... TAKE HARVEY! IT'S HARVEY YOU WANT!
BITE HIM. GO ON. DRINK A LITTLE OF HIS BLOOD. THE BLOOD'S HOT, THE BLOOD'S TASTY.
WHAT ARE YOU WAITING FOR? THIS ISN'T A GAME—IT'S AN EDUCATION.
GRRAAR

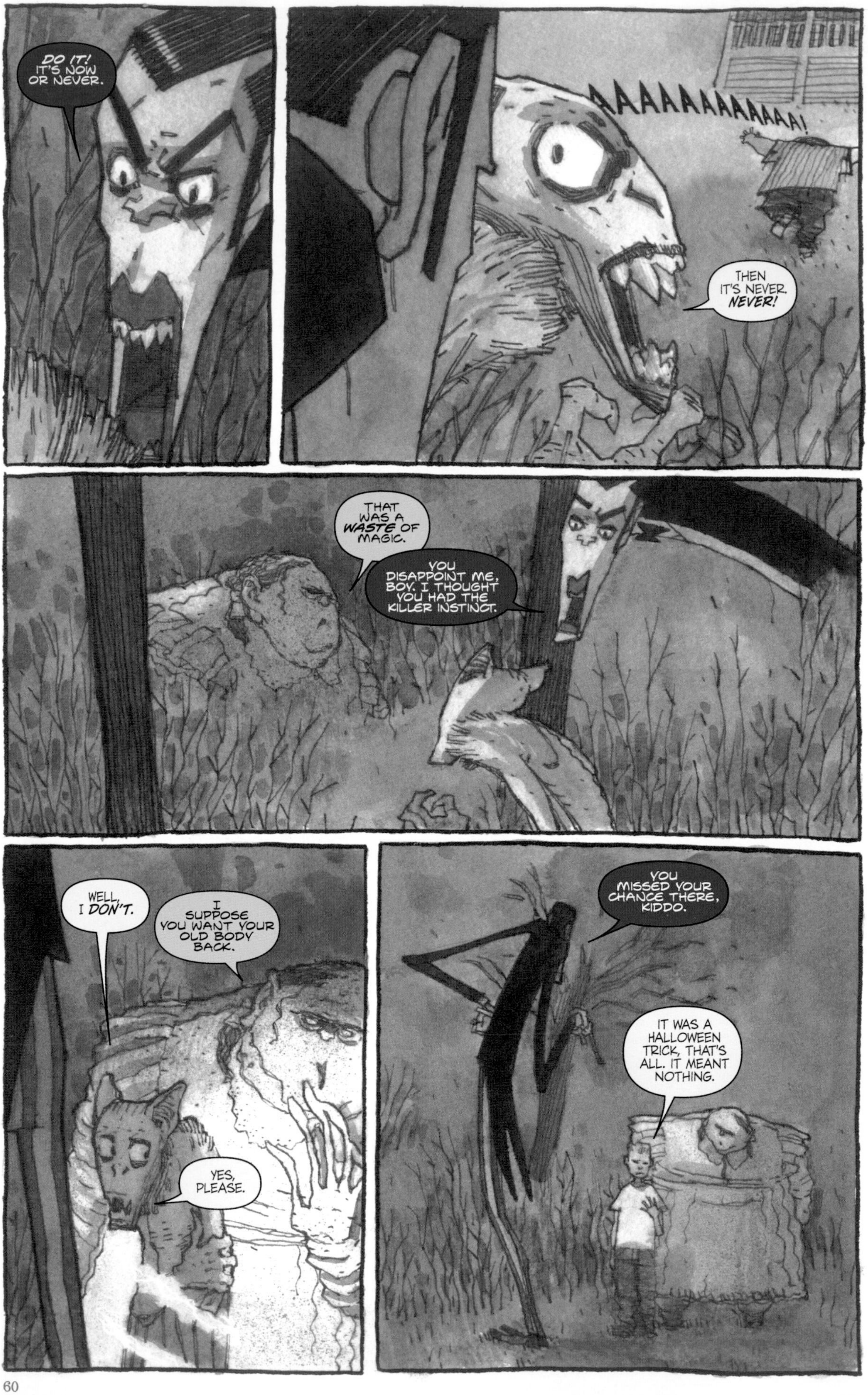
DO IT! IT'S NOW OR NEVER.
AAAAAAAAAAAAA!
THEN IT'S NEVER. NEVER!
THAT WAS A WASTE OF MAGIC.
YOU DISAPPOINT ME, BOY. I THOUGHT YOU HAD THE KILLER INSTINCT.
WELL, I DON'T.
I SUPPOSE YOU WANT YOUR OLD BODY BACK.
YES, PLEASE.
YOU MISSED YOUR CHANCE THERE, KIDDO.
IT WAS A HALLOWEEN TRICK, THAT'S ALL. IT MEANT NOTHING.

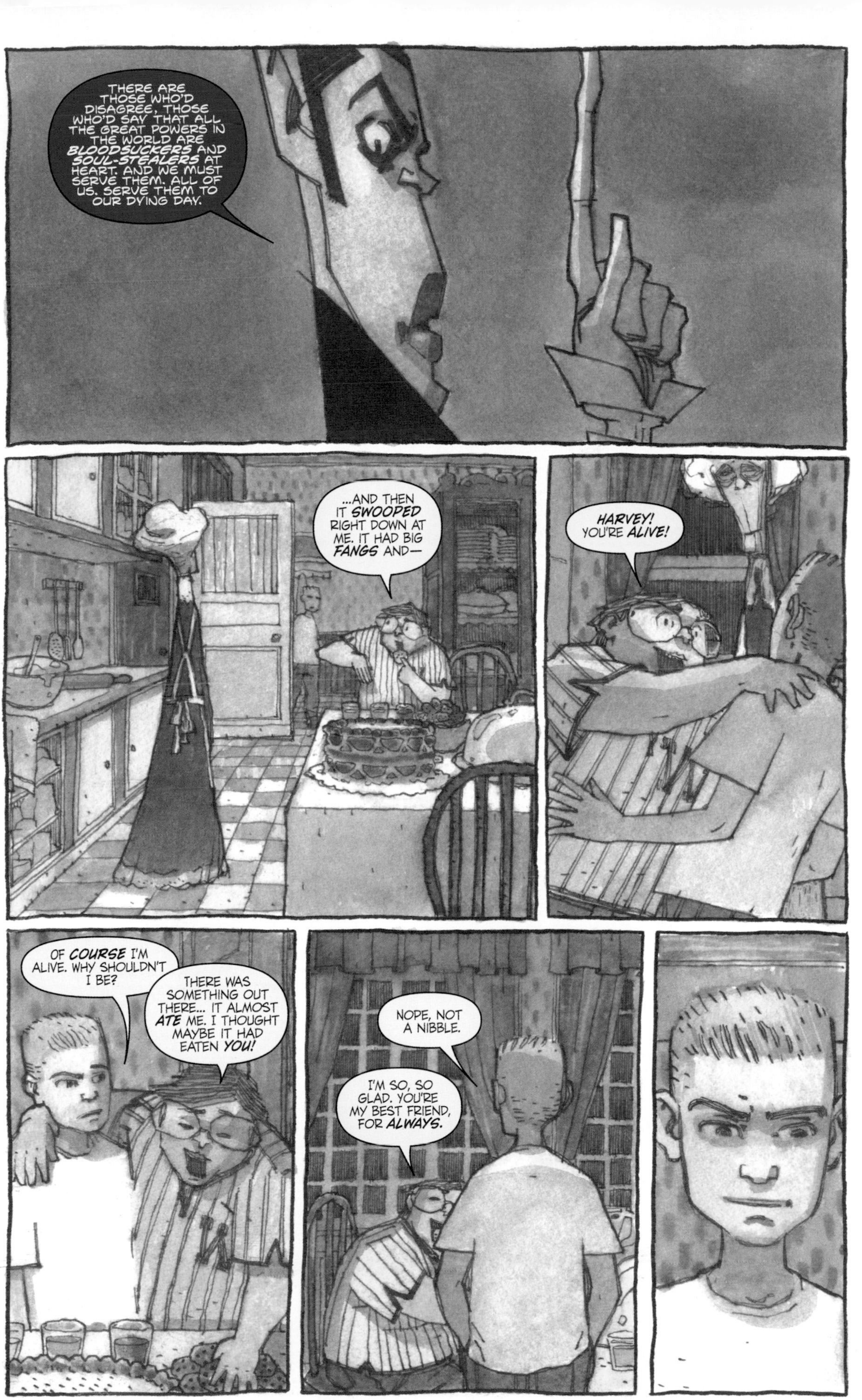
THERE ARE THOSE WHO'D DISAGREE, THOSE WHO'D SAY THAT ALL THE GREAT POWERS IN THE WORLD ARE BLOODSUCKERS AND SOUL-STEALERS AT HEART. AND WE MUST SERVE THEM. ALL OF US. SERVE THEM TO OUR DYING DAY.
...AND THEN IT SWOOPED RIGHT DOWN AT ME. IT HAD BIG FANGS AND—
HARVEY! YOU'RE ALIVE!
OF COURSE I'M ALIVE. WHY SHOULDN'T I BE?
THERE WAS SOMETHING OUT THERE... IT ALMOST ATE ME. I THOUGHT MAYBE IT HAD EATEN YOU!
NOPE, NOT A NIBBLE.
I'M SO, SO GLAD. YOU'RE MY BEST FRIEND, FOR ALWAYS.

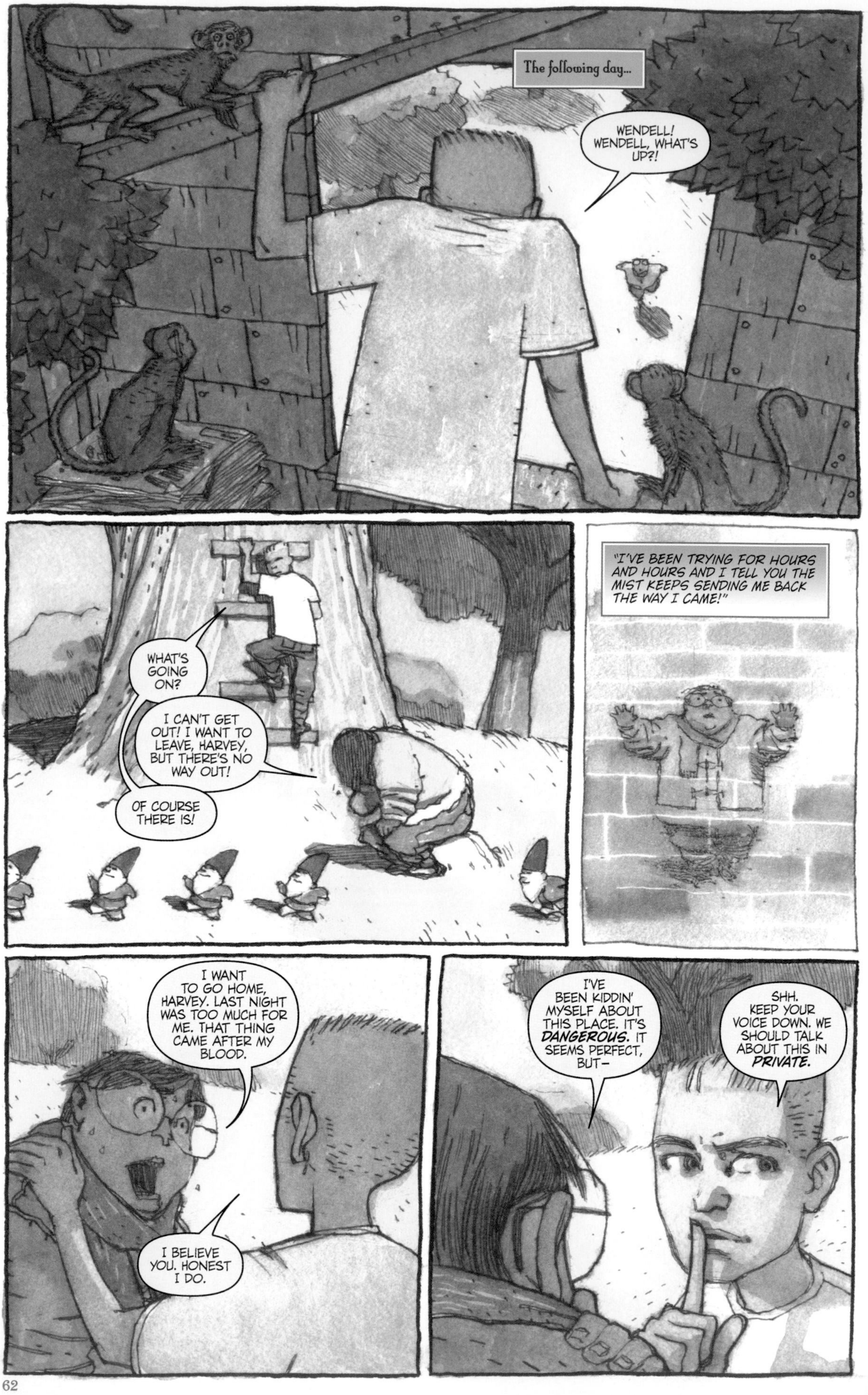
The following day...
WENDELL! WENDELL, WHAT'S UP?!
WHAT'S GOING ON?
I CAN'T GET OUT! I WANT TO LEAVE, HARVEY, BUT THERE'S NO WAY OUT!
OF COURSE THERE IS!
"I'VE BEEN TRYING FOR HOURS AND HOURS AND I TELL YOU THE MIST KEEPS SENDING ME BACK THE WAY I CAME!"
I WANT TO GO HOME, HARVEY. LAST NIGHT WAS TOO MUCH FOR ME. THAT THING CAME AFTER MY BLOOD.
I BELIEVE YOU. HONEST I DO.
I'VE BEEN KIDDIN' MYSELF ABOUT THIS PLACE. IT'S ***DANGEROUS.*** IT SEEMS PERFECT, BUT–
SHH. KEEP YOUR VOICE DOWN. WE SHOULD TALK ABOUT THIS IN ***PRIVATE.***

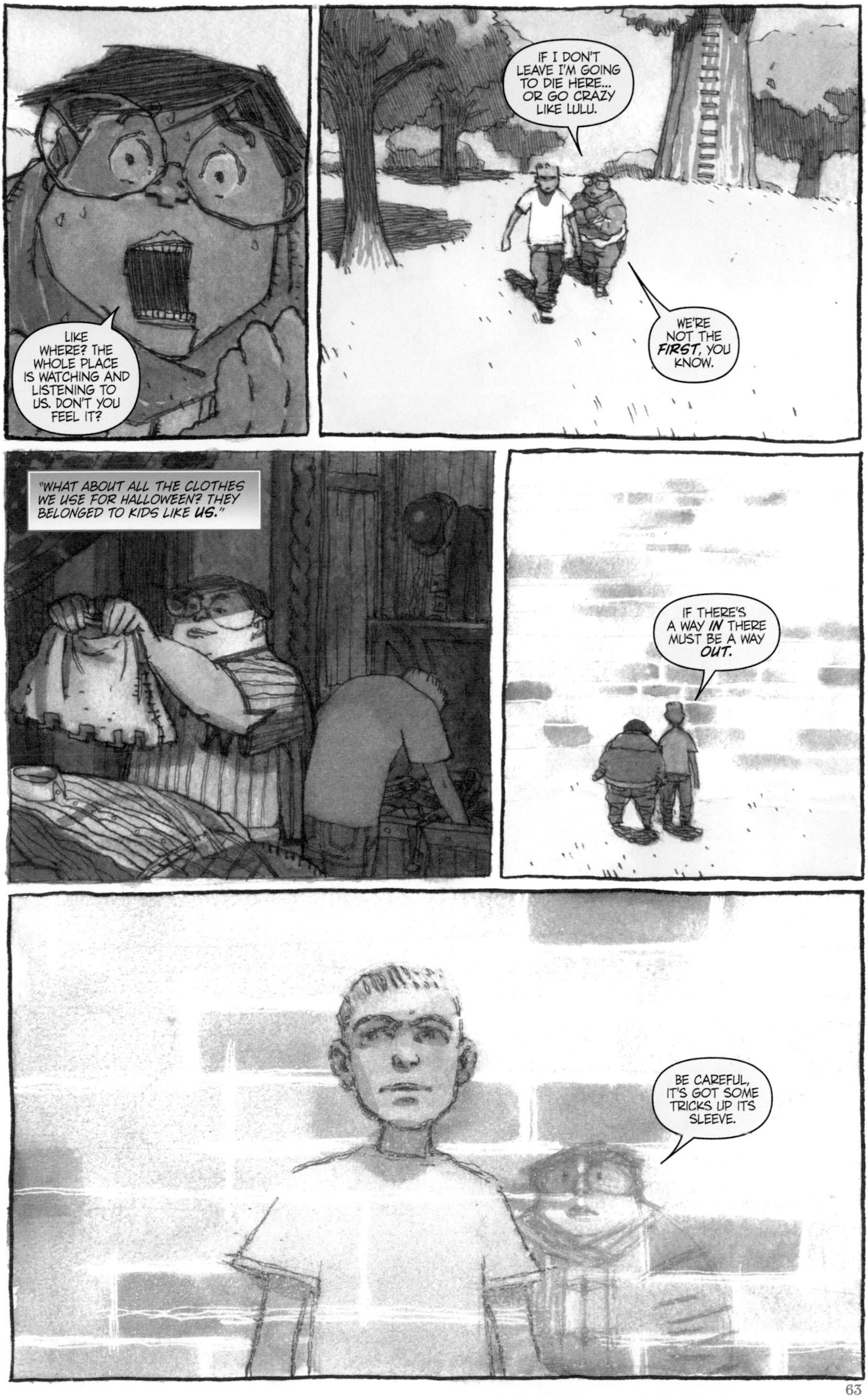
LIKE WHERE? THE WHOLE PLACE IS WATCHING AND LISTENING TO US. DON'T YOU FEEL IT?
IF I DON'T LEAVE I'M GOING TO DIE HERE... OR GO CRAZY LIKE LULU.
WE'RE NOT THE FIRST, YOU KNOW.
"WHAT ABOUT ALL THE CLOTHES WE USE FOR HALLOWEEN? THEY BELONGED TO KIDS LIKE US."
IF THERE'S A WAY IN THERE MUST BE A WAY OUT.
BE CAREFUL, IT'S GOT SOME TRICKS UP ITS SLEEVE.

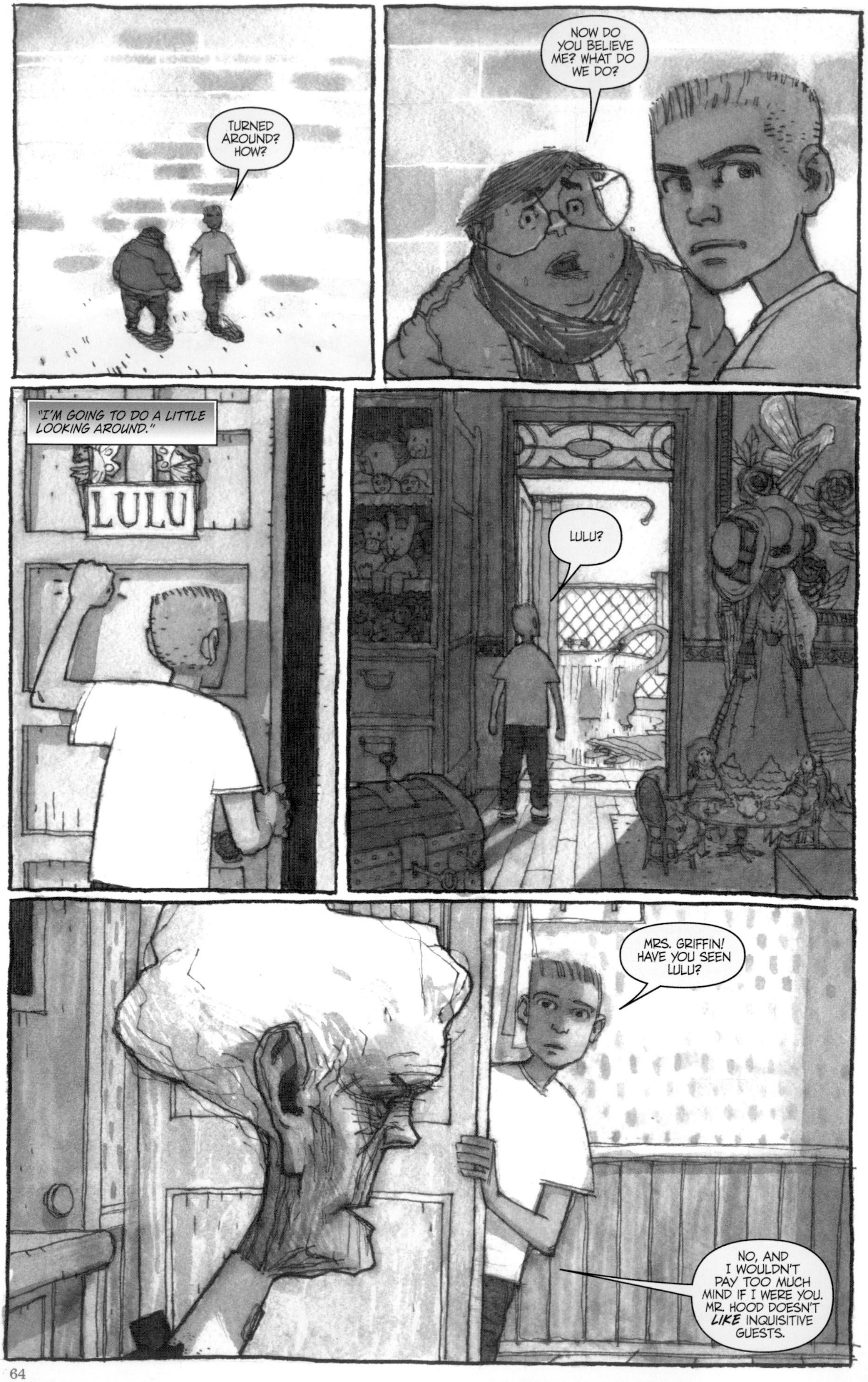
TURNED AROUND? HOW?
NOW DO YOU BELIEVE ME? WHAT DO WE DO?
"I'M GOING TO DO A LITTLE LOOKING AROUND."
LULU
LULU?
MRS. GRIFFIN! HAVE YOU SEEN LULU?
NO, AND I WOULDN'T PAY TOO MUCH MIND IF I WERE YOU. MR. HOOD DOESN'T *LIKE* INQUISITIVE GUESTS.

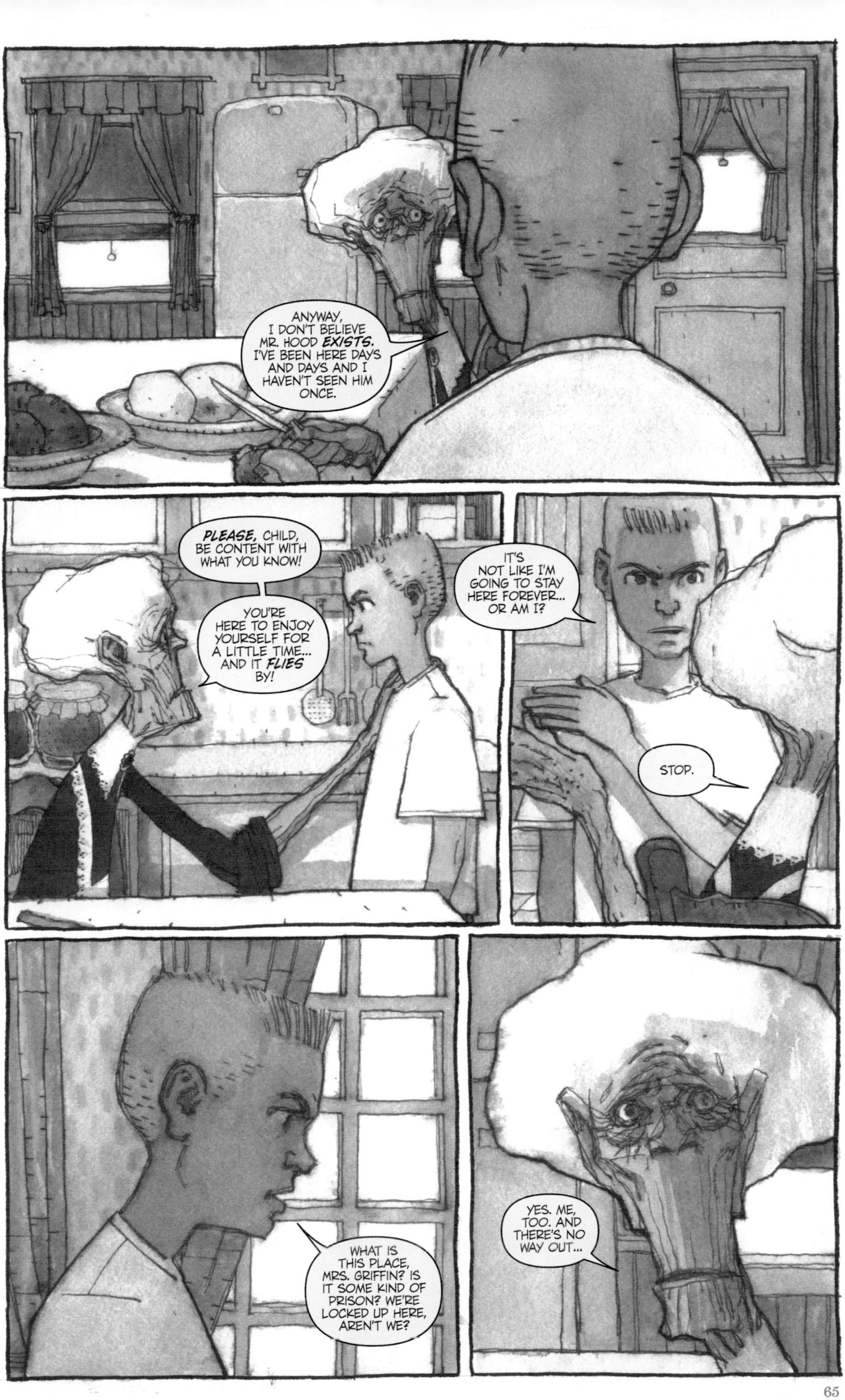
ANYWAY, I DON'T BELIEVE MR. HOOD EXISTS. I'VE BEEN HERE DAYS AND DAYS AND I HAVEN'T SEEN HIM ONCE.
PLEASE, CHILD, BE CONTENT WITH WHAT YOU KNOW!
YOU'RE HERE TO ENJOY YOURSELF FOR A LITTLE TIME... AND IT FLIES BY!
IT'S NOT LIKE I'M GOING TO STAY HERE FOREVER... OR AM I?
STOP.
WHAT IS THIS PLACE, MRS. GRIFFIN? IS IT SOME KIND OF PRISON? WE'RE LOCKED UP HERE, AREN'T WE?
YES. ME, TOO. AND THERE'S NO WAY OUT...

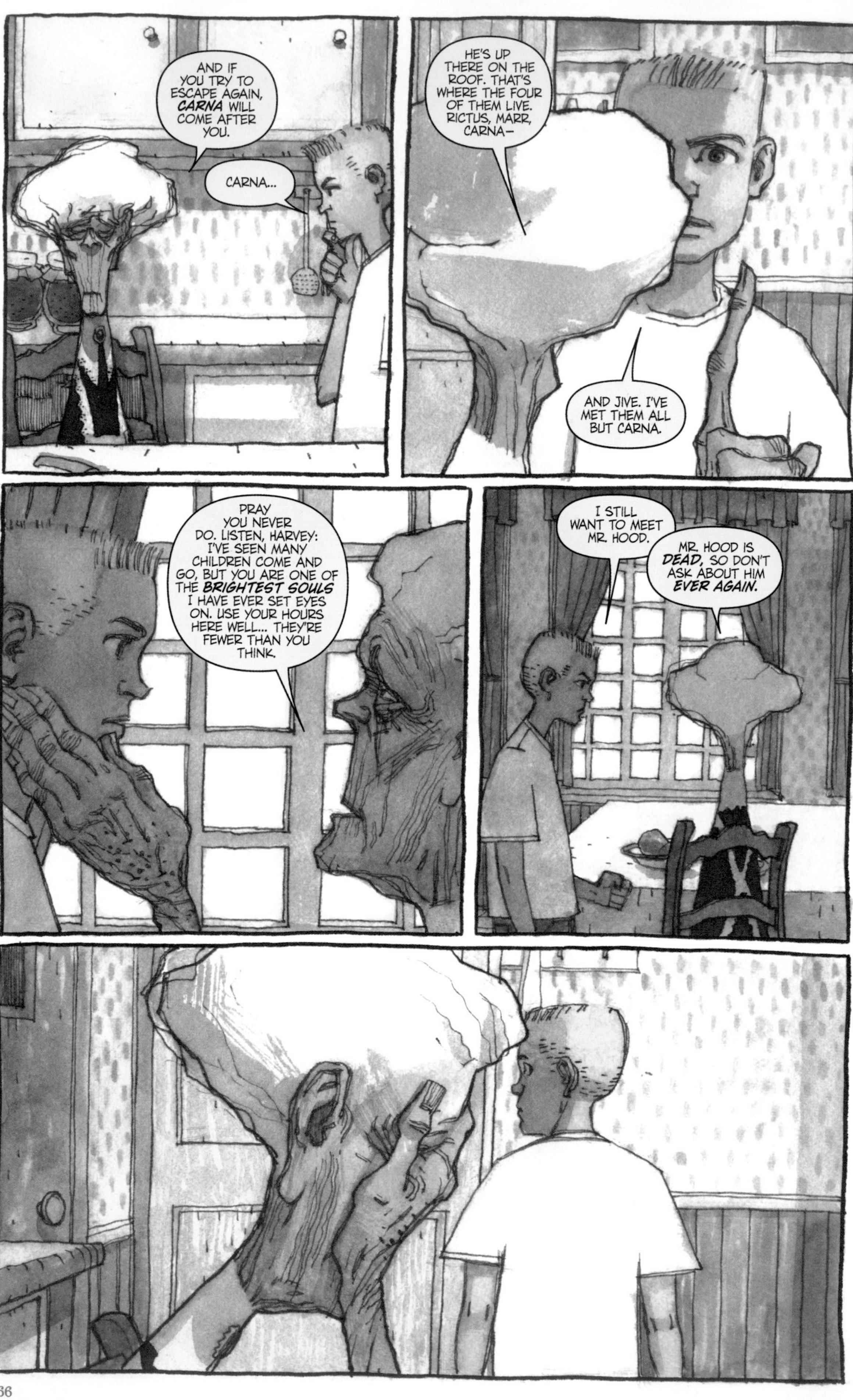
AND IF YOU TRY TO ESCAPE AGAIN, **CARNA** WILL COME AFTER YOU.
CARNA...
HE'S UP THERE ON THE ROOF. THAT'S WHERE THE FOUR OF THEM LIVE. RICTUS, MARR, CARNA–
AND JIVE. I'VE MET THEM ALL BUT CARNA.
PRAY YOU NEVER DO. LISTEN, HARVEY: I'VE SEEN MANY CHILDREN COME AND GO, BUT YOU ARE ONE OF THE **BRIGHTEST SOULS** I HAVE EVER SET EYES ON. USE YOUR HOURS HERE WELL... THEY'RE FEWER THAN YOU THINK.
I STILL WANT TO MEET MR. HOOD.
MR. HOOD IS **DEAD,** SO DON'T ASK ABOUT HIM **EVER AGAIN.**

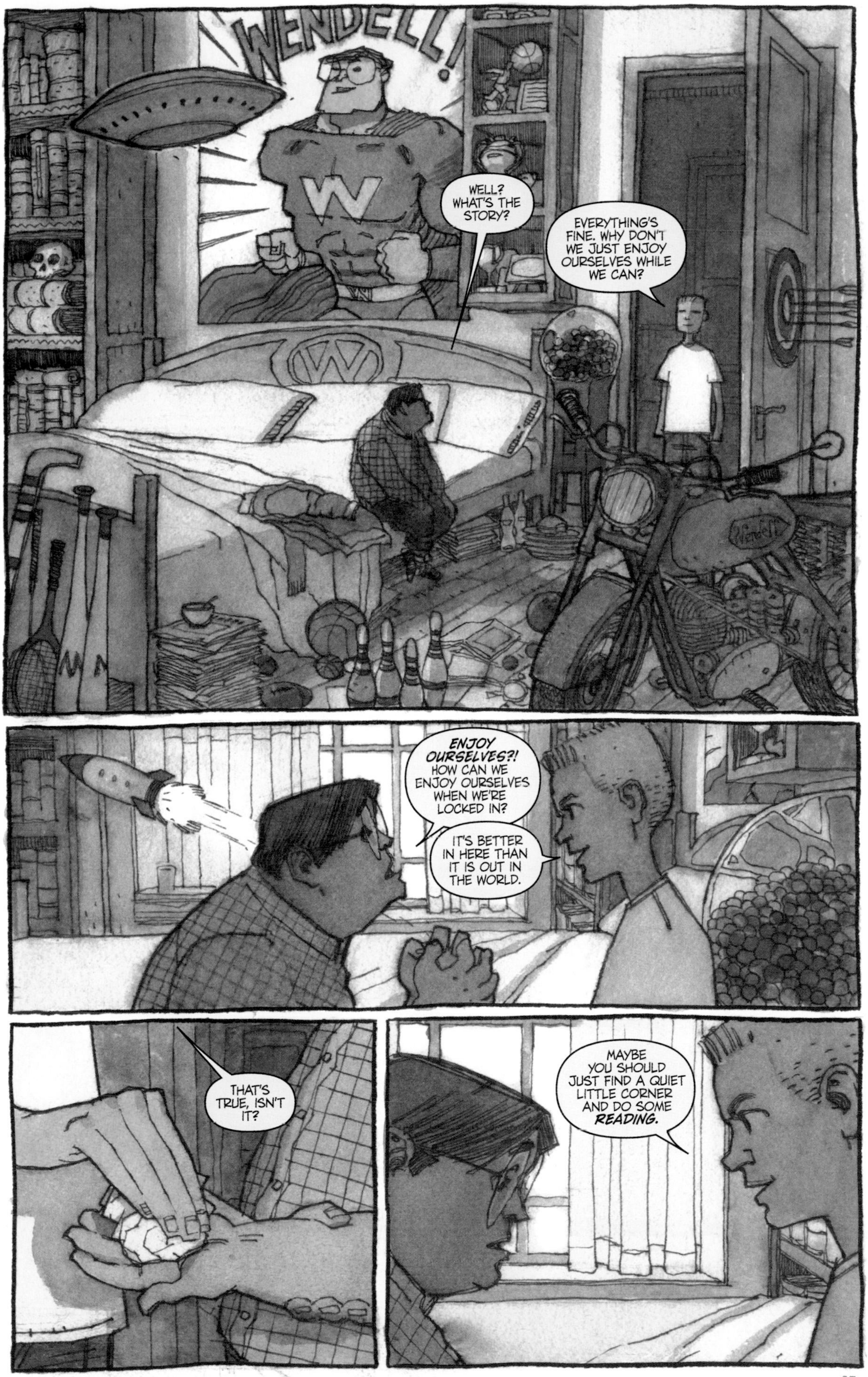
WENDELL!
WELL? WHAT'S THE STORY?
EVERYTHING'S FINE. WHY DON'T WE JUST ENJOY OURSELVES WHILE WE CAN?
Wendell
ENJOY OURSELVES?! HOW CAN WE ENJOY OURSELVES WHEN WE'RE LOCKED IN?
IT'S BETTER IN HERE THAN IT IS OUT IN THE WORLD.
THAT'S TRUE, ISN'T IT?
MAYBE YOU SHOULD JUST FIND A QUIET LITTLE CORNER AND DO SOME READING.

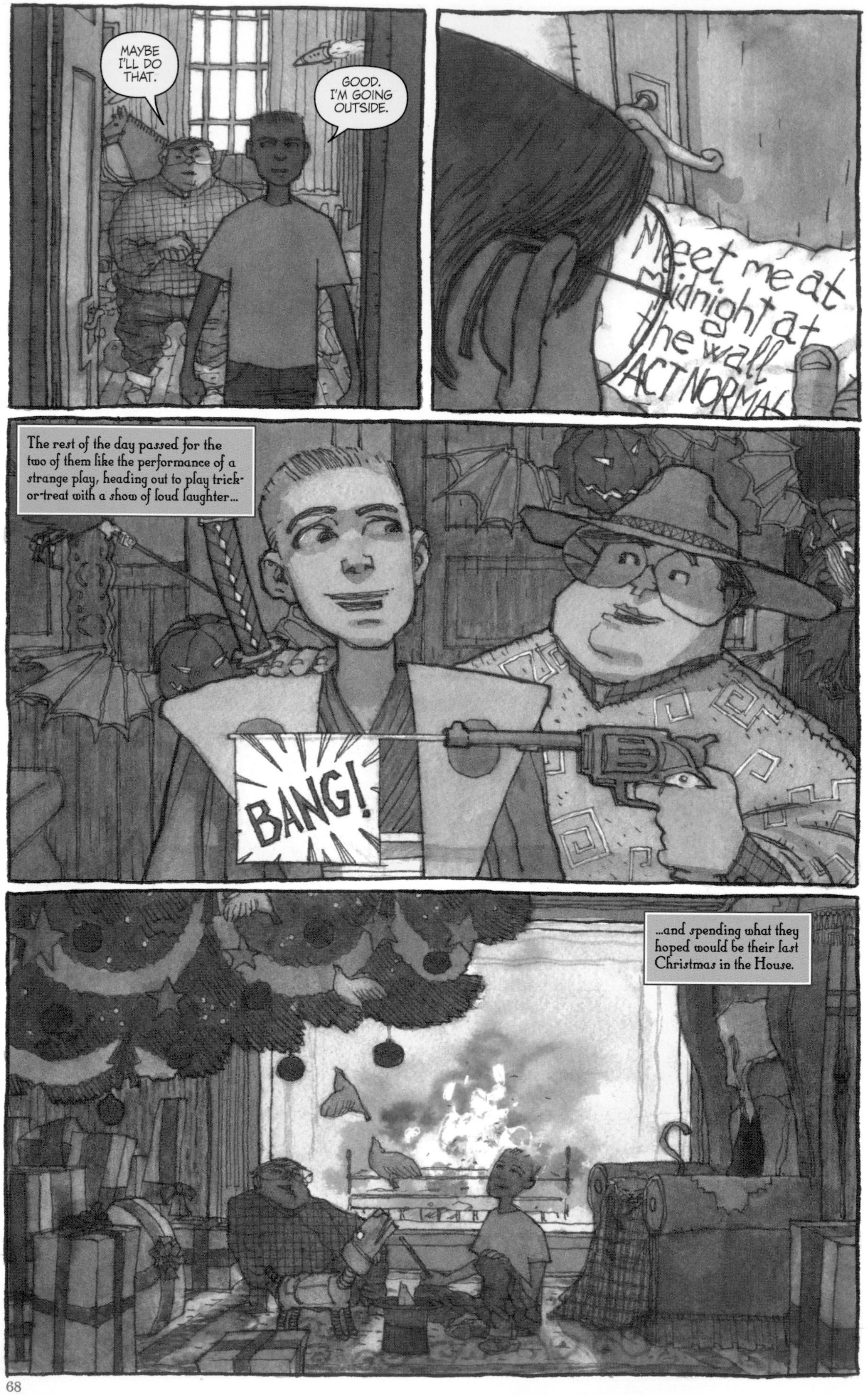
MAYBE I'LL DO THAT.
GOOD. I'M GOING OUTSIDE.
Meet me at midnight at the wall
ACT NORMAL
The rest of the day passed for the two of them like the performance of a strange play, heading out to play trick-or-treat with a show of loud laughter...
BANG!
...and spending what they hoped would be their last Christmas in the House.

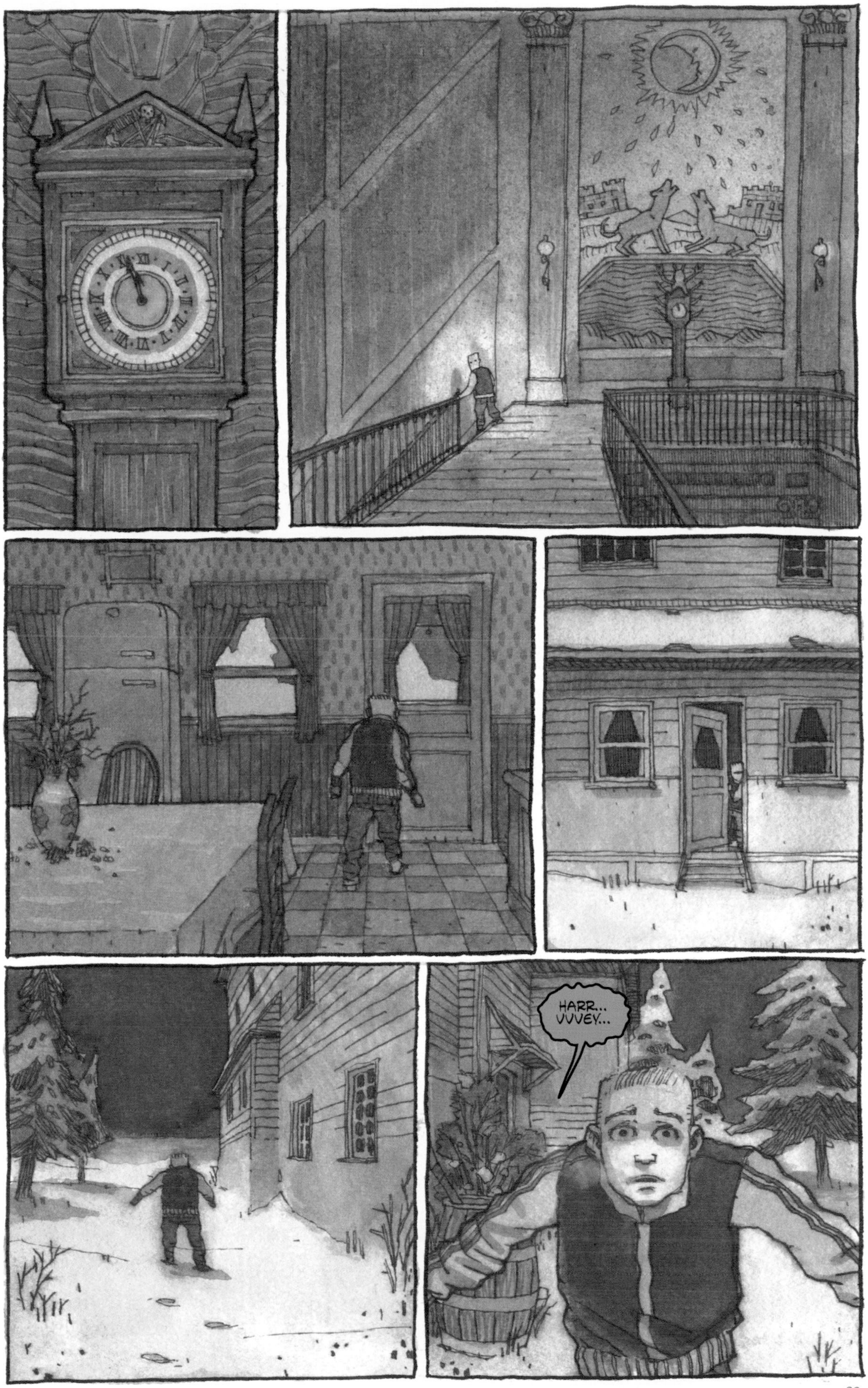
HARR... VVVEY...

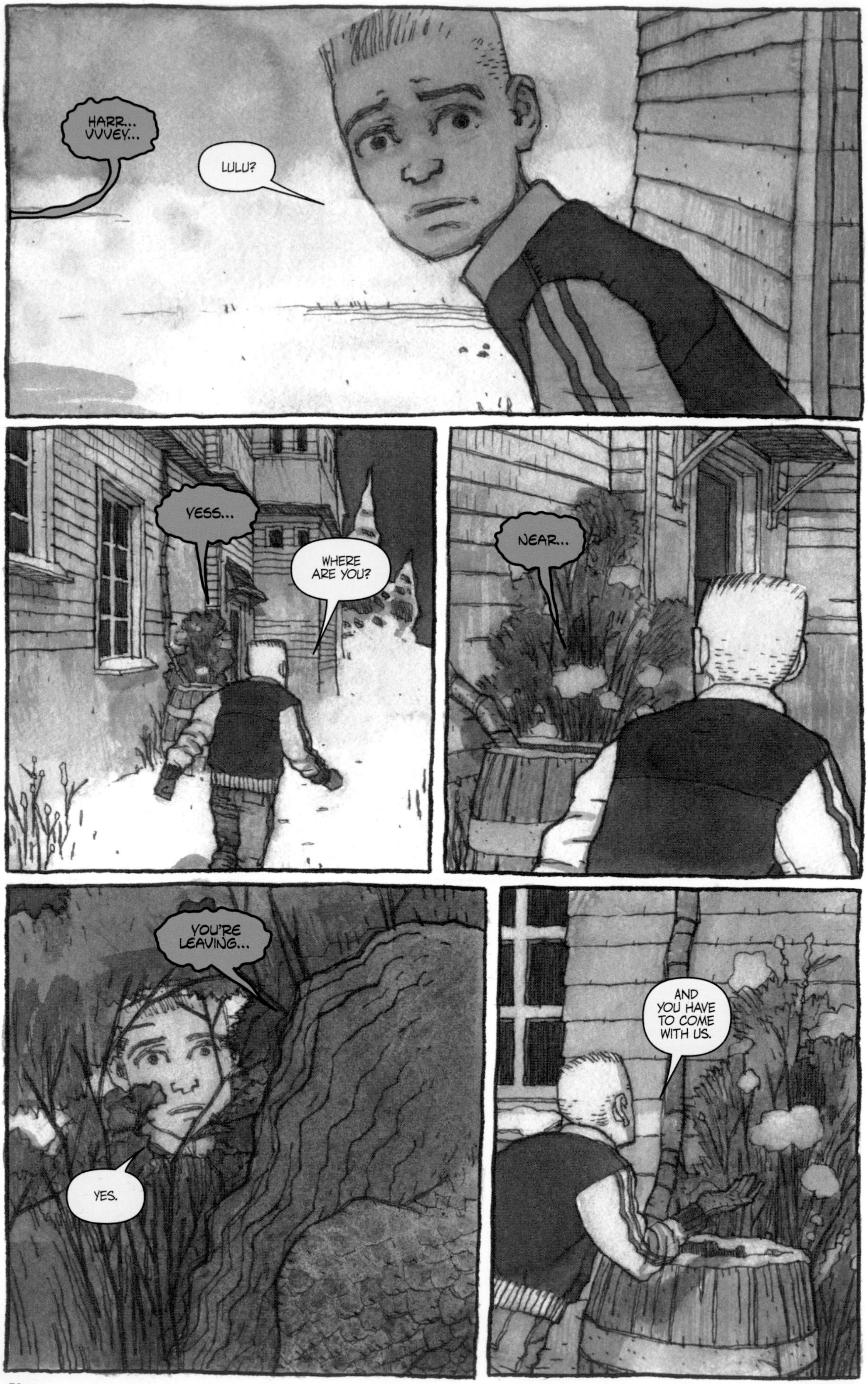
HARR... VVVEY...
LULU?
YESS...
WHERE ARE YOU?
NEAR...
YOU'RE LEAVING...
YES.
AND YOU HAVE TO COME WITH US.

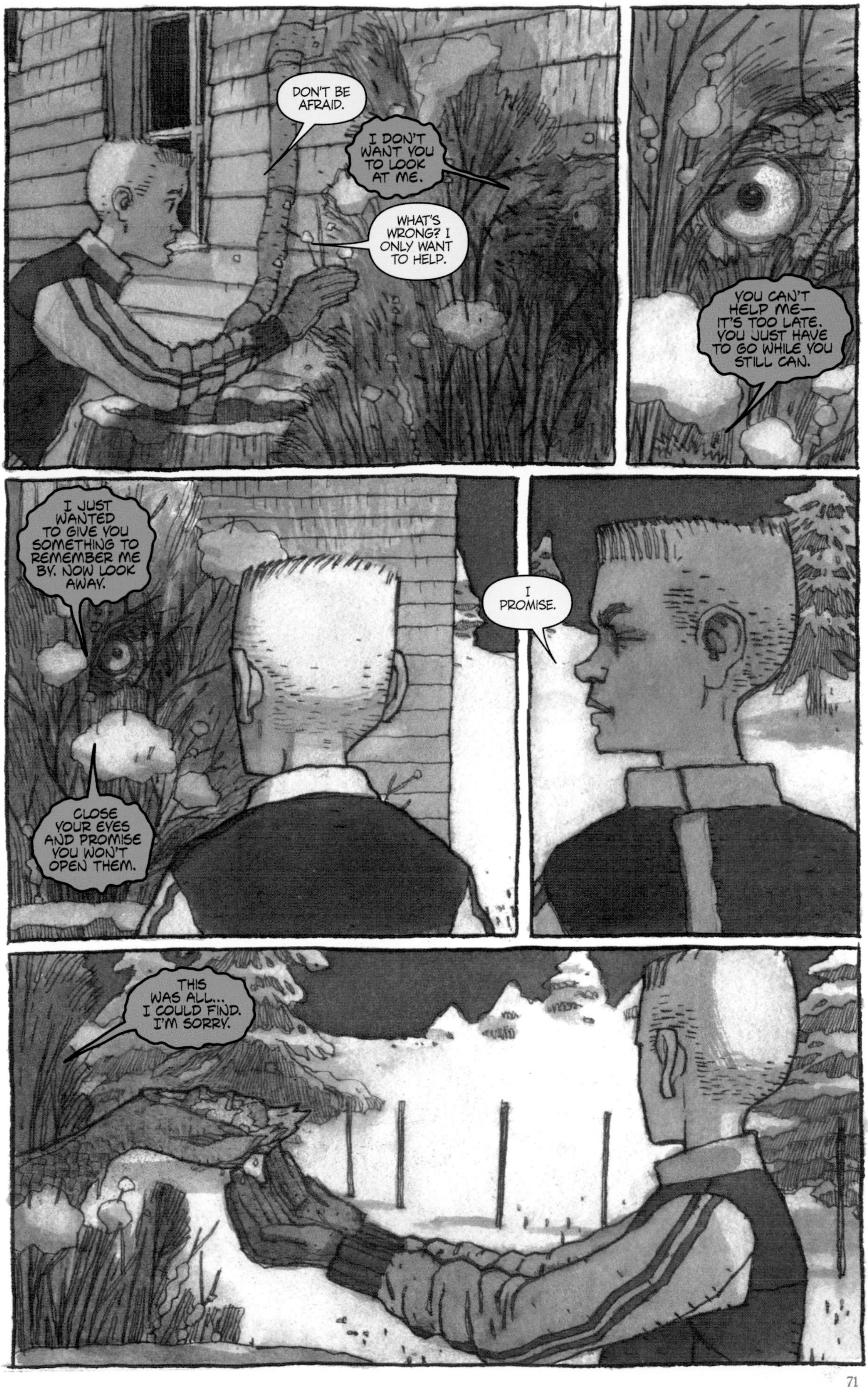
DON'T BE AFRAID.
I DON'T WANT YOU TO LOOK AT ME.
WHAT'S WRONG? I ONLY WANT TO HELP.
YOU CAN'T HELP ME— IT'S TOO LATE. YOU JUST HAVE TO GO WHILE YOU STILL CAN.
I JUST WANTED TO GIVE YOU SOMETHING TO REMEMBER ME BY. NOW LOOK AWAY.
CLOSE YOUR EYES AND PROMISE YOU WON'T OPEN THEM.
I PROMISE.
THIS WAS ALL... I COULD FIND. I'M SORRY.

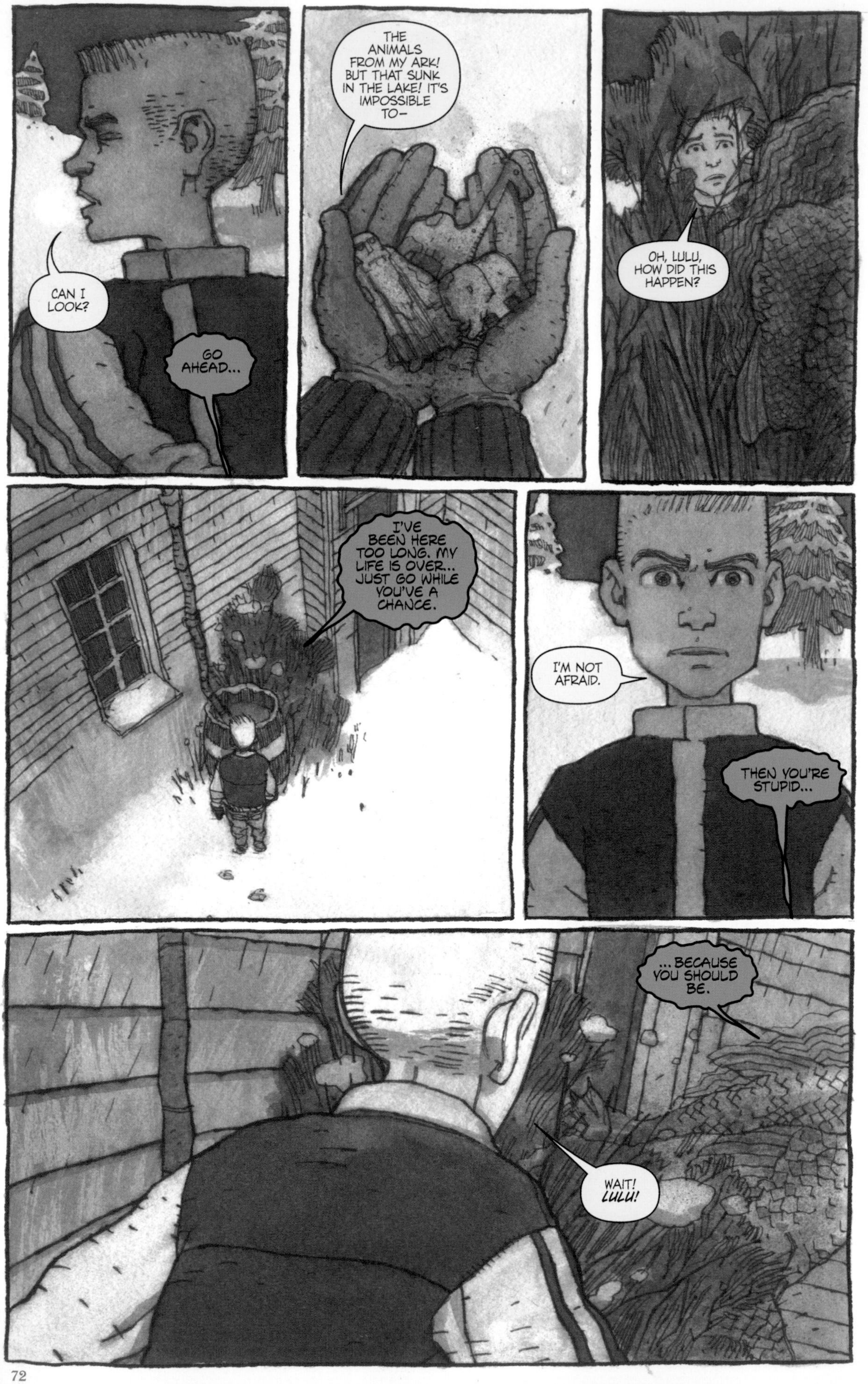
CAN I LOOK?
GO AHEAD...
THE ANIMALS FROM MY ARK! BUT THAT SUNK IN THE LAKE! IT'S IMPOSSIBLE TO–
OH, LULU, HOW DID THIS HAPPEN?
I'VE BEEN HERE TOO LONG. MY LIFE IS OVER... JUST GO WHILE YOU'VE A CHANCE.
I'M NOT AFRAID.
THEN YOU'RE STUPID...
...BECAUSE YOU SHOULD BE.
WAIT! LULU!

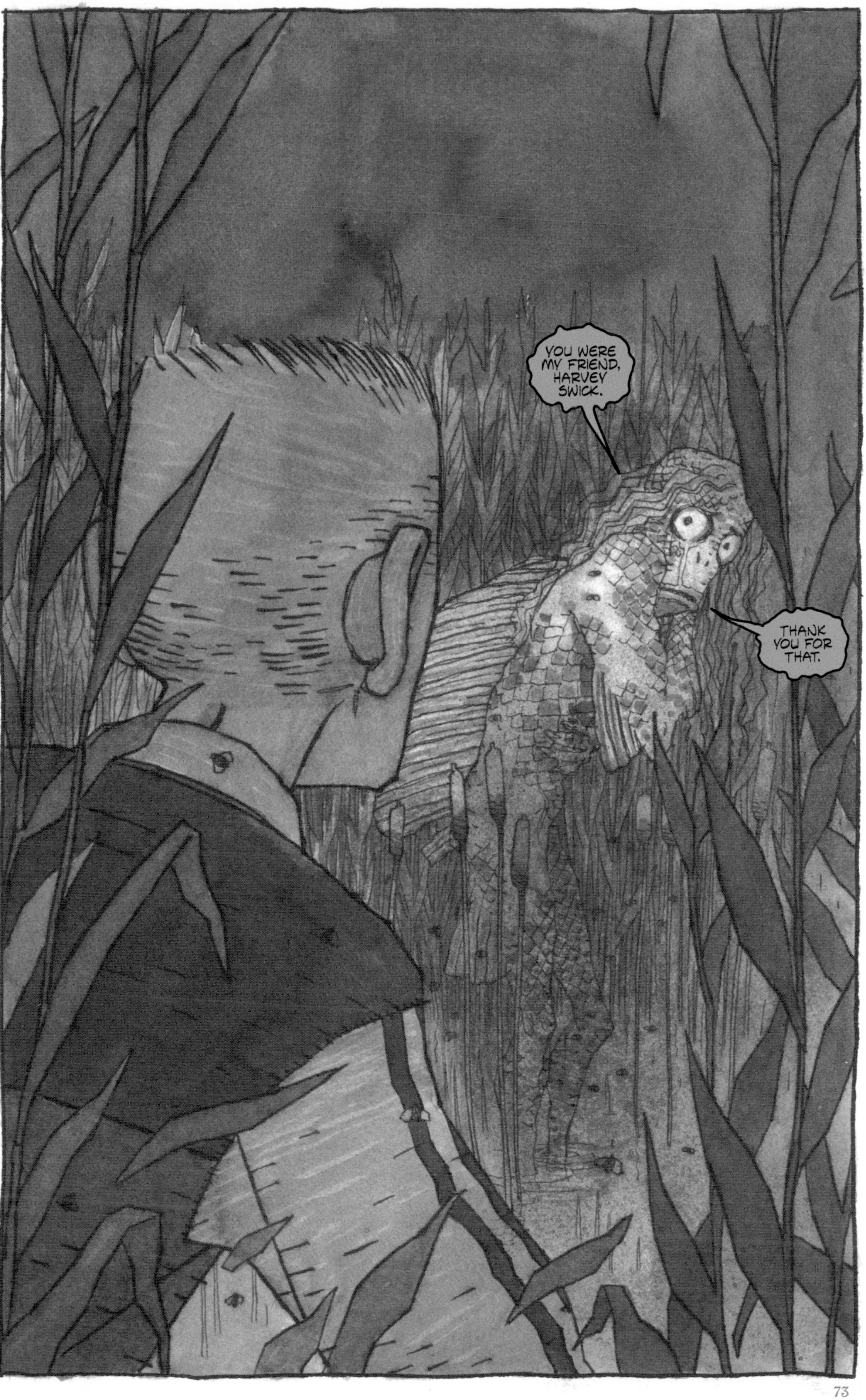
YOU WERE MY FRIEND, HARVEY SWICK.
THANK YOU FOR THAT.

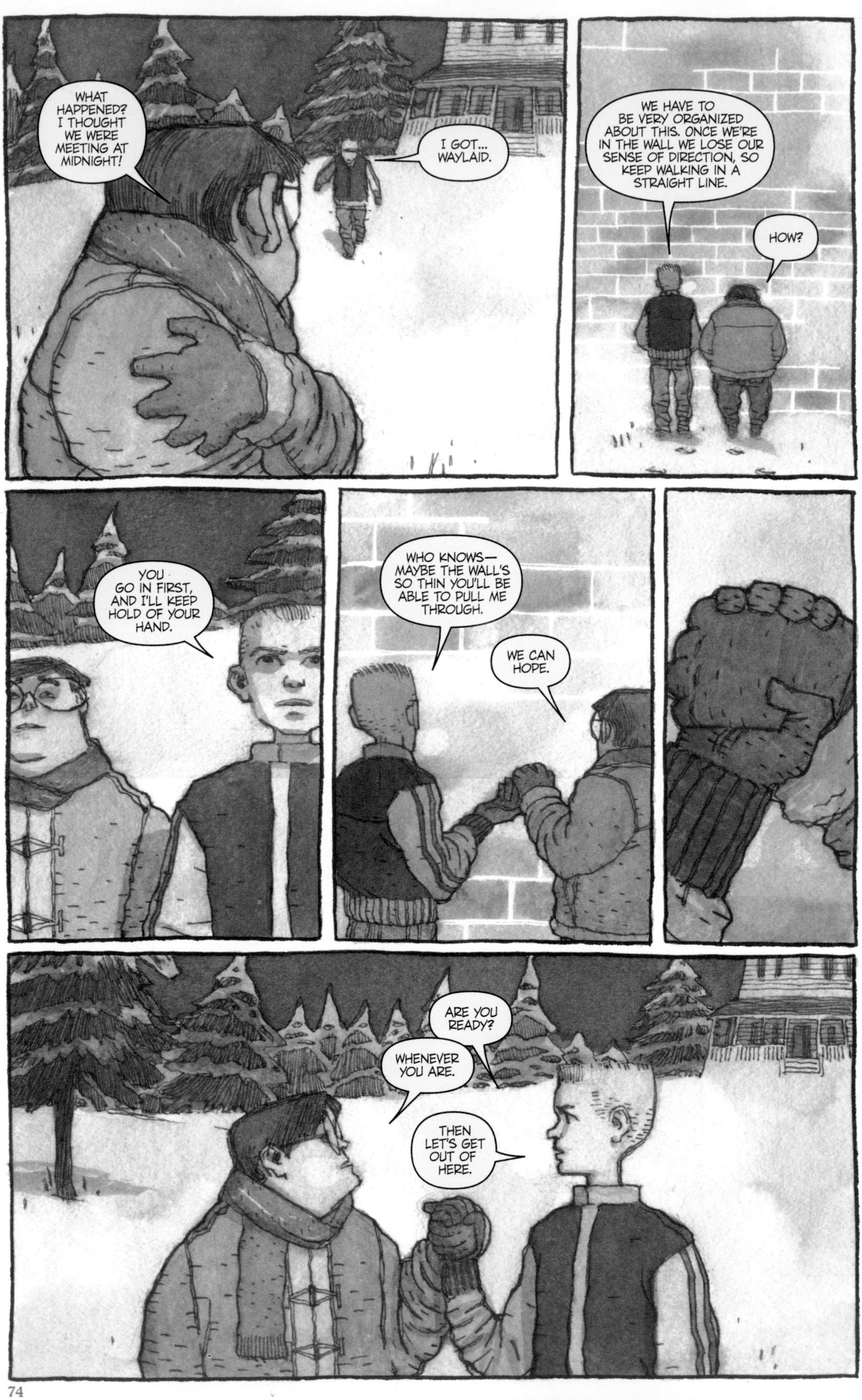
WHAT HAPPENED? I THOUGHT WE WERE MEETING AT MIDNIGHT!
I GOT... WAYLAID.
WE HAVE TO BE VERY ORGANIZED ABOUT THIS. ONCE WE'RE IN THE WALL WE LOSE OUR SENSE OF DIRECTION, SO KEEP WALKING IN A STRAIGHT LINE.
HOW?
YOU GO IN FIRST, AND I'LL KEEP HOLD OF YOUR HAND.
WHO KNOWS— MAYBE THE WALL'S SO THIN YOU'LL BE ABLE TO PULL ME THROUGH.
WE CAN HOPE.
ARE YOU READY?
WHENEVER YOU ARE.
THEN LET'S GET OUT OF HERE.

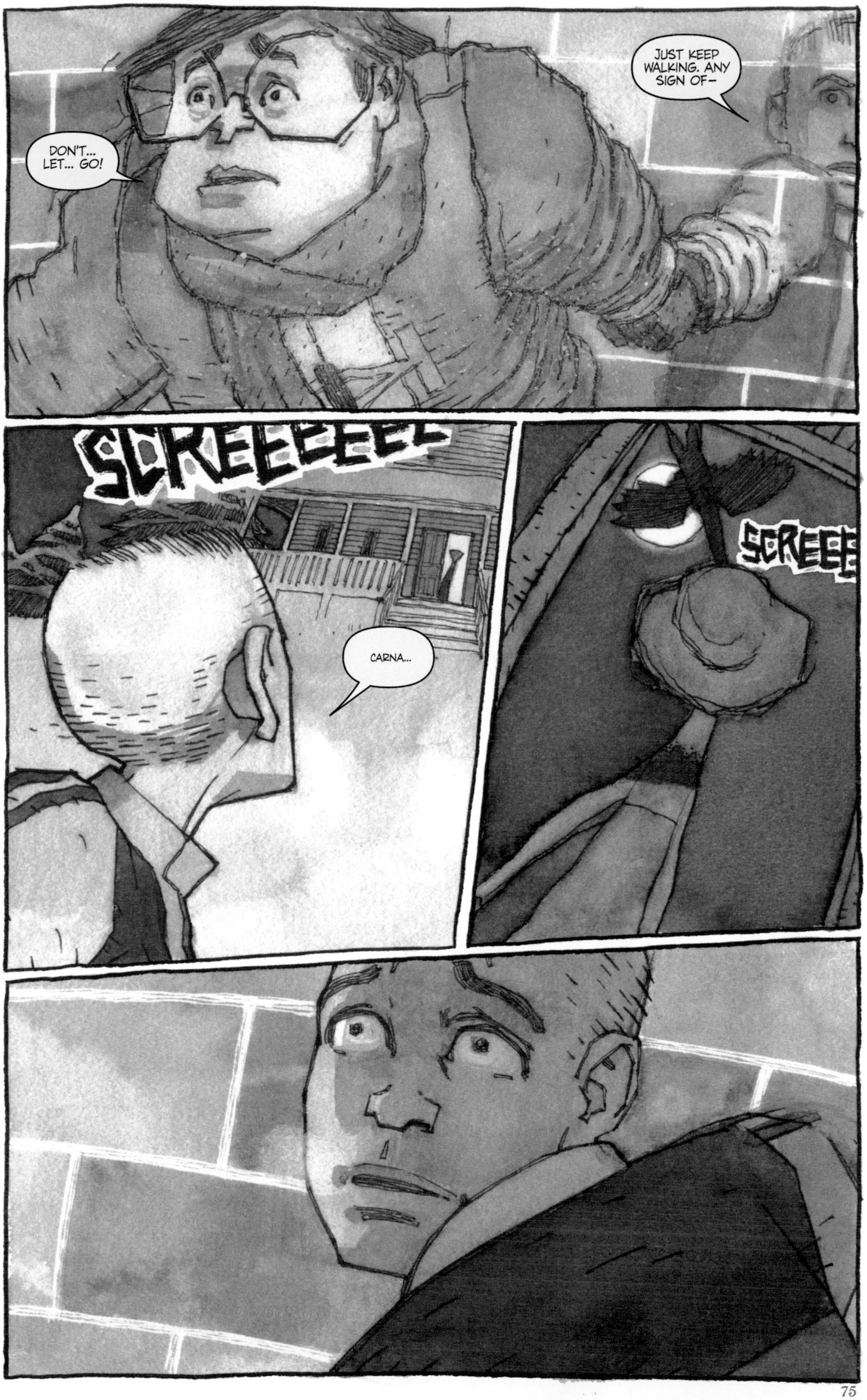
DON'T... LET... GO!
JUST KEEP WALKING. ANY SIGN OF–
SCREEEEEEE
CARNA...
SCREEE

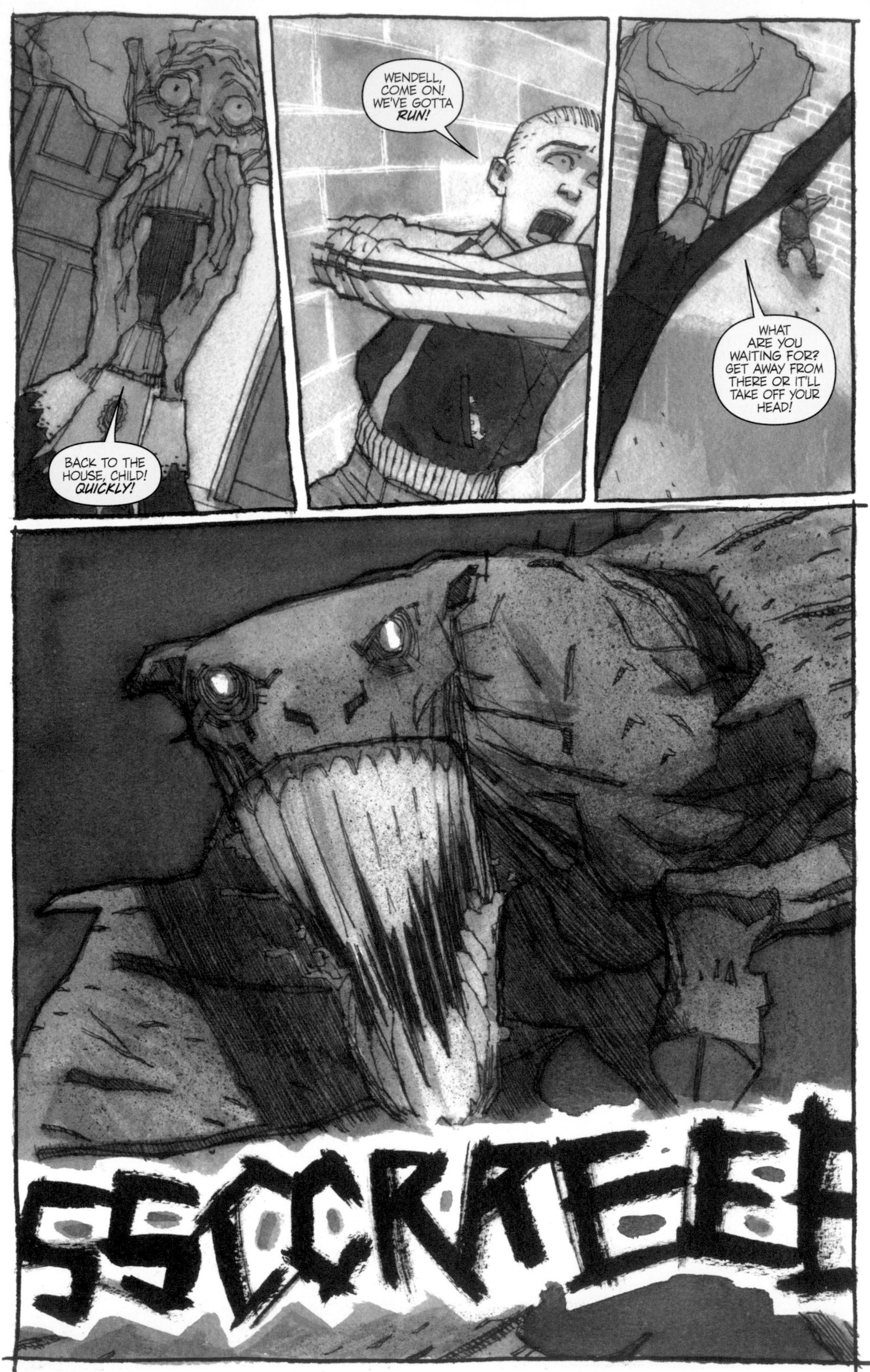
BACK TO THE HOUSE, CHILD! *QUICKLY!*
WENDELL, COME ON! WE'VE GOTTA *RUN!*
WHAT ARE YOU WAITING FOR? GET AWAY FROM THERE OR IT'LL TAKE OFF YOUR HEAD!
SSCCRAEEE

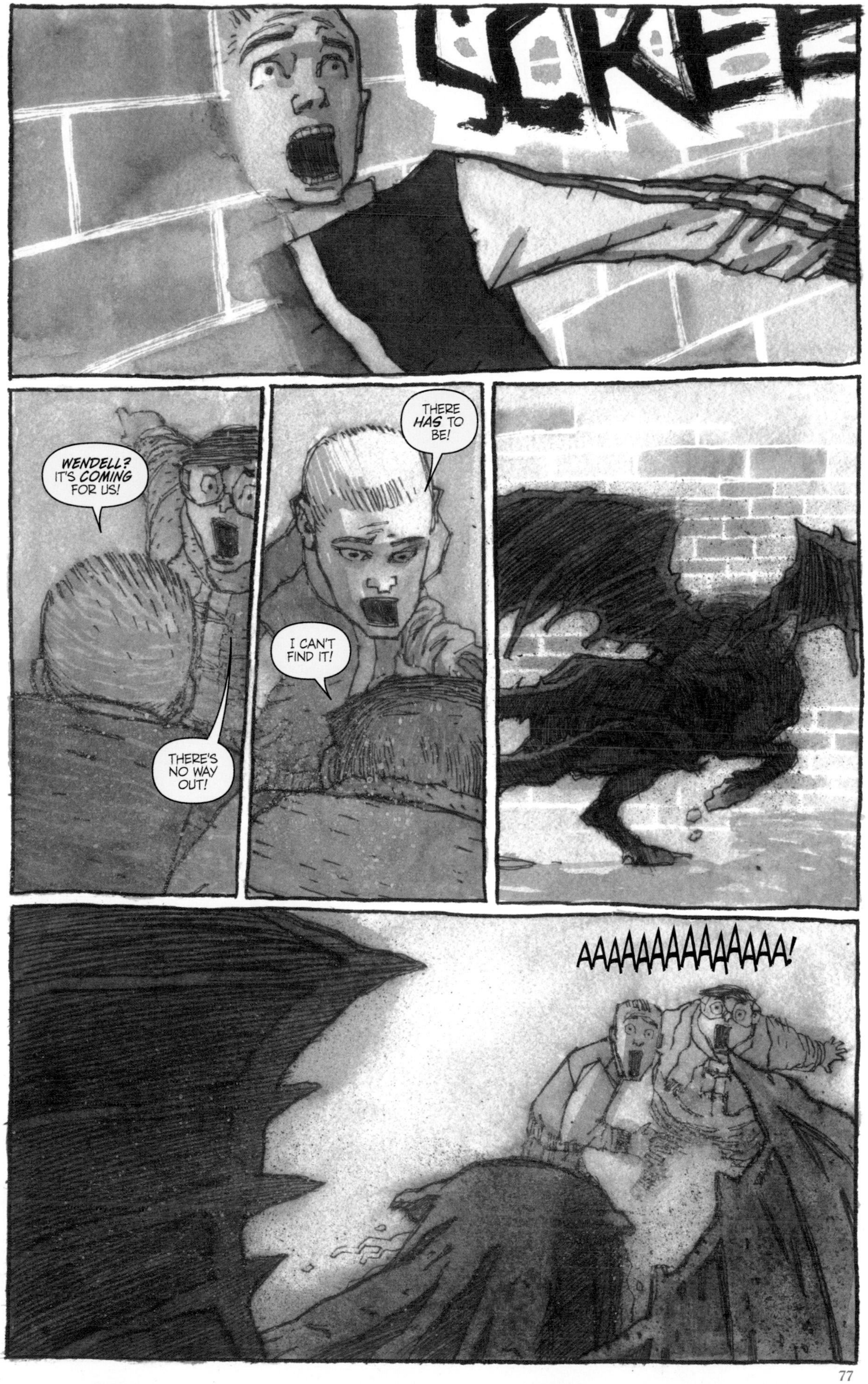
SKREE
WENDELL? IT'S COMING FOR US!
THERE'S NO WAY OUT!
THERE HAS TO BE!
I CAN'T FIND IT!
AAAAAAAAAAAAAA!

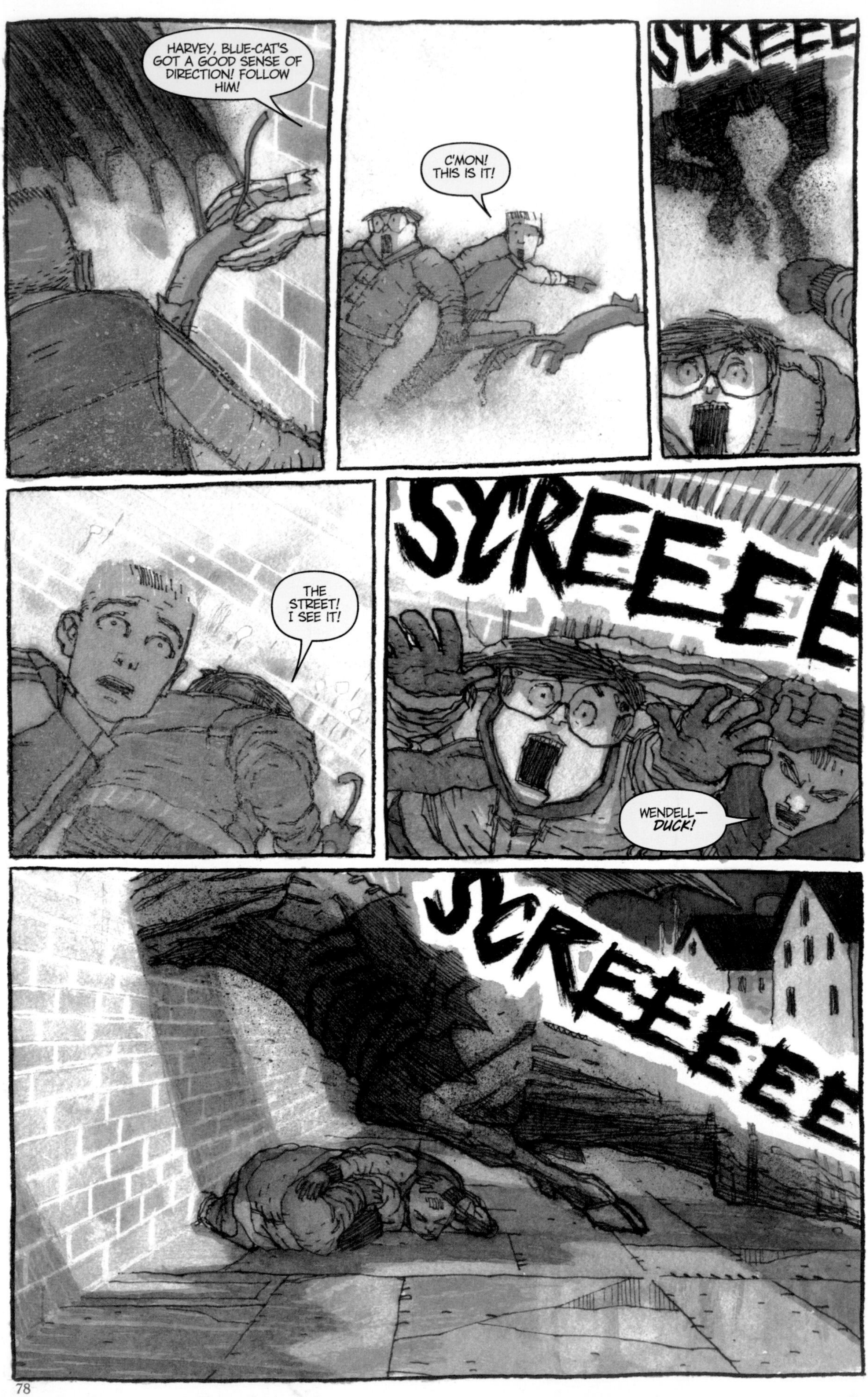
HARVEY, BLUE-CAT'S GOT A GOOD SENSE OF DIRECTION! FOLLOW HIM!
C'MON! THIS IS IT!
SCREEE
THE STREET! I SEE IT!
SCREEEE
WENDELL— DUCK!
SCREEEEEEE

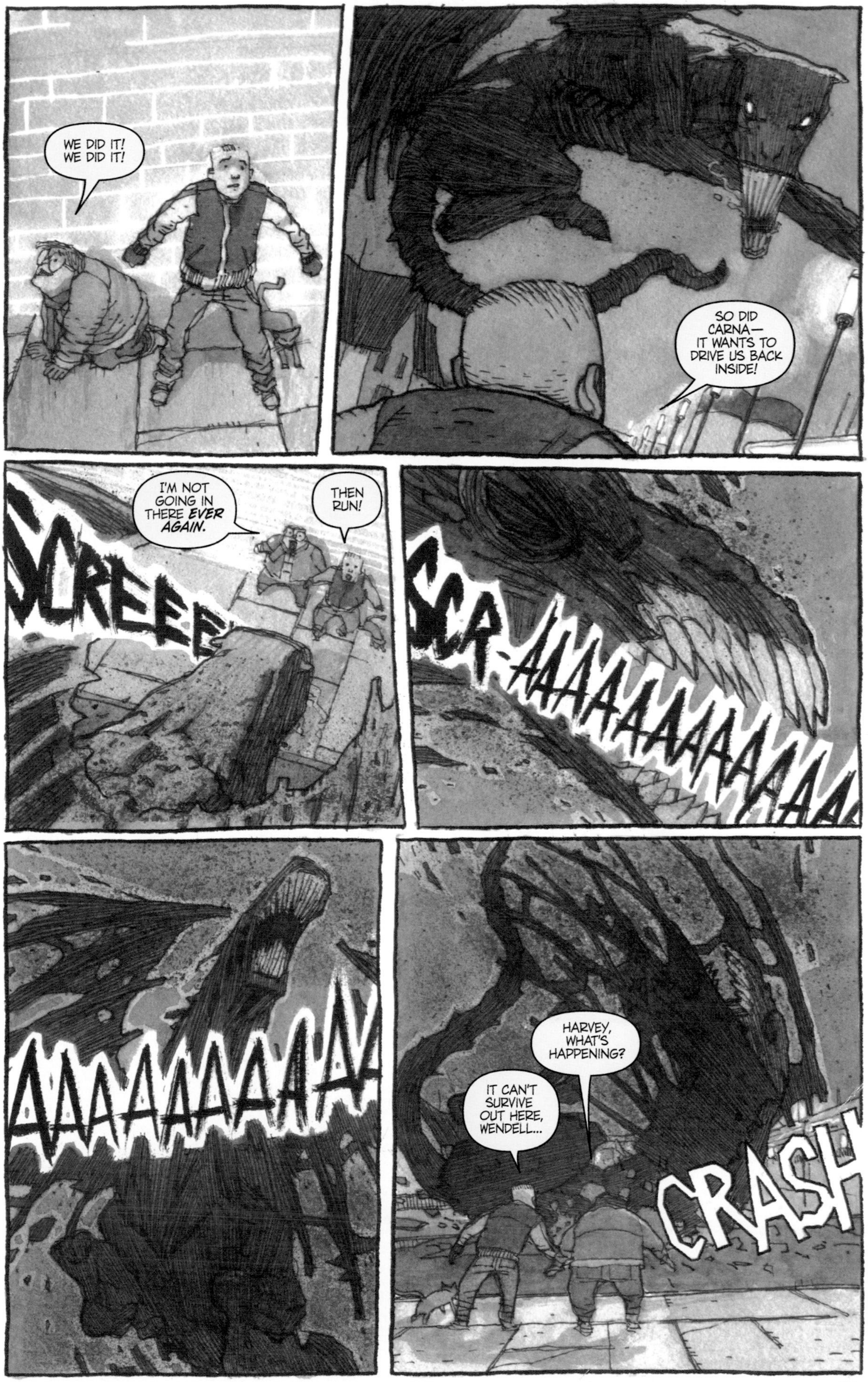
WE DID IT! WE DID IT!
SO DID CARNA— IT WANTS TO DRIVE US BACK INSIDE!
I'M NOT GOING IN THERE EVER AGAIN.
THEN RUN!
SCREEE
SCR-AAAAAAAAAAAAAA
AAAAAAAAAA
HARVEY, WHAT'S HAPPENING?
IT CAN'T SURVIVE OUT HERE, WENDELL...
CRASH

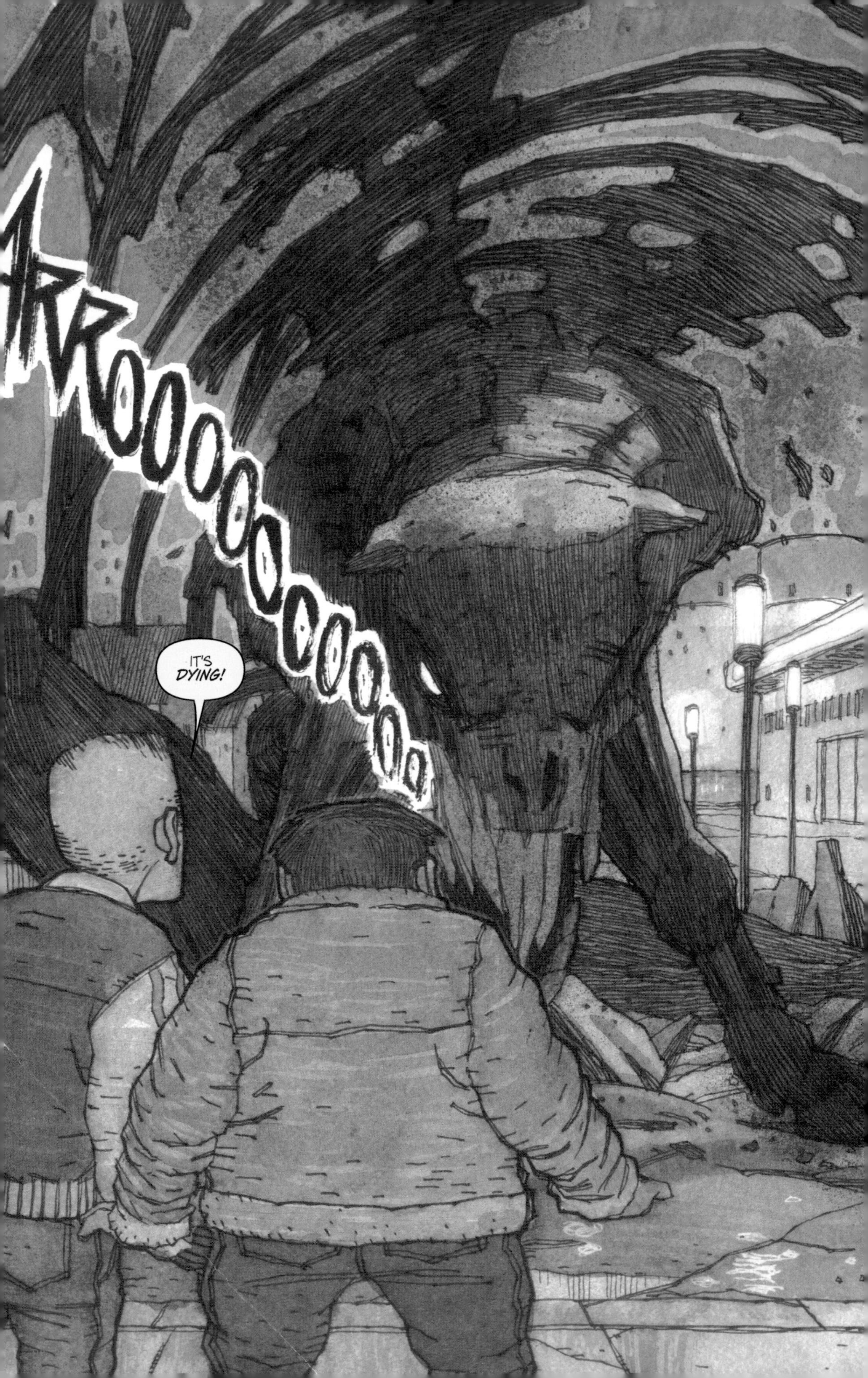
ARROOOOOOOOOO..
IT'S DYING!

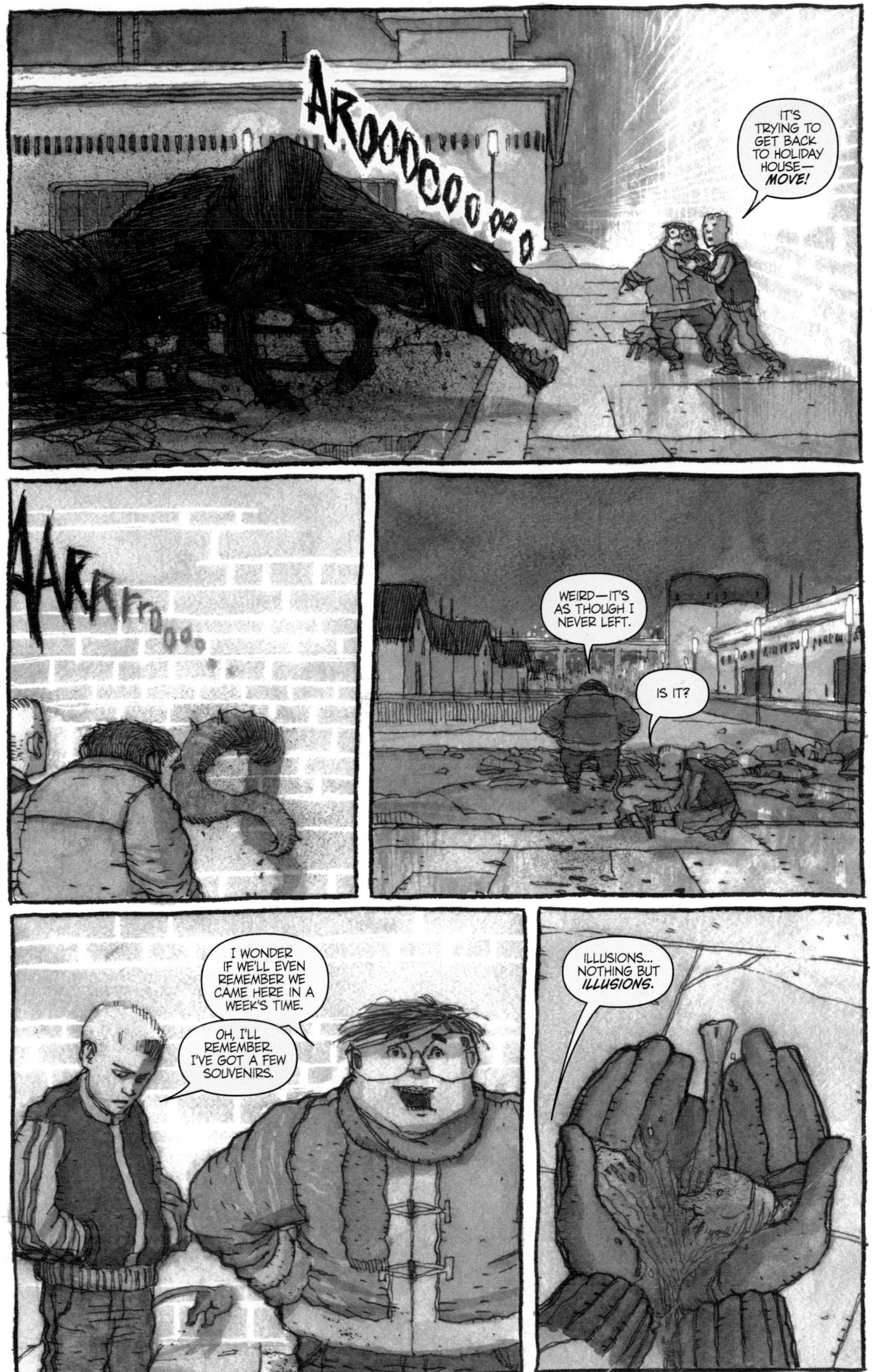
AROOOOOOOOOO
IT'S TRYING TO GET BACK TO HOLIDAY HOUSE—*MOVE!*
AARRRrooo
WEIRD—IT'S AS THOUGH I NEVER LEFT.
IS IT?
I WONDER IF WE'LL EVEN REMEMBER WE CAME HERE IN A WEEK'S TIME.
OH, I'LL REMEMBER. I'VE GOT A FEW SOUVENIRS.
ILLUSIONS... NOTHING BUT *ILLUSIONS.*

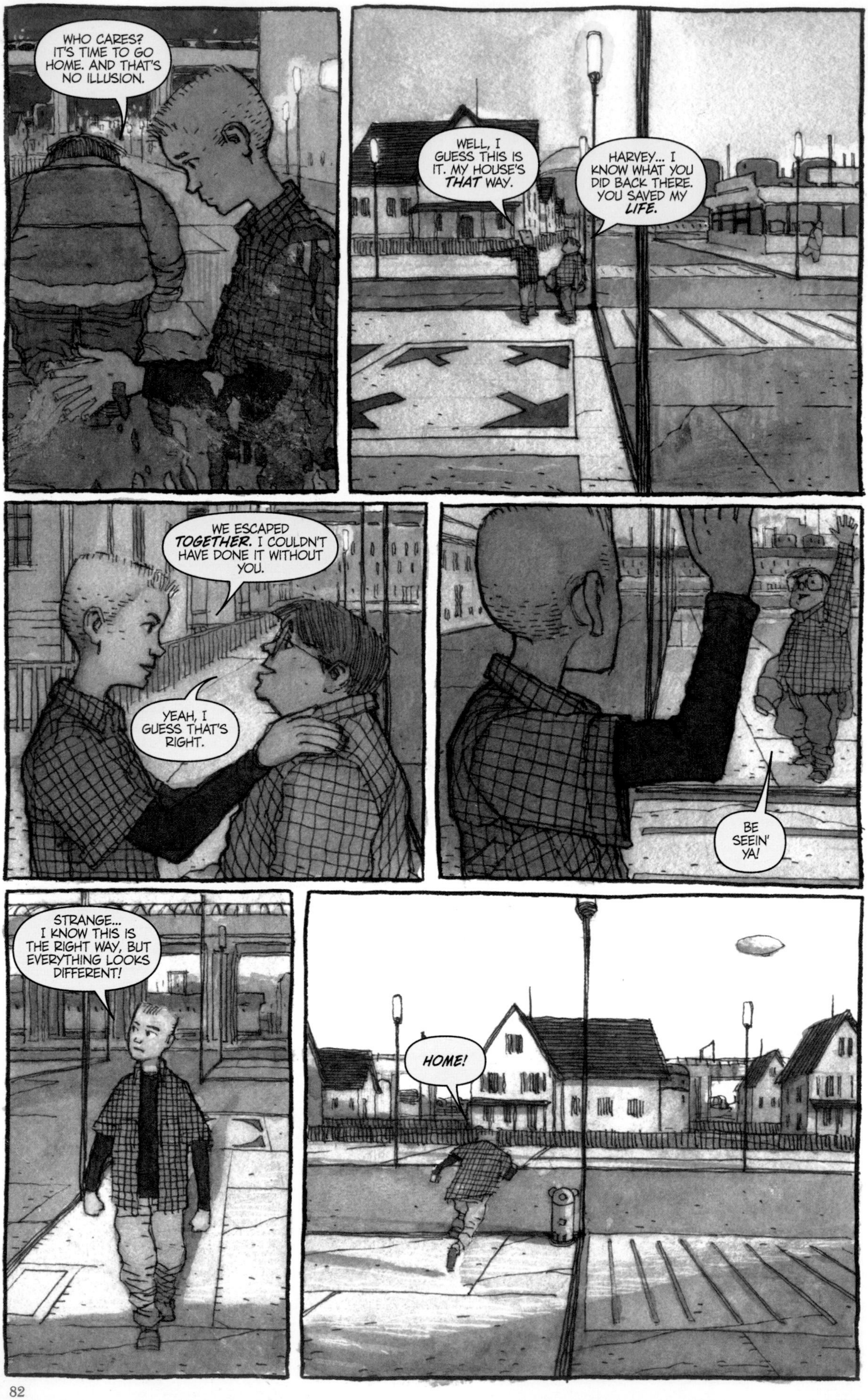
WHO CARES? IT'S TIME TO GO HOME. AND THAT'S NO ILLUSION.
WELL, I GUESS THIS IS IT. MY HOUSE'S THAT WAY.
HARVEY... I KNOW WHAT YOU DID BACK THERE. YOU SAVED MY LIFE.
WE ESCAPED TOGETHER. I COULDN'T HAVE DONE IT WITHOUT YOU.
YEAH, I GUESS THAT'S RIGHT.
BE SEEIN' YA!
STRANGE... I KNOW THIS IS THE RIGHT WAY, BUT EVERYTHING LOOKS DIFFERENT!
HOME!

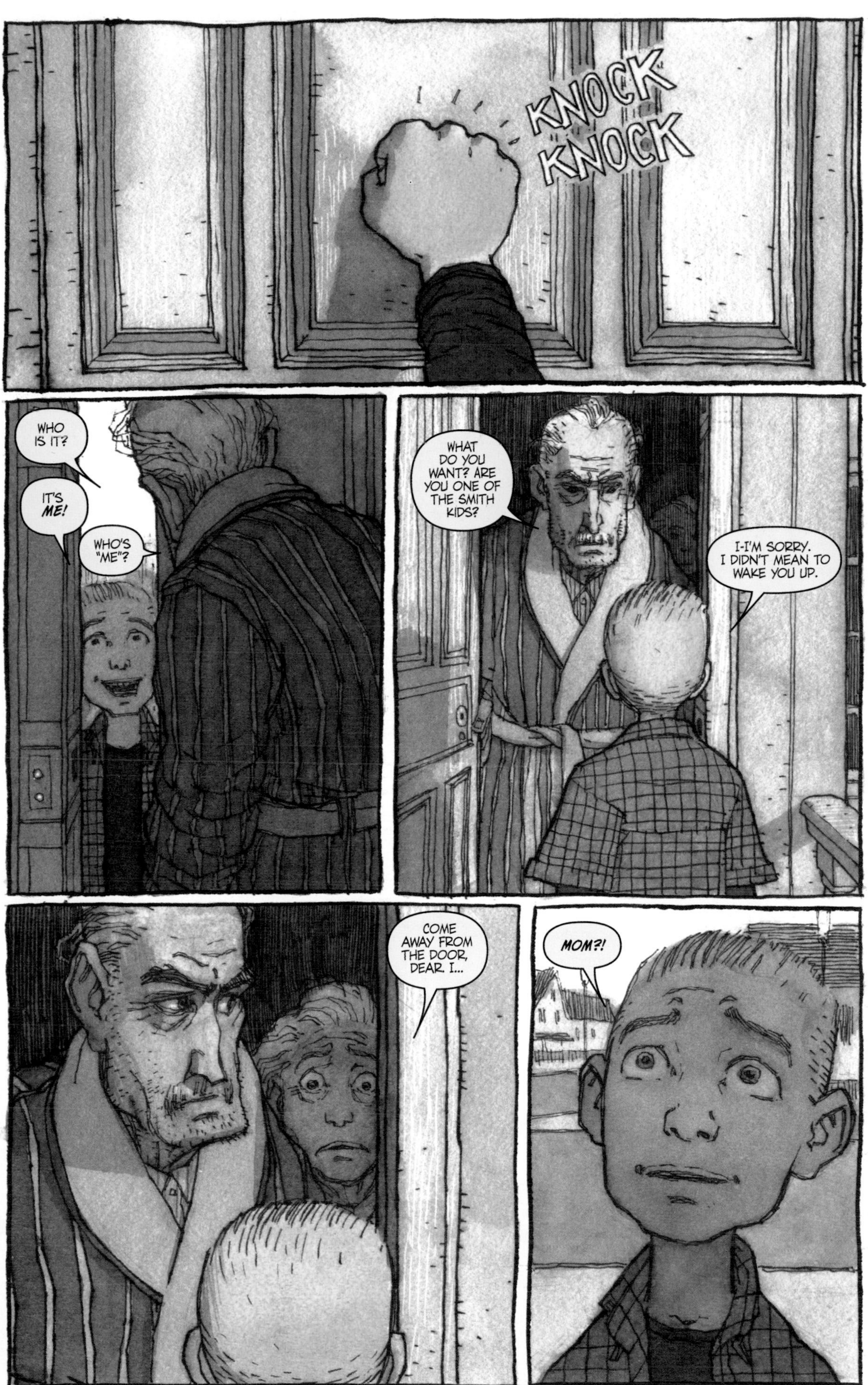
KNOCK KNOCK
WHO IS IT?
IT'S ME!
WHO'S "ME"?
WHAT DO YOU WANT? ARE YOU ONE OF THE SMITH KIDS?
I-I'M SORRY. I DIDN'T MEAN TO WAKE YOU UP.
COME AWAY FROM THE DOOR, DEAR. I...
MOM?!

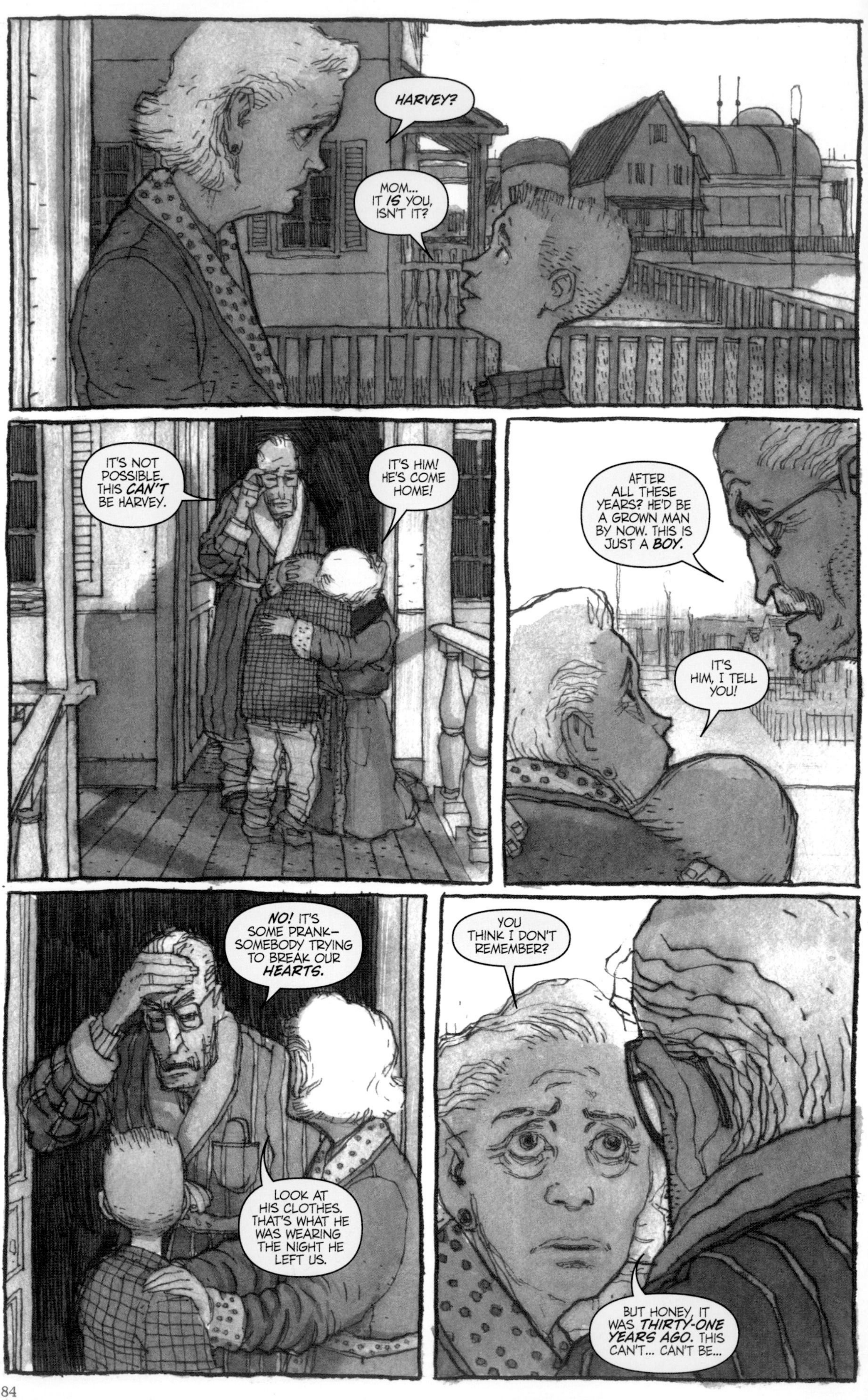
HARVEY?
MOM... IT IS YOU, ISN'T IT?
IT'S NOT POSSIBLE. THIS CAN'T BE HARVEY.
IT'S HIM! HE'S COME HOME!
AFTER ALL THESE YEARS? HE'D BE A GROWN MAN BY NOW. THIS IS JUST A BOY.
IT'S HIM, I TELL YOU!
NO! IT'S SOME PRANK— SOMEBODY TRYING TO BREAK OUR HEARTS.
LOOK AT HIS CLOTHES. THAT'S WHAT HE WAS WEARING THE NIGHT HE LEFT US.
YOU THINK I DON'T REMEMBER?
BUT HONEY, IT WAS THIRTY-ONE YEARS AGO. THIS CAN'T... CAN'T BE...

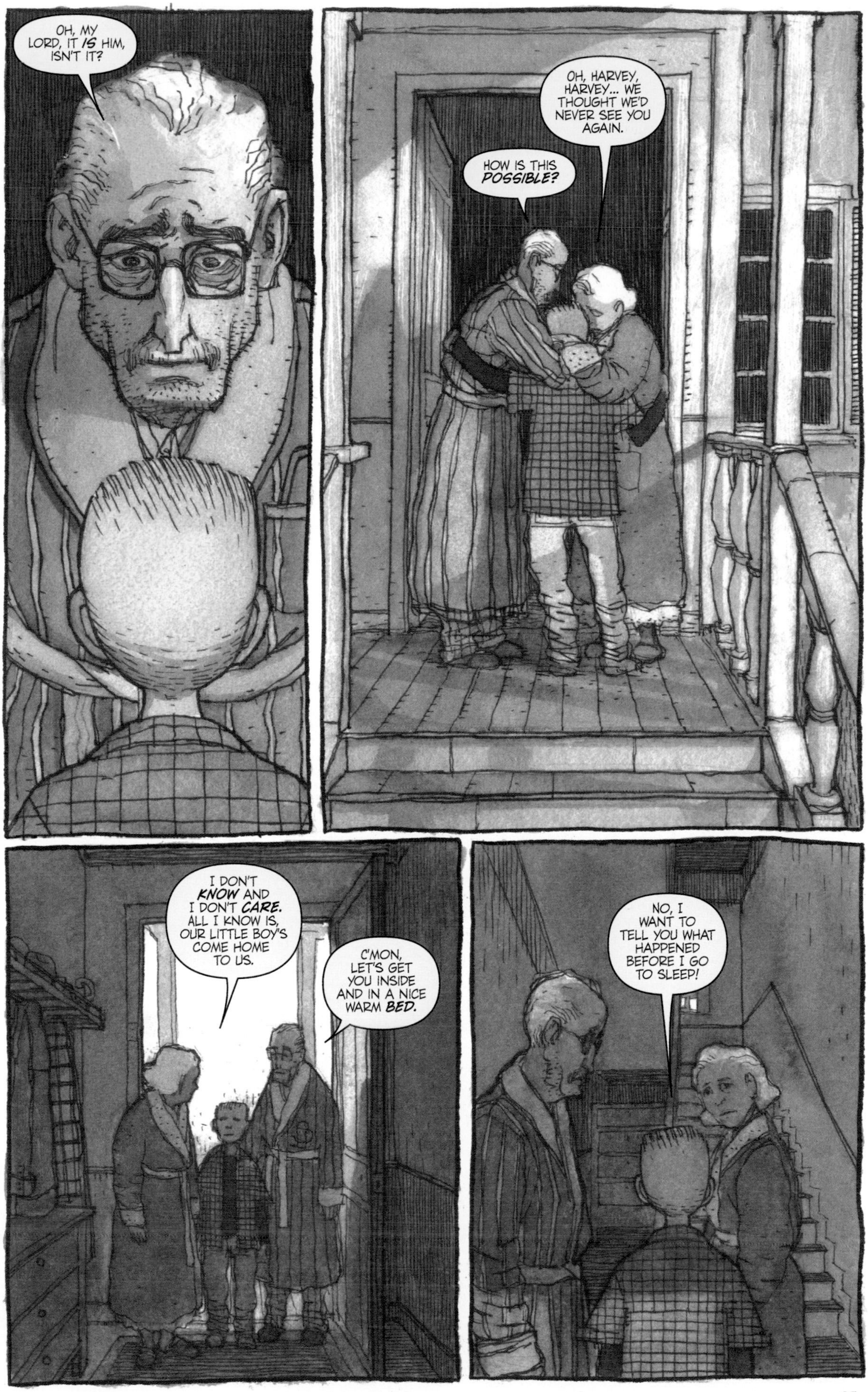
OH, MY LORD, IT *IS* HIM, ISN'T IT?
OH, HARVEY, HARVEY... WE THOUGHT WE'D NEVER SEE YOU AGAIN.
HOW IS THIS *POSSIBLE?*
I DON'T *KNOW* AND I DON'T *CARE.* ALL I KNOW IS, OUR LITTLE BOY'S COME HOME TO US.
C'MON, LET'S GET YOU INSIDE AND IN A NICE WARM *BED.*
NO, I WANT TO TELL YOU WHAT HAPPENED BEFORE I GO TO SLEEP!

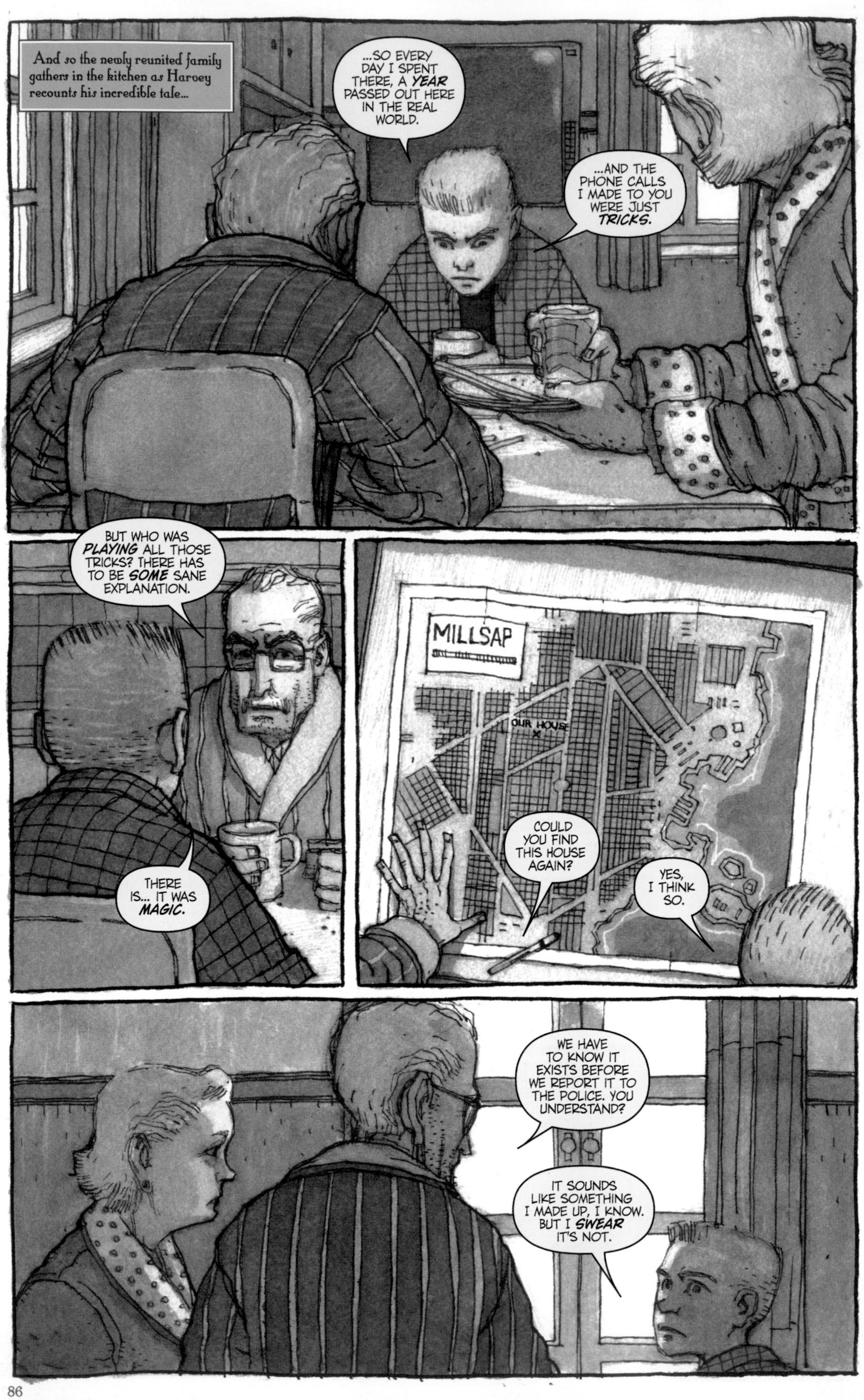
And so the newly reunited family gathers in the kitchen as Harvey recounts his incredible tale...
...SO EVERY DAY I SPENT THERE, A YEAR PASSED OUT HERE IN THE REAL WORLD.
...AND THE PHONE CALLS I MADE TO YOU WERE JUST TRICKS.
BUT WHO WAS PLAYING ALL THOSE TRICKS? THERE HAS TO BE SOME SANE EXPLANATION.
THERE IS... IT WAS MAGIC.
MILLSAP
OUR HOUSE
COULD YOU FIND THIS HOUSE AGAIN?
YES, I THINK SO.
WE HAVE TO KNOW IT EXISTS BEFORE WE REPORT IT TO THE POLICE. YOU UNDERSTAND?
IT SOUNDS LIKE SOMETHING I MADE UP, I KNOW. BUT I SWEAR IT'S NOT.

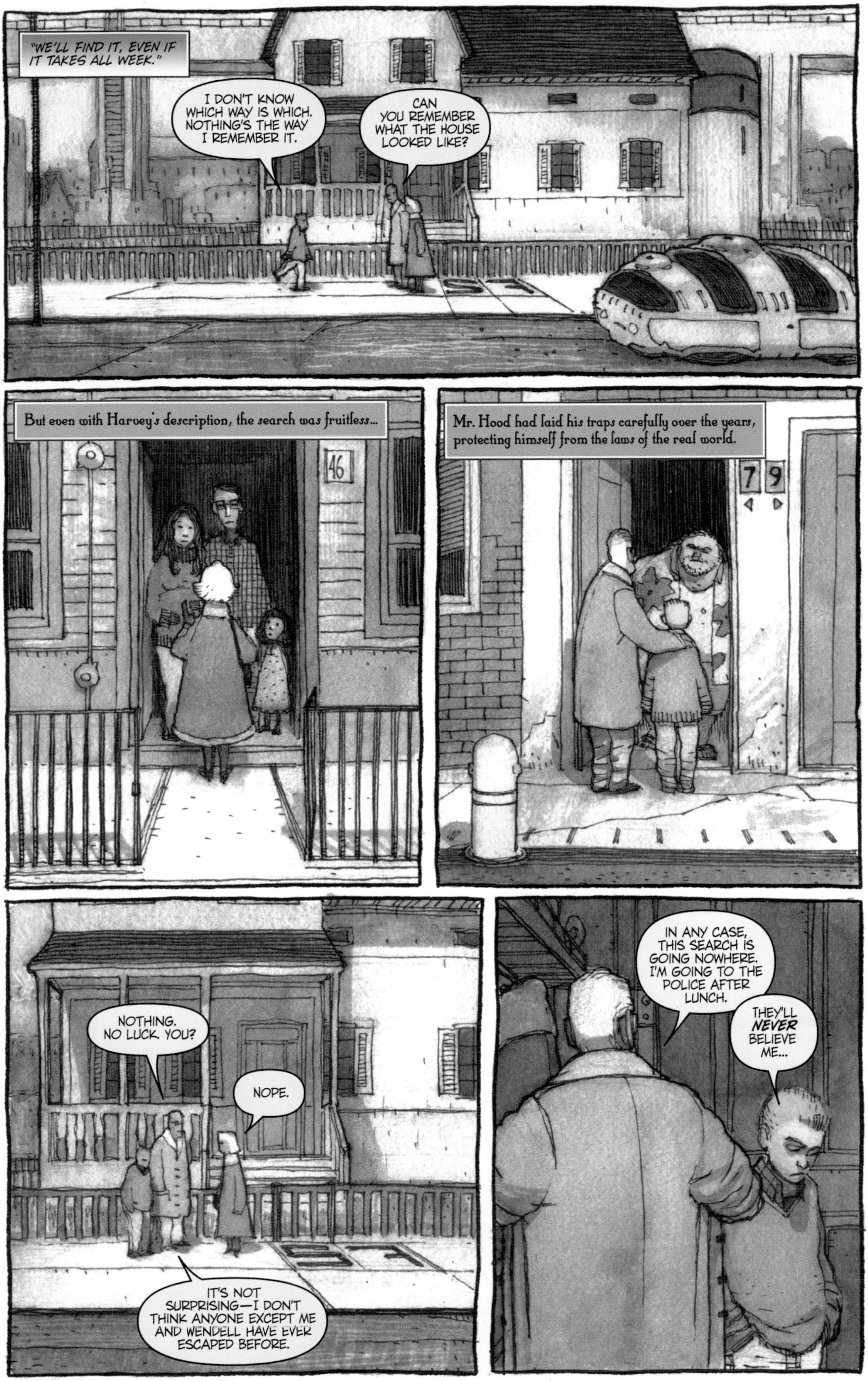

"WE'LL FIND IT, EVEN IF IT TAKES ALL WEEK."
I DON'T KNOW WHICH WAY IS WHICH. NOTHING'S THE WAY I REMEMBER IT.
CAN YOU REMEMBER WHAT THE HOUSE LOOKED LIKE?
But even with Harvey's description, the search was fruitless...
46
Mr. Hood had laid his traps carefully over the years, protecting himself from the laws of the real world.
79
NOTHING. NO LUCK. YOU?
NOPE.
IT'S NOT SURPRISING—I DON'T THINK ANYONE EXCEPT ME AND WENDELL HAVE EVER ESCAPED BEFORE.
IN ANY CASE, THIS SEARCH IS GOING NOWHERE. I'M GOING TO THE POLICE AFTER LUNCH.
THEY'LL ***NEVER*** BELIEVE ME...

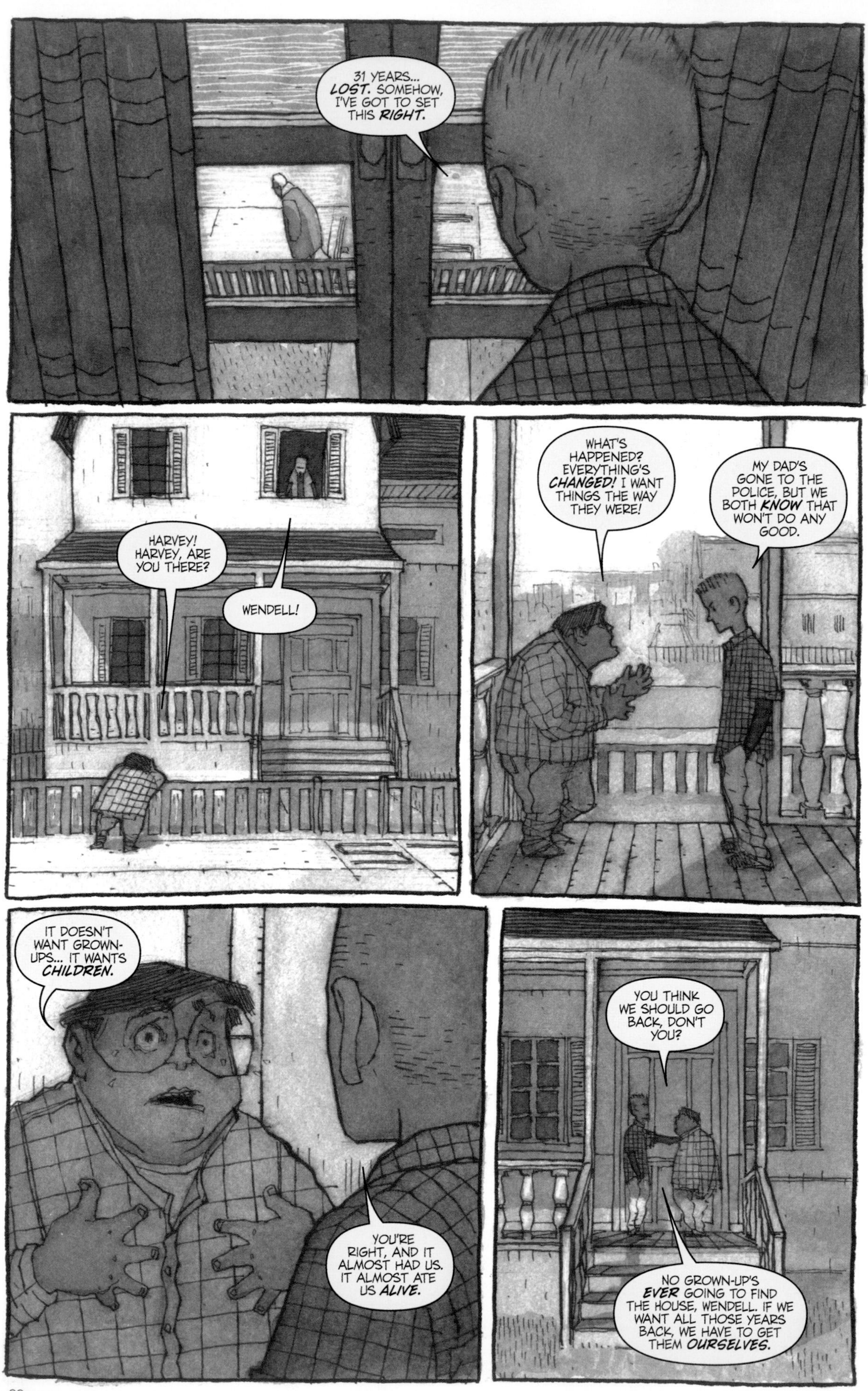
31 YEARS... LOST. SOMEHOW, I'VE GOT TO SET THIS RIGHT.
HARVEY! HARVEY, ARE YOU THERE?
WENDELL!
WHAT'S HAPPENED? EVERYTHING'S CHANGED! I WANT THINGS THE WAY THEY WERE!
MY DAD'S GONE TO THE POLICE, BUT WE BOTH KNOW THAT WON'T DO ANY GOOD.
IT DOESN'T WANT GROWN-UPS... IT WANTS CHILDREN.
YOU'RE RIGHT, AND IT ALMOST HAD US. IT ALMOST ATE US ALIVE.
YOU THINK WE SHOULD GO BACK, DON'T YOU?
NO GROWN-UP'S EVER GOING TO FIND THE HOUSE, WENDELL. IF WE WANT ALL THOSE YEARS BACK, WE HAVE TO GET THEM OURSELVES.

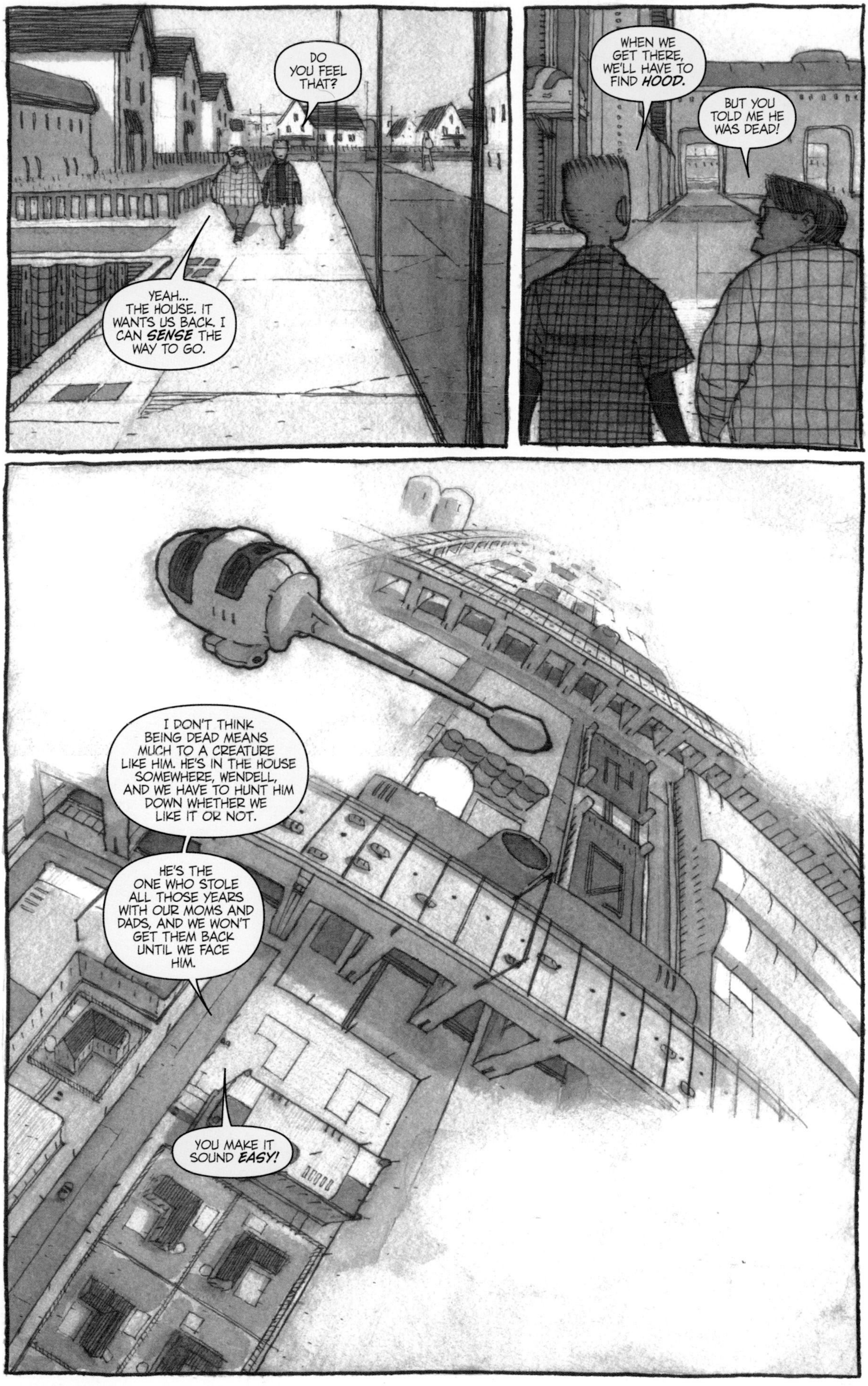
DO YOU FEEL THAT?
YEAH... THE HOUSE. IT WANTS US BACK. I CAN SENSE THE WAY TO GO.
WHEN WE GET THERE, WE'LL HAVE TO FIND HOOD.
BUT YOU TOLD ME HE WAS DEAD!
I DON'T THINK BEING DEAD MEANS MUCH TO A CREATURE LIKE HIM. HE'S IN THE HOUSE SOMEWHERE, WENDELL, AND WE HAVE TO HUNT HIM DOWN WHETHER WE LIKE IT OR NOT.
HE'S THE ONE WHO STOLE ALL THOSE YEARS WITH OUR MOMS AND DADS, AND WE WON'T GET THEM BACK UNTIL WE FACE HIM.
YOU MAKE IT SOUND EASY!

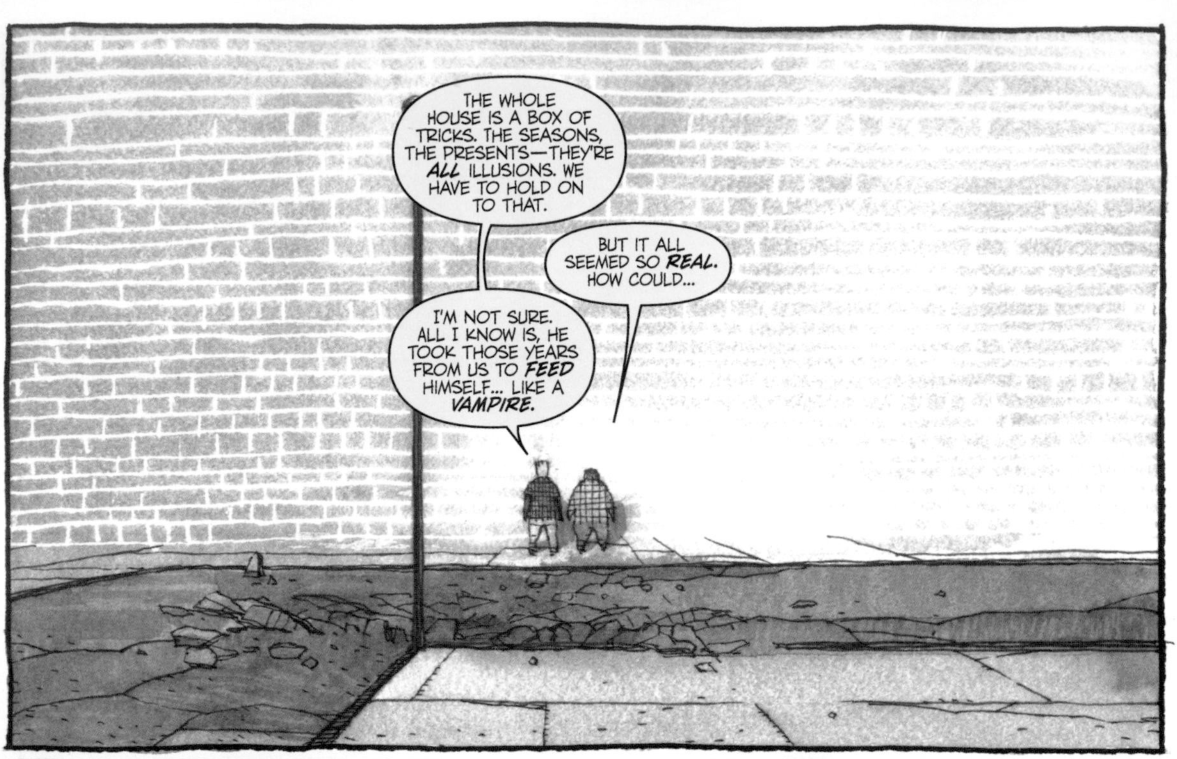
THE WHOLE HOUSE IS A BOX OF TRICKS. THE SEASONS, THE PRESENTS—THEY'RE ALL ILLUSIONS. WE HAVE TO HOLD ON TO THAT.
BUT IT ALL SEEMED SO REAL. HOW COULD...
I'M NOT SURE. ALL I KNOW IS, HE TOOK THOSE YEARS FROM US TO FEED HIMSELF... LIKE A VAMPIRE.

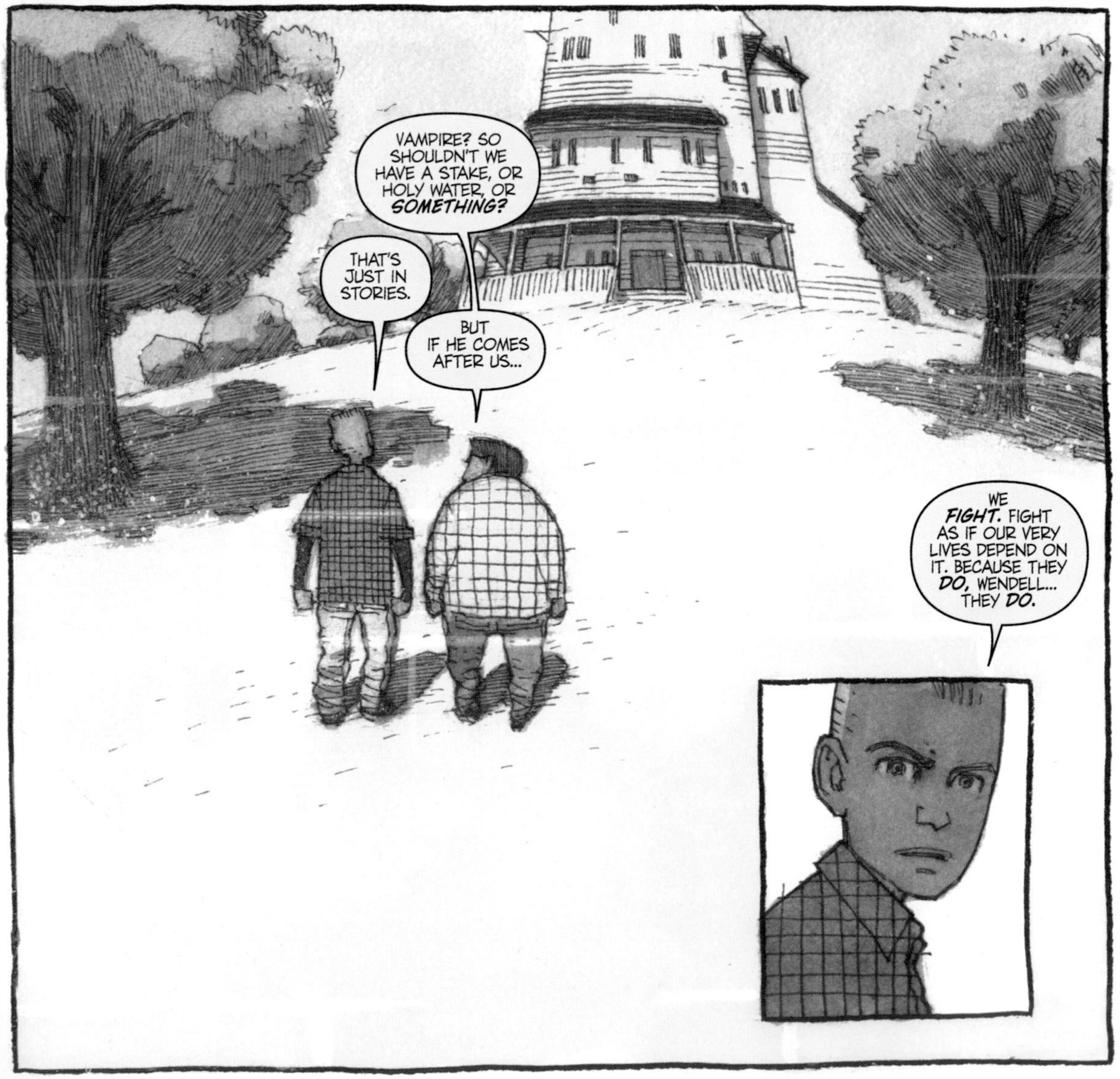
VAMPIRE? SO SHOULDN'T WE HAVE A STAKE, OR HOLY WATER, OR SOMETHING?
THAT'S JUST IN STORIES.
BUT IF HE COMES AFTER US...
WE FIGHT. FIGHT AS IF OUR VERY LIVES DEPEND ON IT. BECAUSE THEY DO, WENDELL... THEY DO.

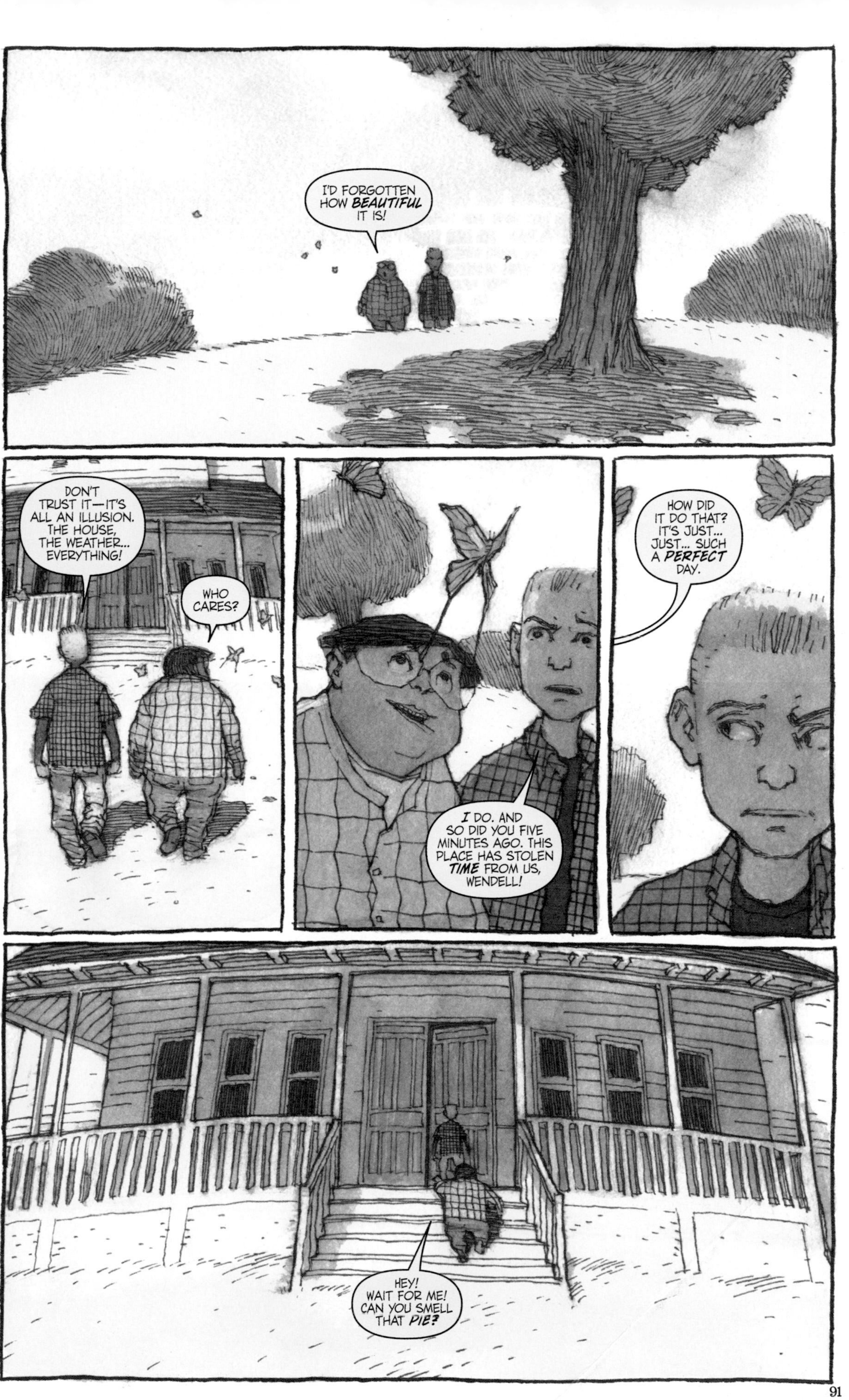
I'D FORGOTTEN HOW BEAUTIFUL IT IS!
DON'T TRUST IT—IT'S ALL AN ILLUSION. THE HOUSE, THE WEATHER... EVERYTHING!
WHO CARES?
I DO. AND SO DID YOU FIVE MINUTES AGO. THIS PLACE HAS STOLEN TIME FROM US, WENDELL!
HOW DID IT DO THAT? IT'S JUST... JUST... SUCH A PERFECT DAY.
HEY! WAIT FOR ME! CAN YOU SMELL THAT PIE?

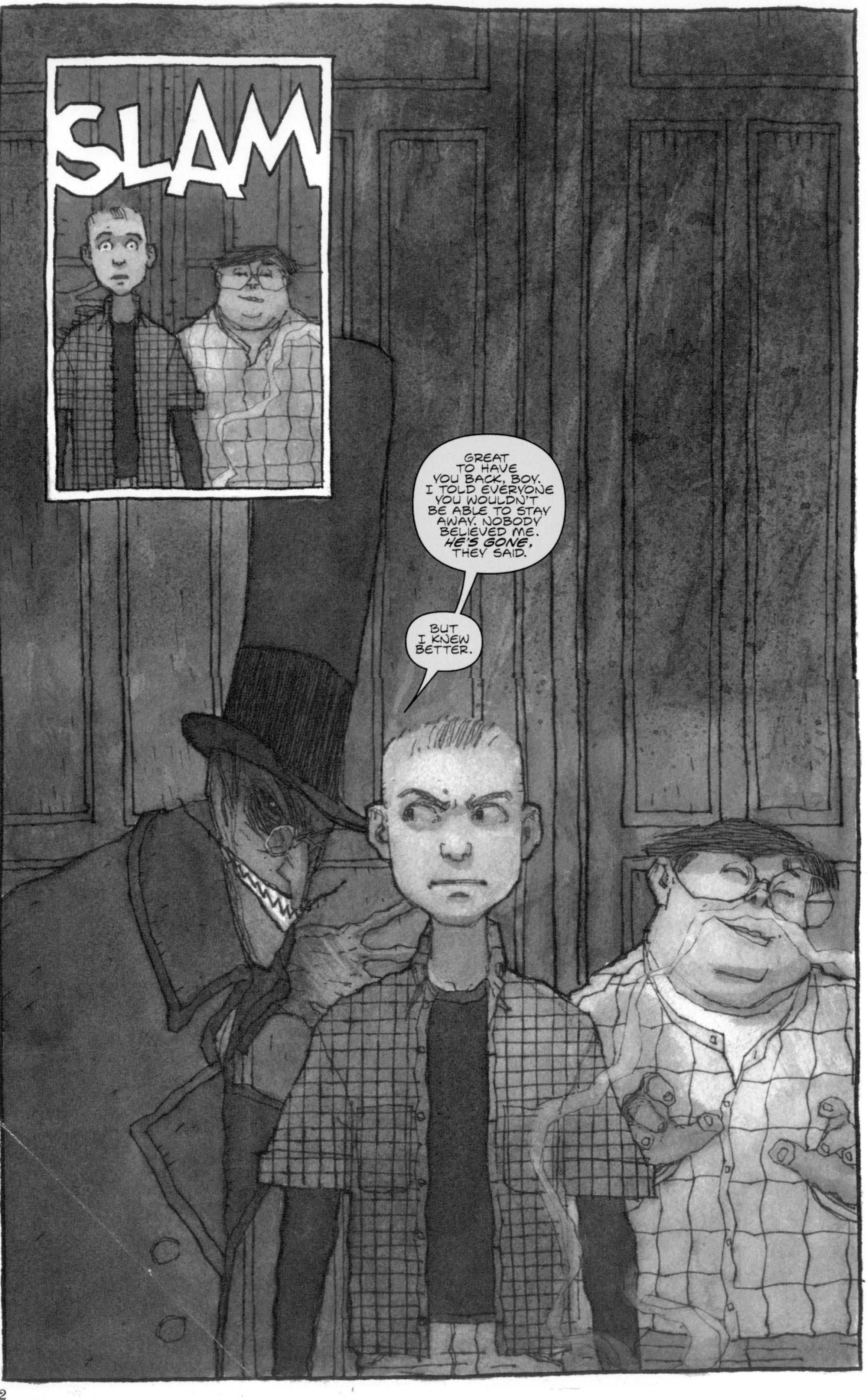
SLAM
GREAT TO HAVE YOU BACK, BOY. I TOLD EVERYONE YOU WOULDN'T BE ABLE TO STAY AWAY. NOBODY BELIEVED ME. HE'S GONE, THEY SAID.
BUT I KNEW BETTER.

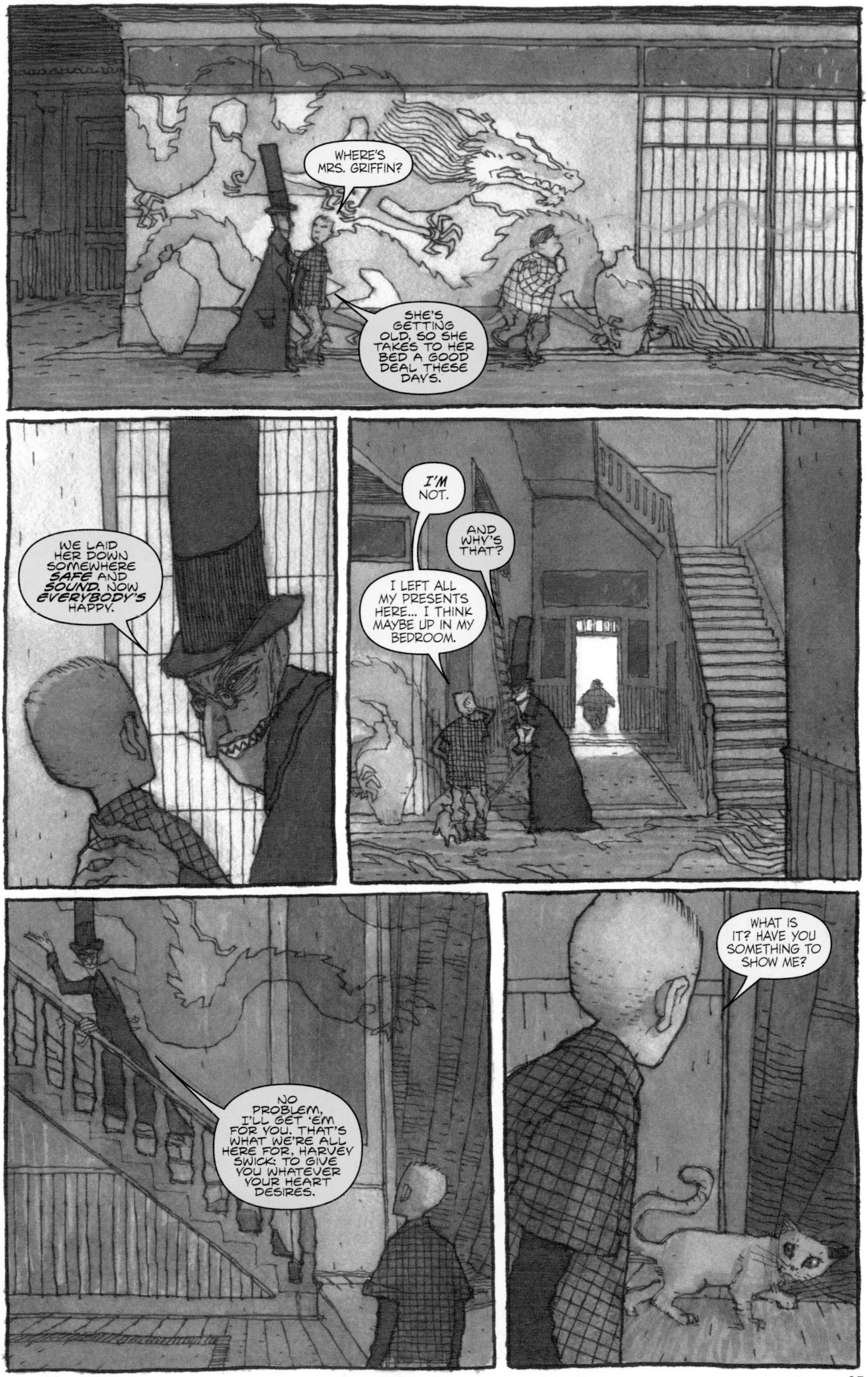
WHERE'S MRS. GRIFFIN?
SHE'S GETTING OLD, SO SHE TAKES TO HER BED A GOOD DEAL THESE DAYS.
WE LAID HER DOWN SOMEWHERE SAFE AND SOUND. NOW EVERYBODY'S HAPPY.
I'M NOT.
AND WHY'S THAT?
I LEFT ALL MY PRESENTS HERE... I THINK MAYBE UP IN MY BEDROOM.
NO PROBLEM, I'LL GET 'EM FOR YOU. THAT'S WHAT WE'RE ALL HERE FOR, HARVEY SWICK: TO GIVE YOU WHATEVER YOUR HEART DESIRES.
WHAT IS IT? HAVE YOU SOMETHING TO SHOW ME?

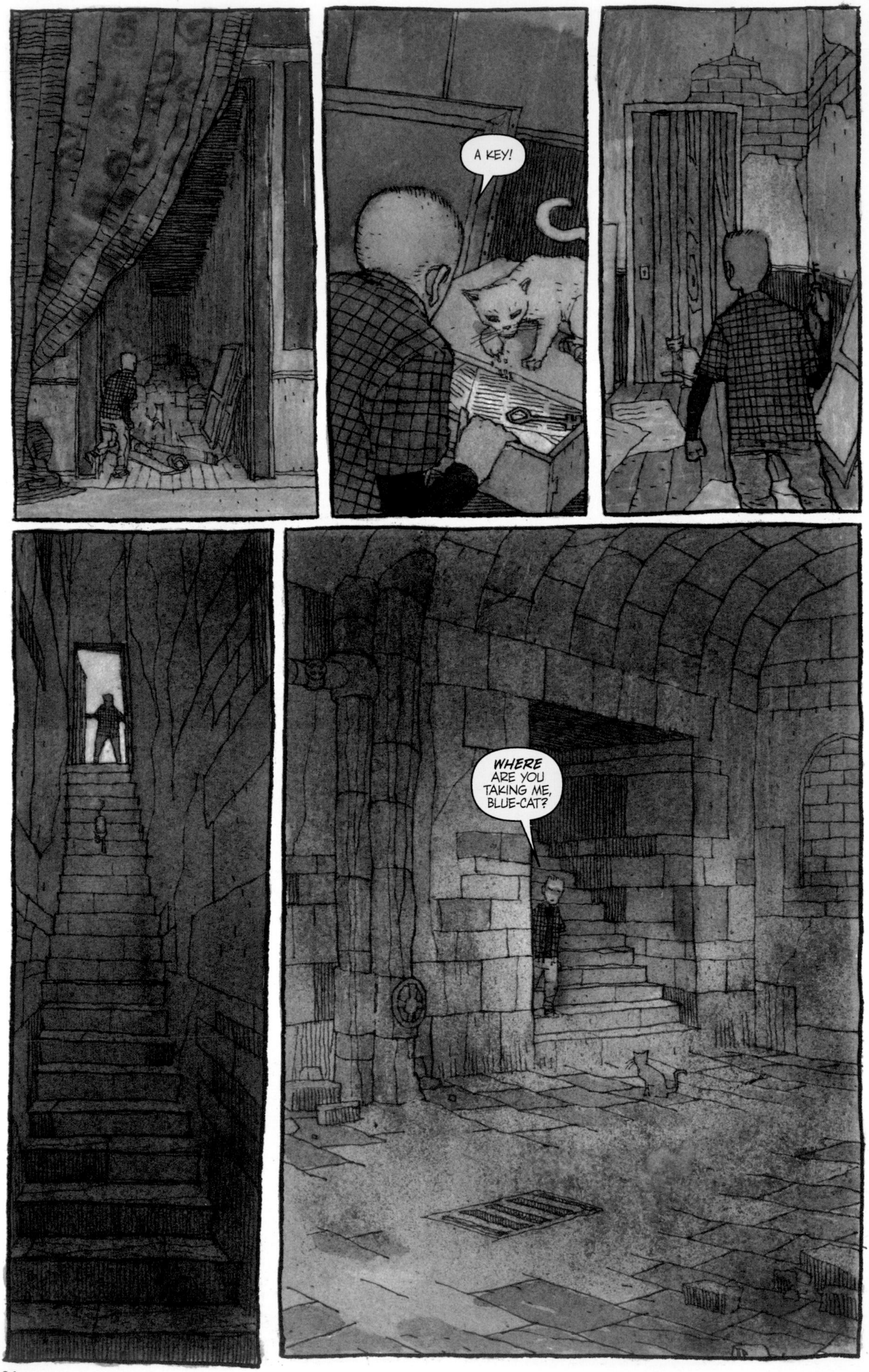
A KEY!
WHERE ARE YOU TAKING ME, BLUE-CAT?

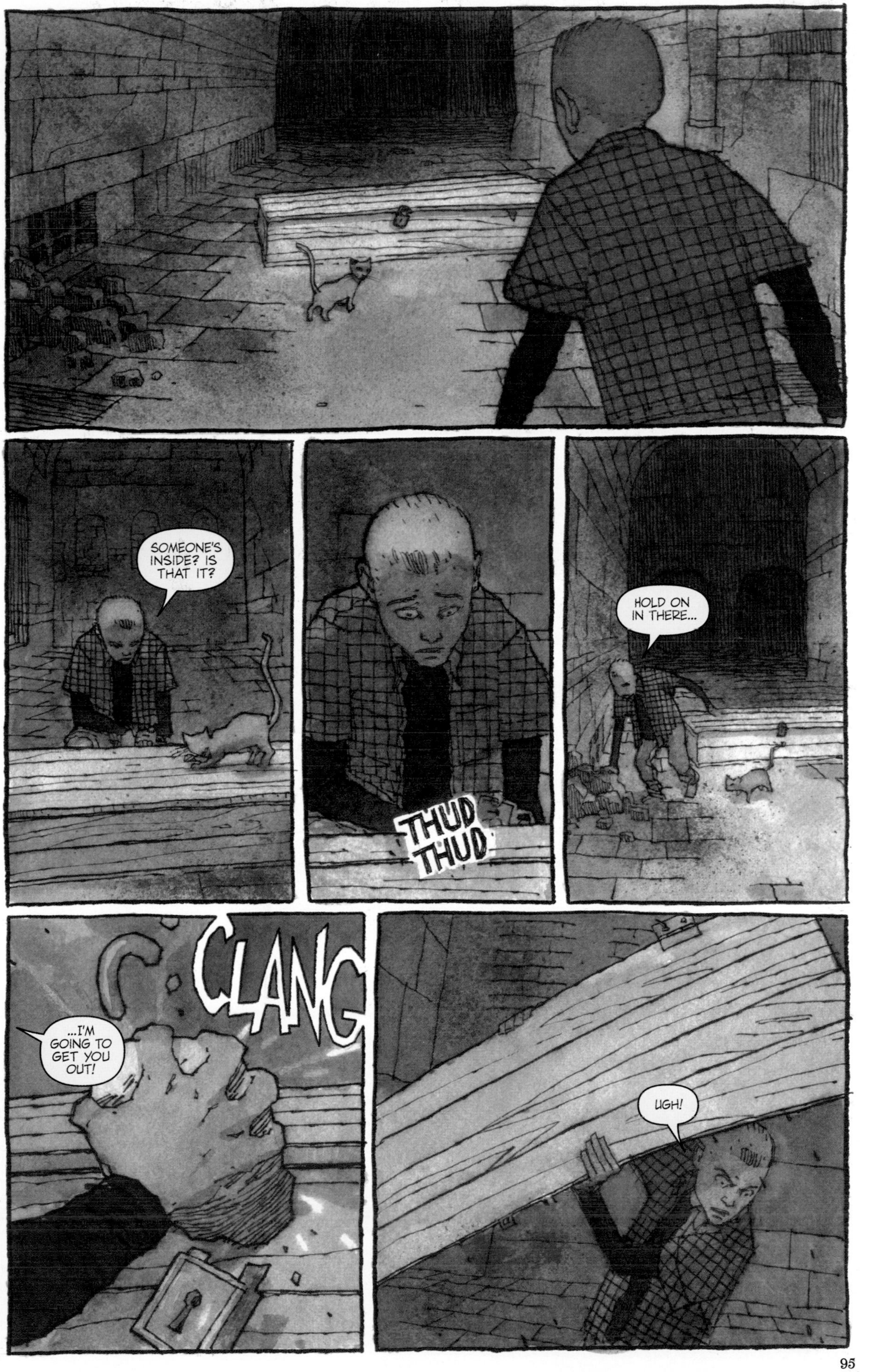
SOMEONE'S INSIDE? IS THAT IT?
THUD THUD
HOLD ON IN THERE...
CLANG
...I'M GOING TO GET YOU OUT!
UGH!

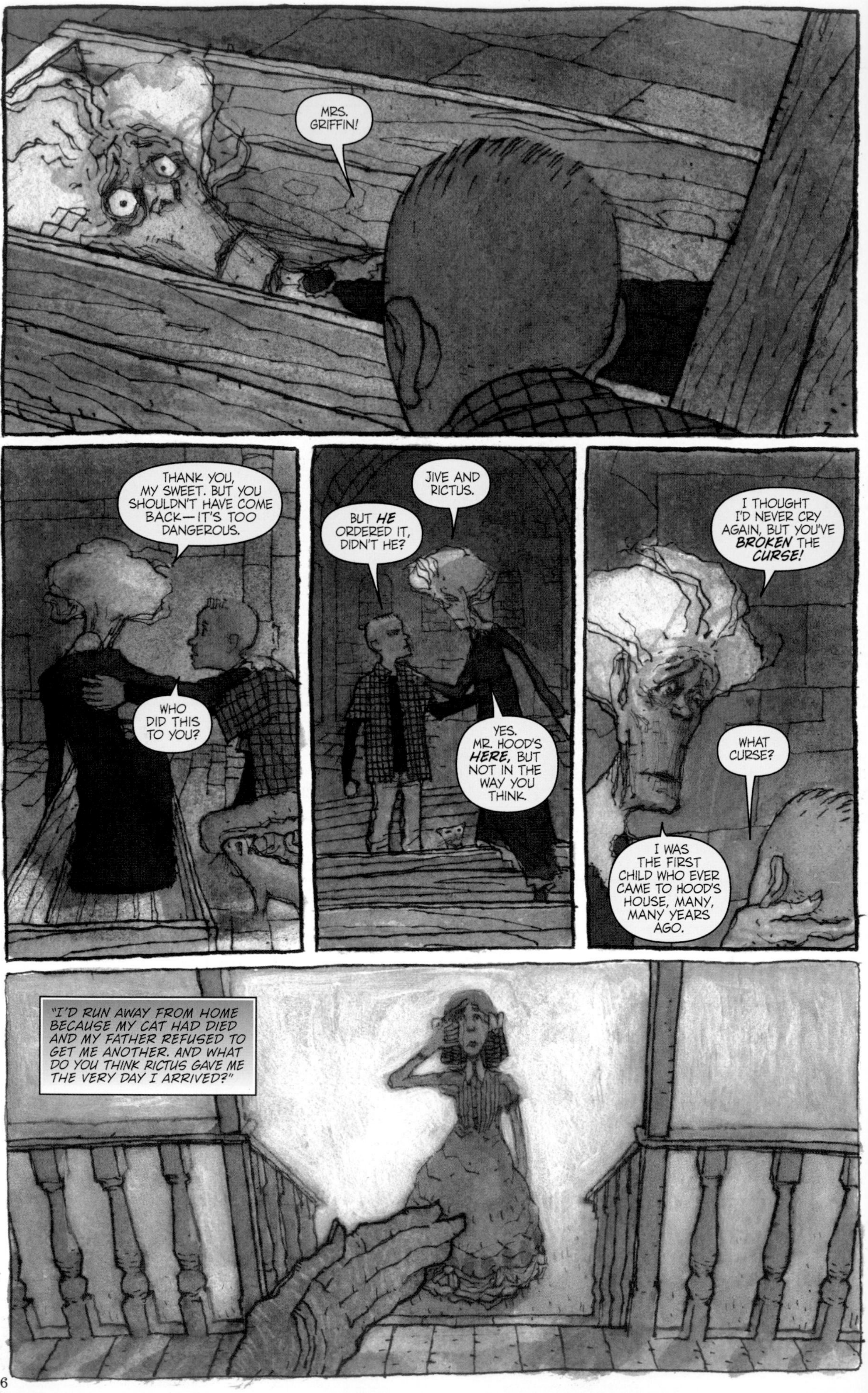
MRS. GRIFFIN!
THANK YOU, MY SWEET. BUT YOU SHOULDN'T HAVE COME BACK—IT'S TOO DANGEROUS.
WHO DID THIS TO YOU?
JIVE AND RICTUS.
BUT **HE** ORDERED IT, DIDN'T HE?
YES. MR. HOOD'S **HERE,** BUT NOT IN THE WAY YOU THINK.
I THOUGHT I'D NEVER CRY AGAIN, BUT YOU'VE **BROKEN** THE **CURSE!**
WHAT CURSE?
I WAS THE FIRST CHILD WHO EVER CAME TO HOOD'S HOUSE, MANY, MANY YEARS AGO.
"I'D RUN AWAY FROM HOME BECAUSE MY CAT HAD DIED AND MY FATHER REFUSED TO GET ME ANOTHER. AND WHAT DO YOU THINK RICTUS GAVE ME THE VERY DAY I ARRIVED?"

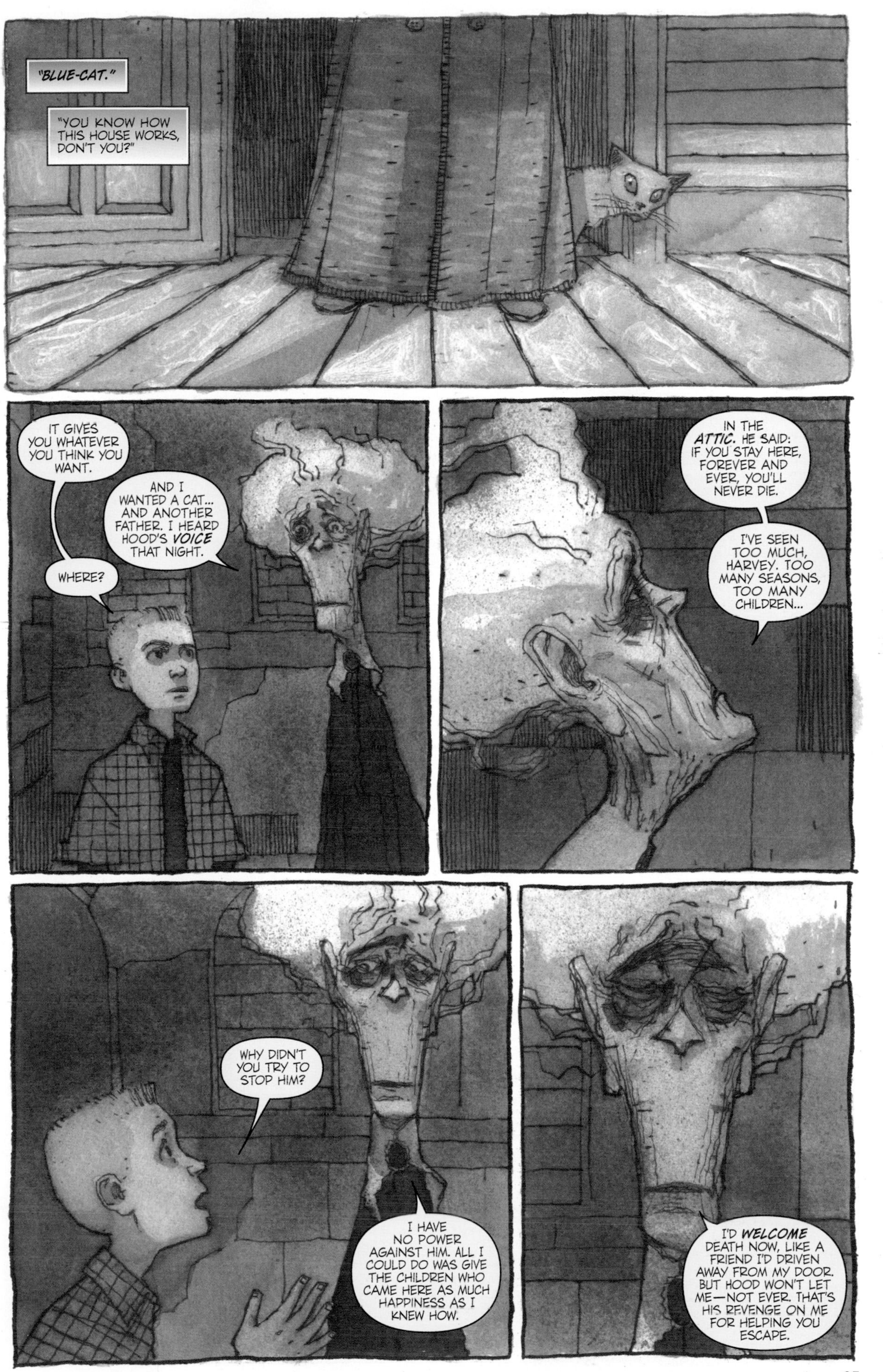
"BLUE-CAT."
"YOU KNOW HOW THIS HOUSE WORKS, DON'T YOU?"
IT GIVES YOU WHATEVER YOU THINK YOU WANT.
AND I WANTED A CAT... AND ANOTHER FATHER. I HEARD HOOD'S VOICE THAT NIGHT.
WHERE?
IN THE ATTIC. HE SAID: IF YOU STAY HERE, FOREVER AND EVER, YOU'LL NEVER DIE.
I'VE SEEN TOO MUCH, HARVEY. TOO MANY SEASONS, TOO MANY CHILDREN...
WHY DIDN'T YOU TRY TO STOP HIM?
I HAVE NO POWER AGAINST HIM. ALL I COULD DO WAS GIVE THE CHILDREN WHO CAME HERE AS MUCH HAPPINESS AS I KNEW HOW.
I'D WELCOME DEATH NOW, LIKE A FRIEND I'D DRIVEN AWAY FROM MY DOOR. BUT HOOD WON'T LET ME—NOT EVER. THAT'S HIS REVENGE ON ME FOR HELPING YOU ESCAPE.

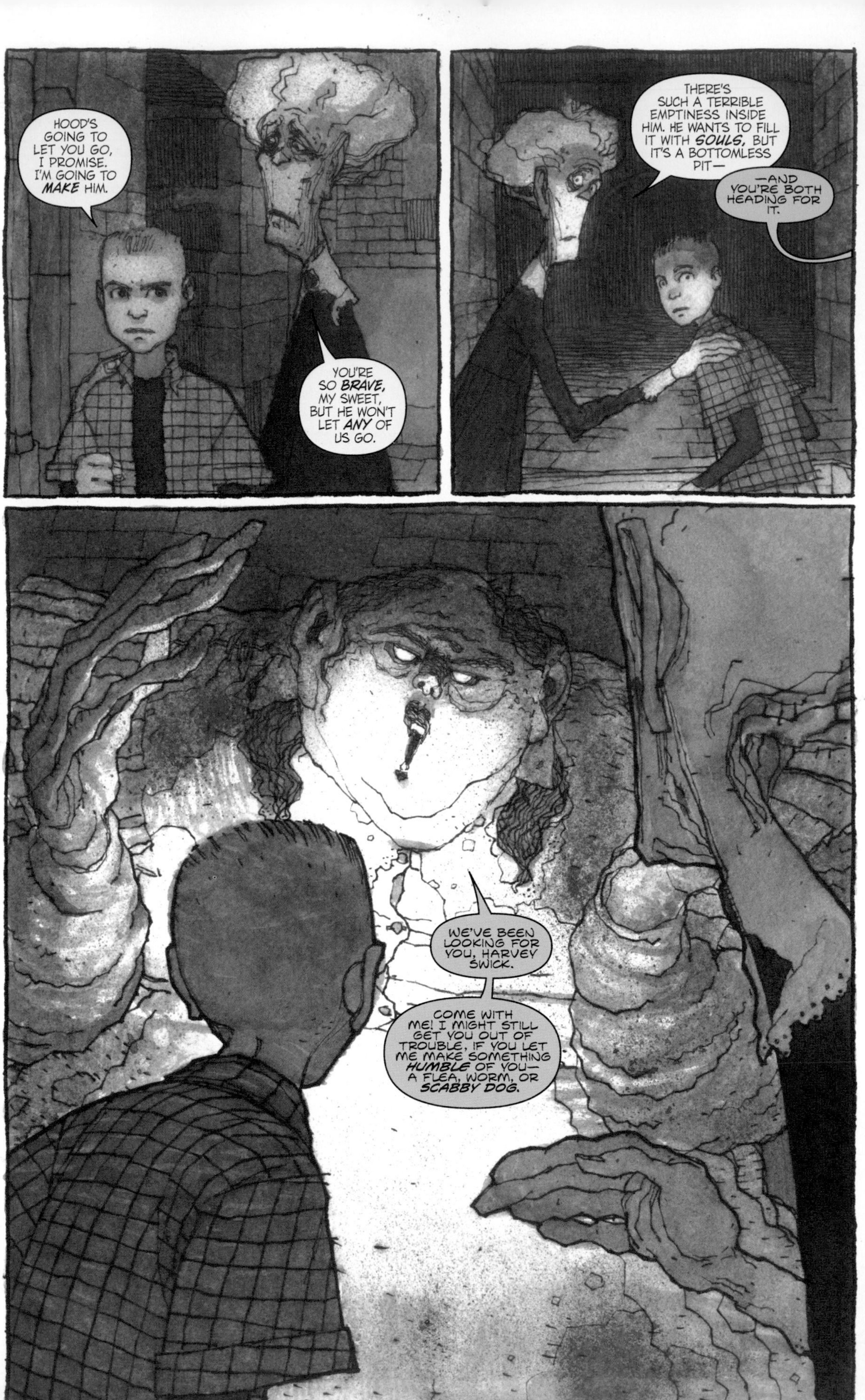
HOOD'S GOING TO LET YOU GO, I PROMISE. I'M GOING TO MAKE HIM.
YOU'RE SO BRAVE, MY SWEET, BUT HE WON'T LET ANY OF US GO.
THERE'S SUCH A TERRIBLE EMPTINESS INSIDE HIM. HE WANTS TO FILL IT WITH SOULS, BUT IT'S A BOTTOMLESS PIT—
—AND YOU'RE BOTH HEADING FOR IT.
WE'VE BEEN LOOKING FOR YOU, HARVEY SWICK.
COME WITH ME! I MIGHT STILL GET YOU OUT OF TROUBLE, IF YOU LET ME MAKE SOMETHING HUMBLE OF YOU— A FLEA, WORM, OR SCABBY DOG.

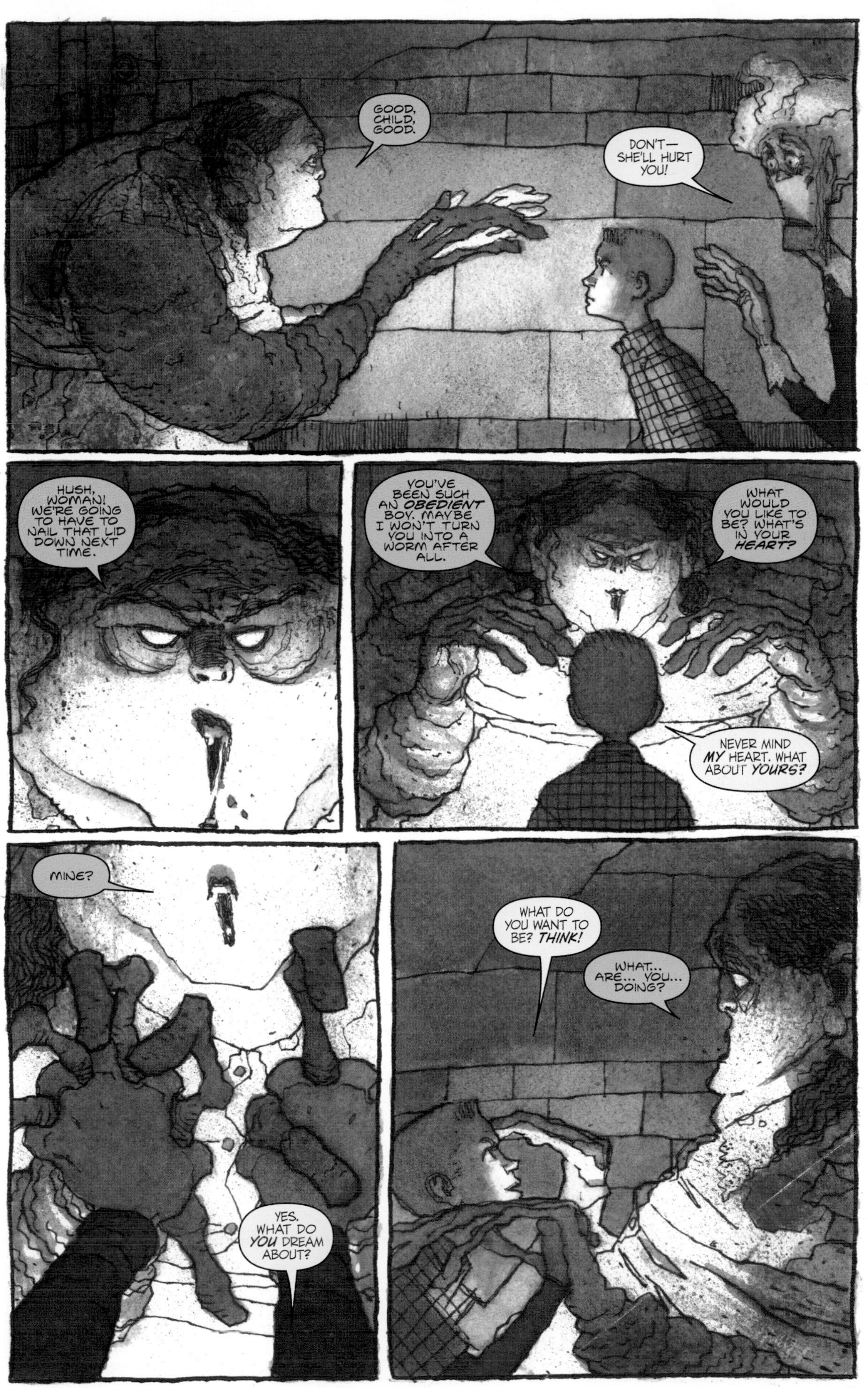
GOOD, CHILD, GOOD.
DON'T— SHE'LL HURT YOU!
HUSH, WOMAN! WE'RE GOING TO HAVE TO NAIL THAT LID DOWN NEXT TIME.
YOU'VE BEEN SUCH AN *OBEDIENT* BOY. MAYBE I WON'T TURN YOU INTO A WORM AFTER ALL.
WHAT WOULD YOU LIKE TO BE? WHAT'S IN YOUR *HEART?*
NEVER MIND *MY* HEART. WHAT ABOUT *YOURS?*
MINE?
YES. WHAT DO *YOU* DREAM ABOUT?
WHAT DO YOU WANT TO BE? *THINK!*
WHAT... ARE... YOU... DOING?

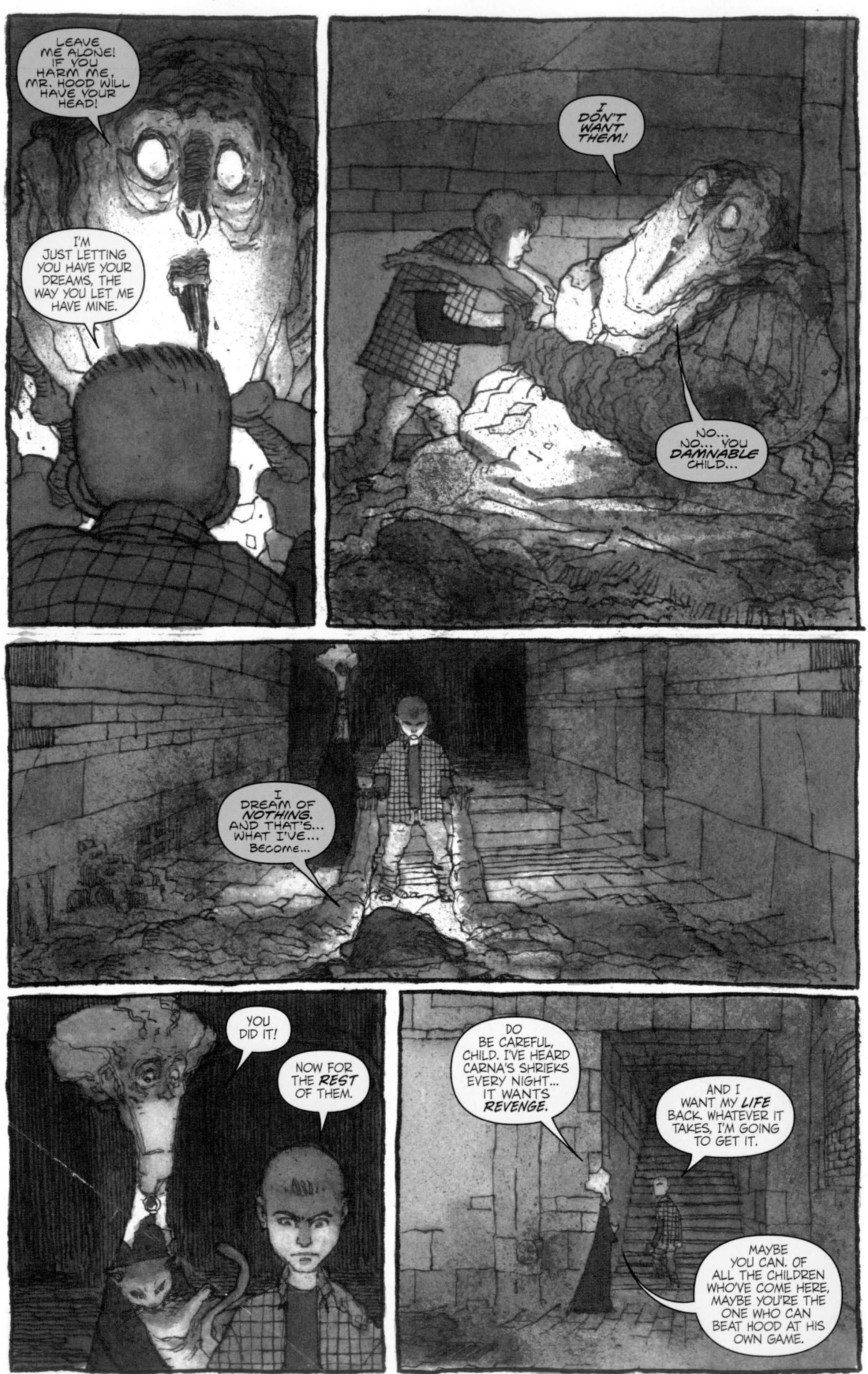
LEAVE ME ALONE! IF YOU HARM ME, MR. HOOD WILL HAVE YOUR HEAD!
I'M JUST LETTING YOU HAVE YOUR DREAMS, THE WAY YOU LET ME HAVE MINE.
I DON'T WANT THEM!
NO... NO... YOU DAMNABLE CHILD...
I DREAM OF NOTHING. AND THAT'S... WHAT I'VE... BECOME...
YOU DID IT!
NOW FOR THE REST OF THEM.
DO BE CAREFUL, CHILD. I'VE HEARD CARNA'S SHRIEKS EVERY NIGHT... IT WANTS REVENGE.
AND I WANT MY LIFE BACK. WHATEVER IT TAKES, I'M GOING TO GET IT.
MAYBE YOU CAN. OF ALL THE CHILDREN WHO'VE COME HERE, MAYBE YOU'RE THE ONE WHO CAN BEAT HOOD AT HIS OWN GAME.

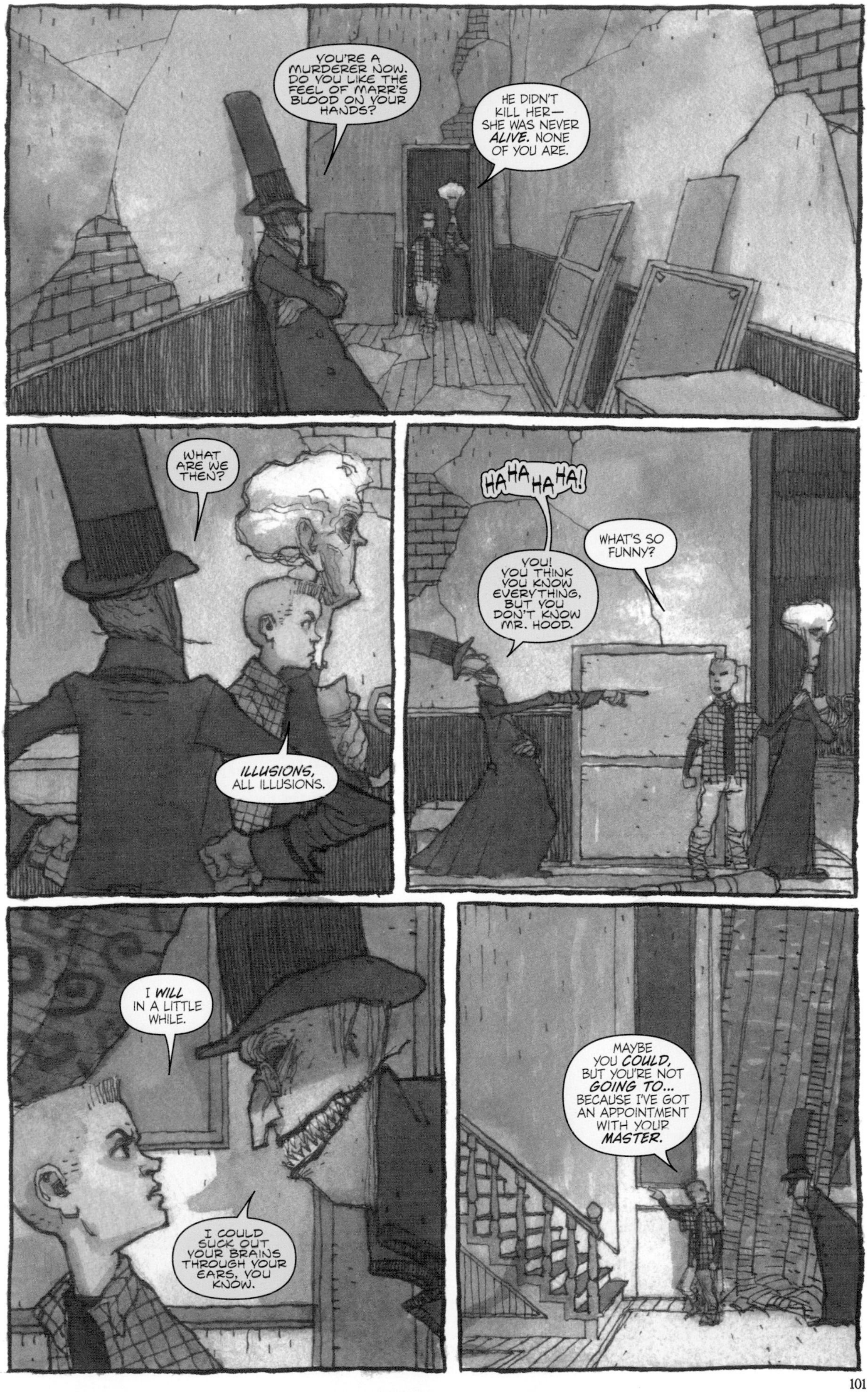
YOU'RE A MURDERER NOW. DO YOU LIKE THE FEEL OF MARR'S BLOOD ON YOUR HANDS?
HE DIDN'T KILL HER— SHE WAS NEVER ALIVE. NONE OF YOU ARE.
WHAT ARE WE THEN?
ILLUSIONS, ALL ILLUSIONS.
HAHAHAHA!
YOU! YOU THINK YOU KNOW EVERYTHING, BUT YOU DON'T KNOW MR. HOOD.
WHAT'S SO FUNNY?
I WILL IN A LITTLE WHILE.
I COULD SUCK OUT YOUR BRAINS THROUGH YOUR EARS, YOU KNOW.
MAYBE YOU COULD, BUT YOU'RE NOT GOING TO... BECAUSE I'VE GOT AN APPOINTMENT WITH YOUR MASTER.

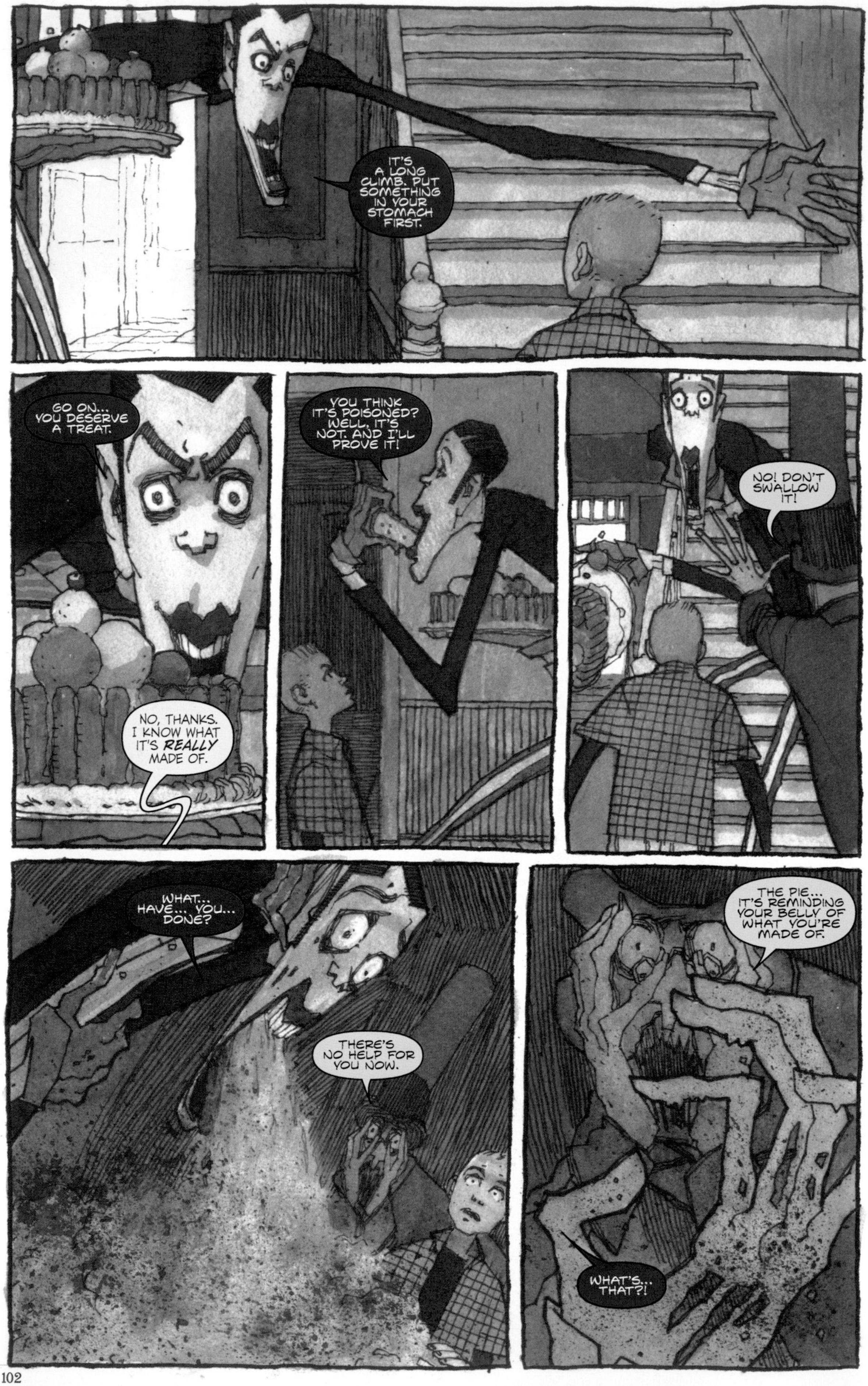
IT'S A LONG CLIMB. PUT SOMETHING IN YOUR STOMACH FIRST.
GO ON... YOU DESERVE A TREAT.
NO, THANKS. I KNOW WHAT IT'S REALLY MADE OF.
YOU THINK IT'S POISONED? WELL, IT'S NOT. AND I'LL PROVE IT!
NO! DON'T SWALLOW IT!
WHAT... HAVE... YOU... DONE?
THERE'S NO HELP FOR YOU NOW.
THE PIE... IT'S REMINDING YOUR BELLY OF WHAT YOU'RE MADE OF.
WHAT'S... THAT?!

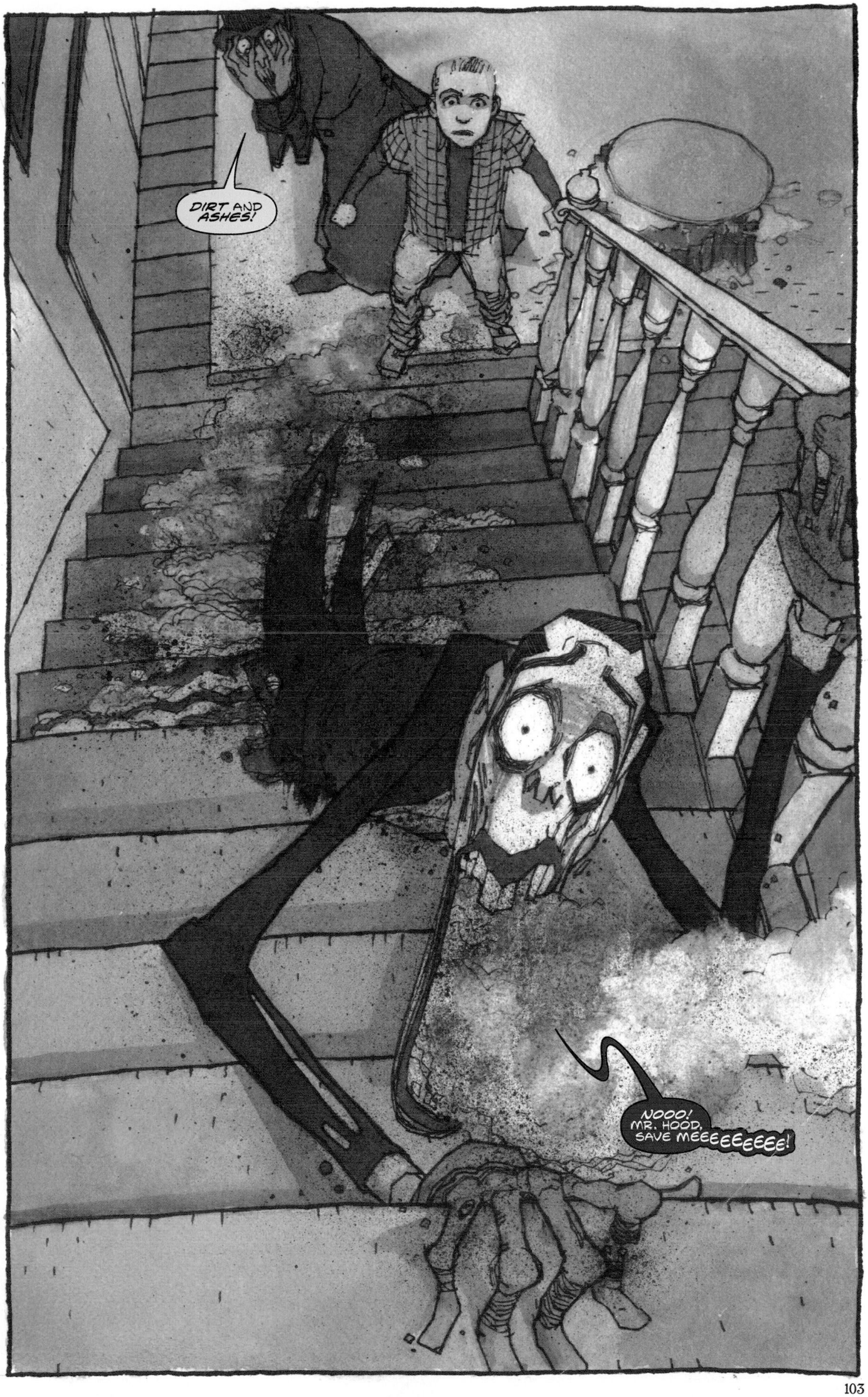
DIRT AND ASHES!
NOOO! MR. HOOD, SAVE MEEEEEEEEEE!

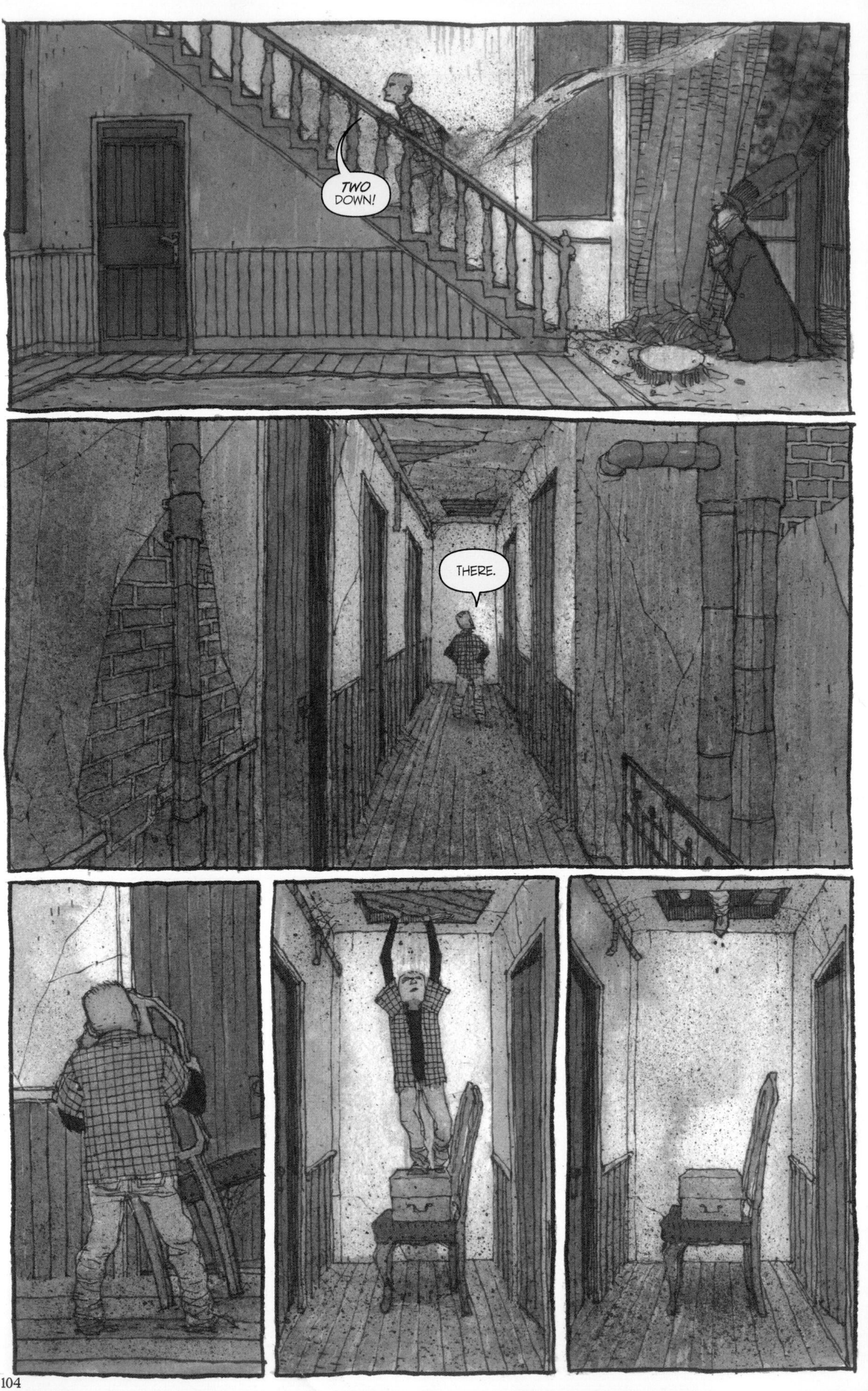
TWO DOWN!
THERE.

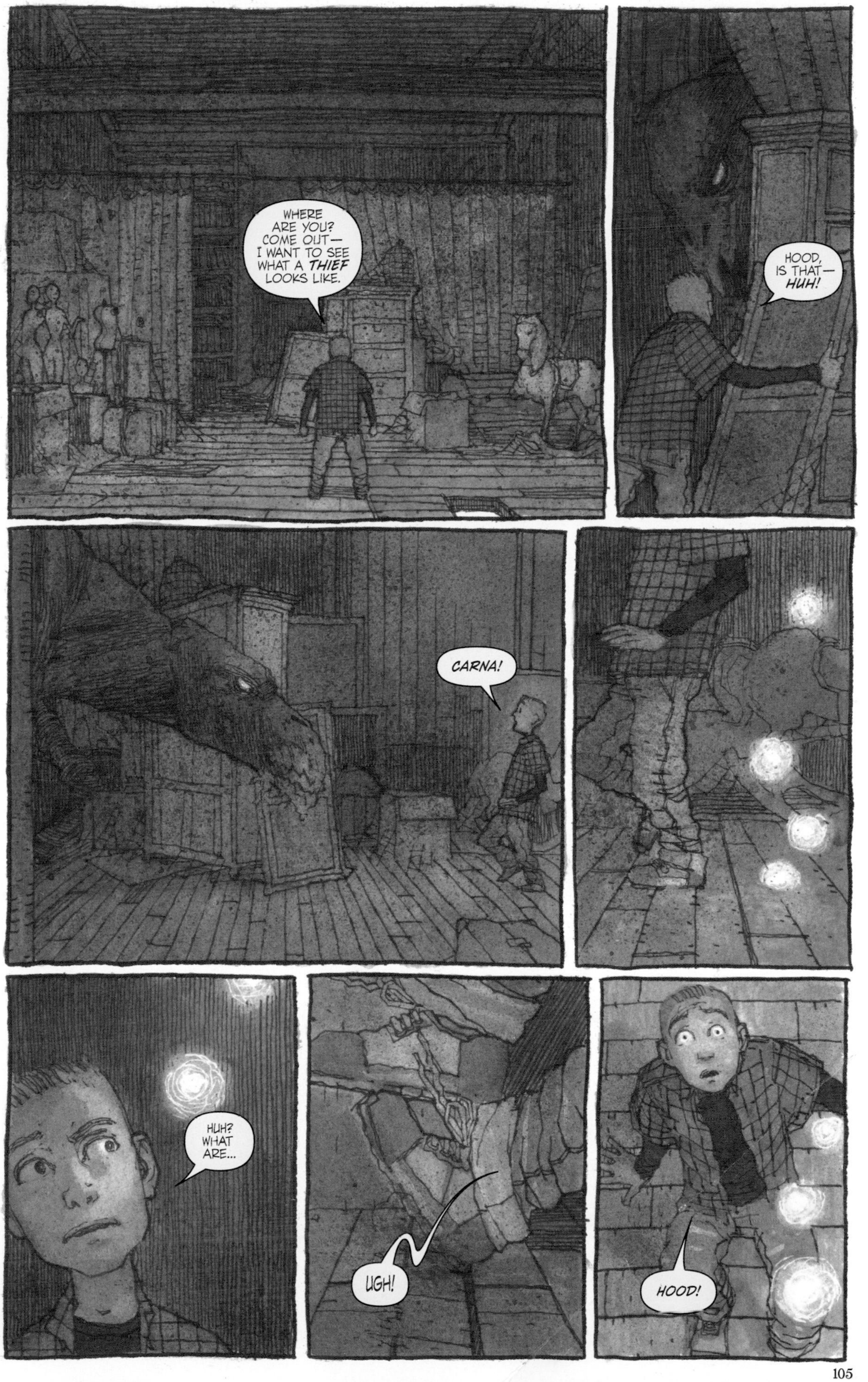
WHERE ARE YOU? COME OUT— I WANT TO SEE WHAT A THIEF LOOKS LIKE.
HOOD, IS THAT— HUH!
CARNA!
HUH? WHAT ARE...
UGH!
HOOD!

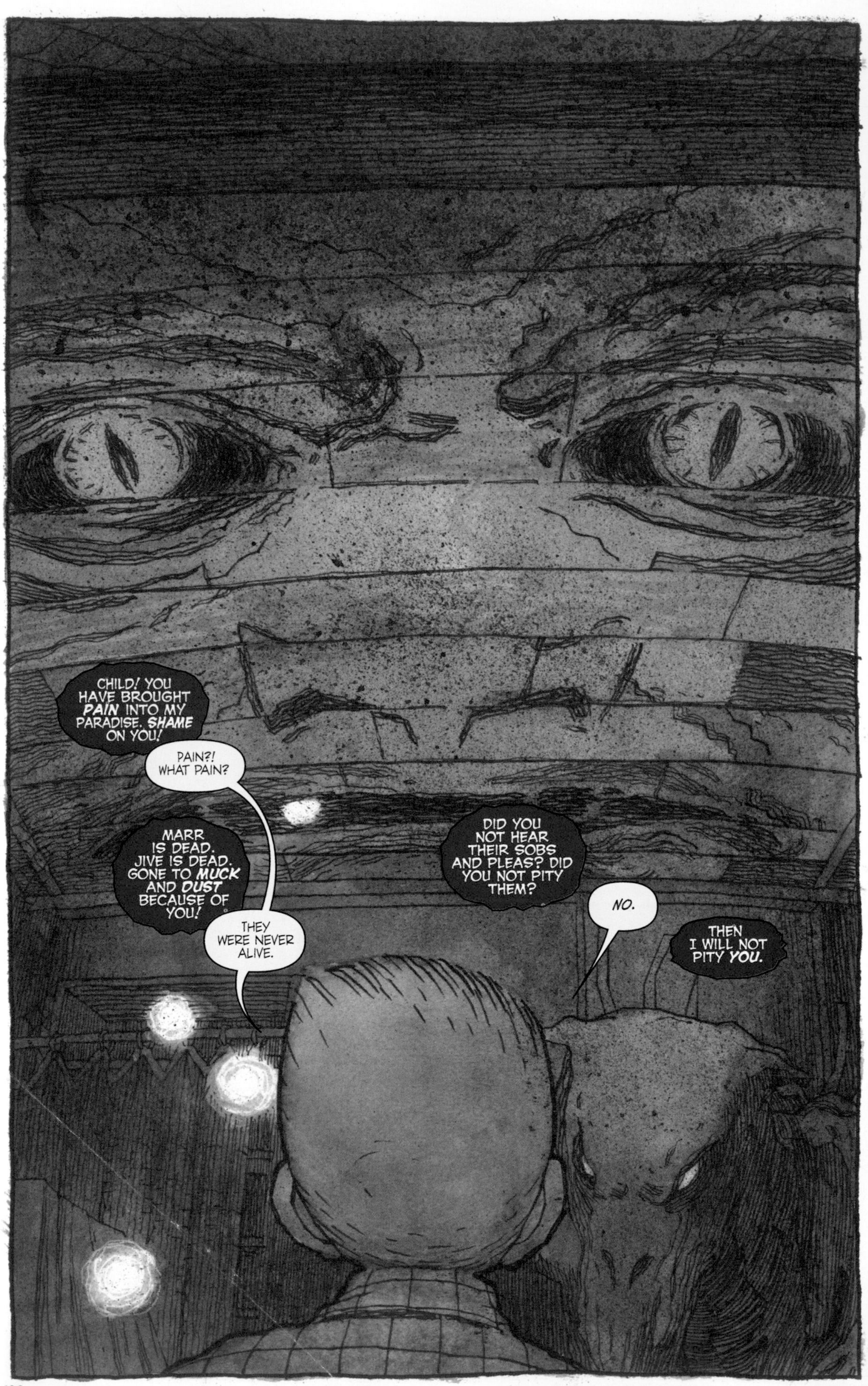
CHILD! YOU HAVE BROUGHT PAIN INTO MY PARADISE. SHAME ON YOU!
PAIN?! WHAT PAIN?
MARR IS DEAD. JIVE IS DEAD. GONE TO MUCK AND DUST BECAUSE OF YOU!
THEY WERE NEVER ALIVE.
DID YOU NOT HEAR THEIR SOBS AND PLEAS? DID YOU NOT PITY THEM?
NO.
THEN I WILL NOT PITY YOU.

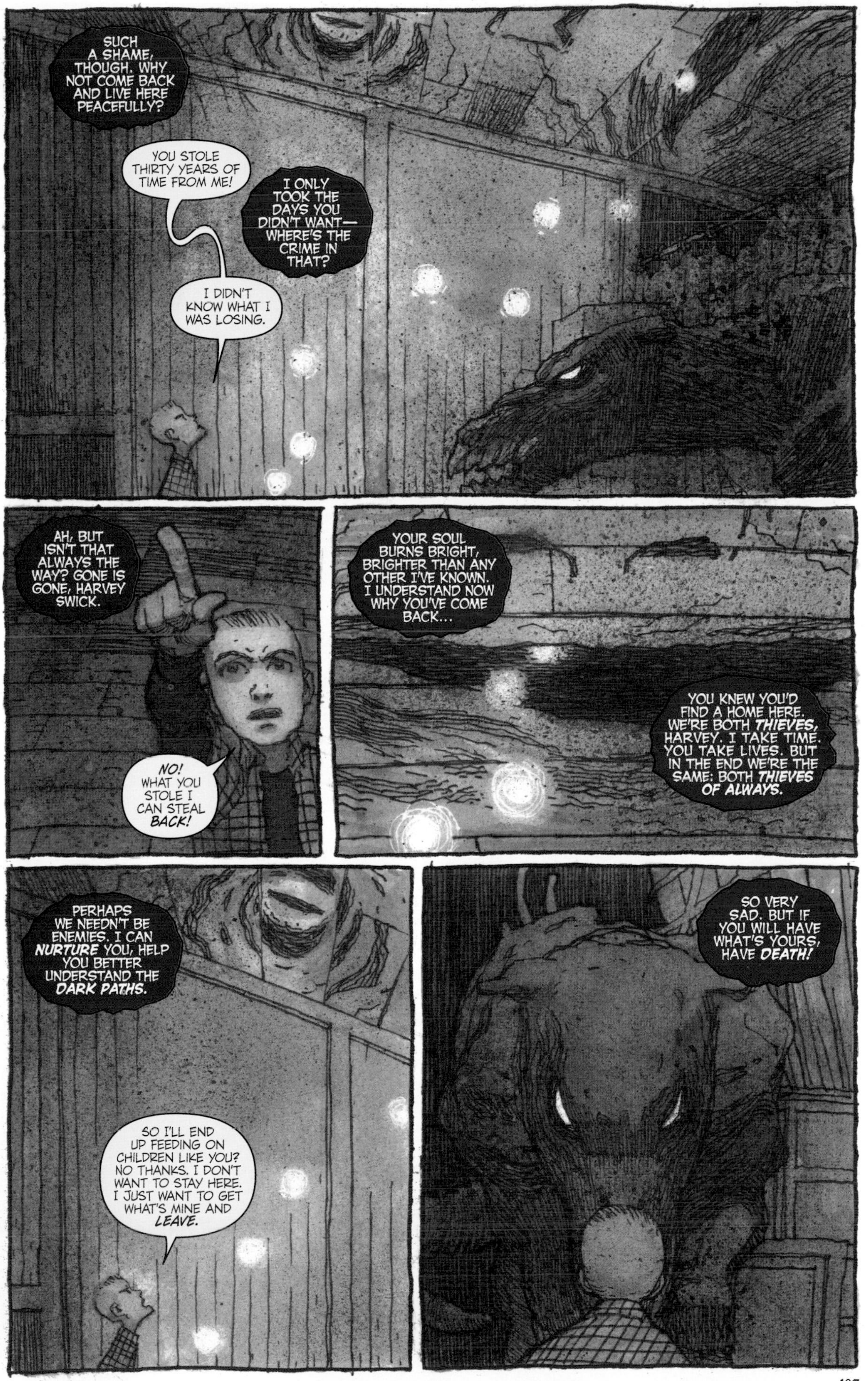

SUCH A SHAME, THOUGH. WHY NOT COME BACK AND LIVE HERE PEACEFULLY?
YOU STOLE THIRTY YEARS OF TIME FROM ME!
I ONLY TOOK THE DAYS YOU DIDN'T WANT— WHERE'S THE CRIME IN THAT?
I DIDN'T KNOW WHAT I WAS LOSING.
AH, BUT ISN'T THAT ALWAYS THE WAY? GONE IS GONE, HARVEY SWICK.
NO! WHAT YOU STOLE I CAN STEAL BACK!
YOUR SOUL BURNS BRIGHT, BRIGHTER THAN ANY OTHER I'VE KNOWN. I UNDERSTAND NOW WHY YOU'VE COME BACK...
YOU KNEW YOU'D FIND A HOME HERE. WE'RE BOTH THIEVES, HARVEY. I TAKE TIME. YOU TAKE LIVES. BUT IN THE END WE'RE THE SAME: BOTH THIEVES OF ALWAYS.
PERHAPS WE NEEDN'T BE ENEMIES. I CAN NURTURE YOU, HELP YOU BETTER UNDERSTAND THE DARK PATHS.
SO I'LL END UP FEEDING ON CHILDREN LIKE YOU? NO THANKS. I DON'T WANT TO STAY HERE. I JUST WANT TO GET WHAT'S MINE AND LEAVE.
SO VERY SAD. BUT IF YOU WILL HAVE WHAT'S YOURS, HAVE DEATH!

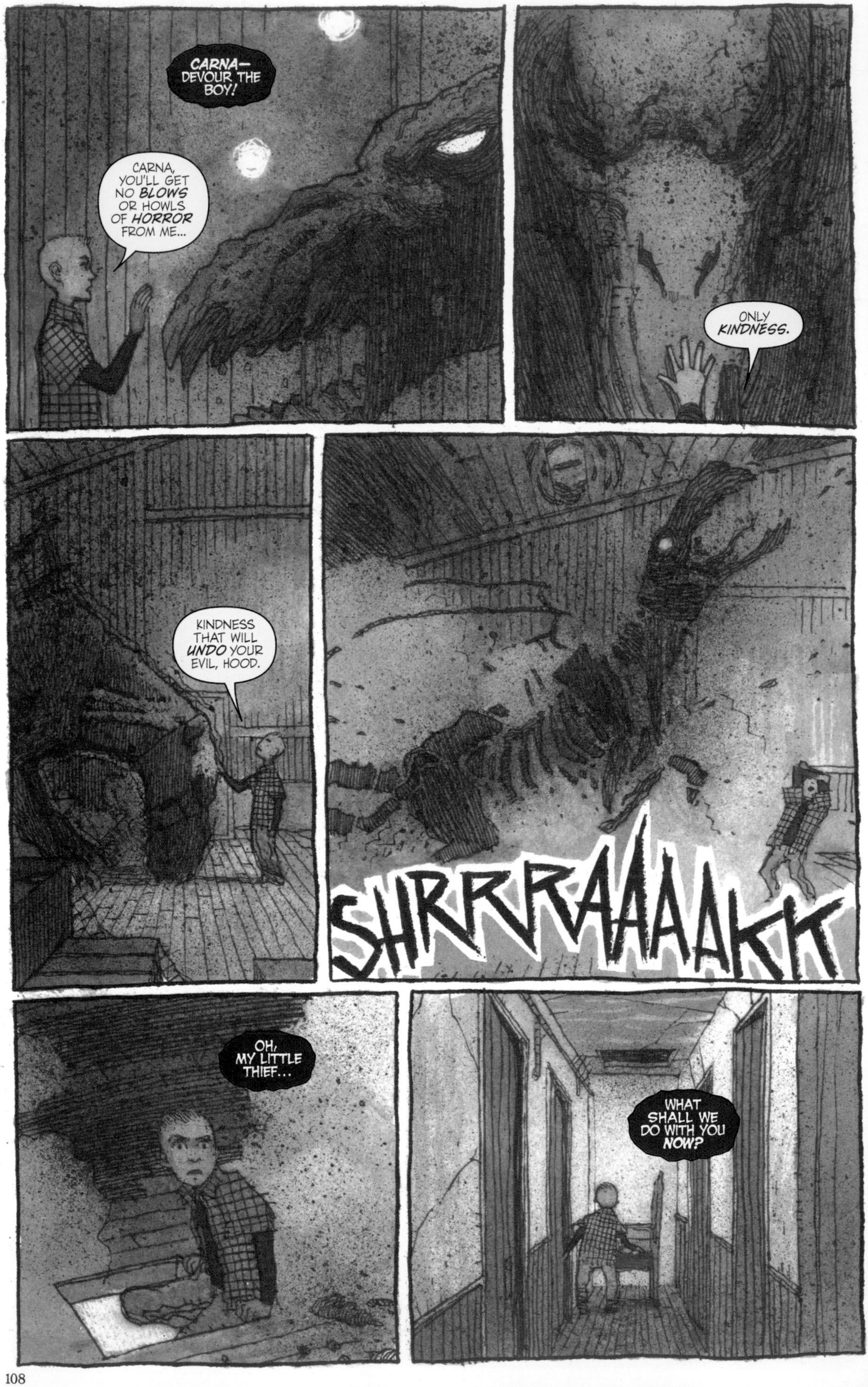
CARNA— DEVOUR THE BOY!
CARNA, YOU'LL GET NO BLOWS OR HOWLS OF HORROR FROM ME...
ONLY KINDNESS.
KINDNESS THAT WILL UNDO YOUR EVIL, HOOD.
SHRRRAAAAKK
OH, MY LITTLE THIEF...
WHAT SHALL WE DO WITH YOU NOW?

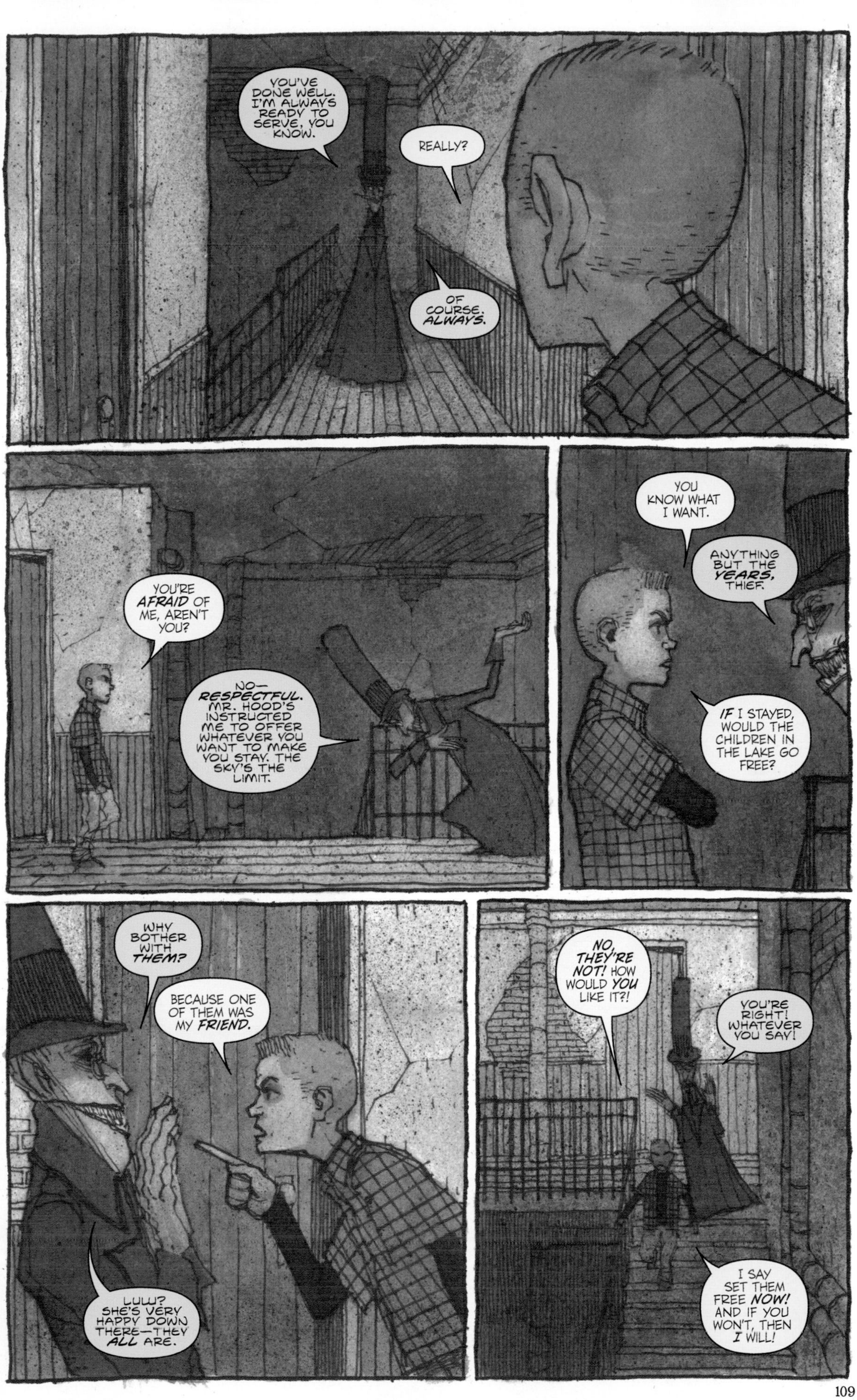

YOU'VE DONE WELL. I'M ALWAYS READY TO SERVE, YOU KNOW.
REALLY?
OF COURSE. *ALWAYS.*
YOU'RE *AFRAID* OF ME, AREN'T YOU?
NO— *RESPECTFUL.* MR. HOOD'S INSTRUCTED ME TO OFFER WHATEVER YOU WANT TO MAKE YOU STAY. THE SKY'S THE LIMIT.
YOU KNOW WHAT I WANT.
ANYTHING BUT THE *YEARS,* THIEF.
IF I STAYED, WOULD THE CHILDREN IN THE LAKE GO FREE?
WHY BOTHER WITH *THEM?*
BECAUSE ONE OF THEM WAS MY *FRIEND.*
LULU? SHE'S VERY HAPPY DOWN THERE—THEY *ALL* ARE.
NO, THEY'RE NOT! HOW WOULD *YOU* LIKE IT?!
YOU'RE RIGHT! WHATEVER YOU SAY!
I SAY SET THEM FREE *NOW!* AND IF YOU WON'T, THEN *I* WILL!

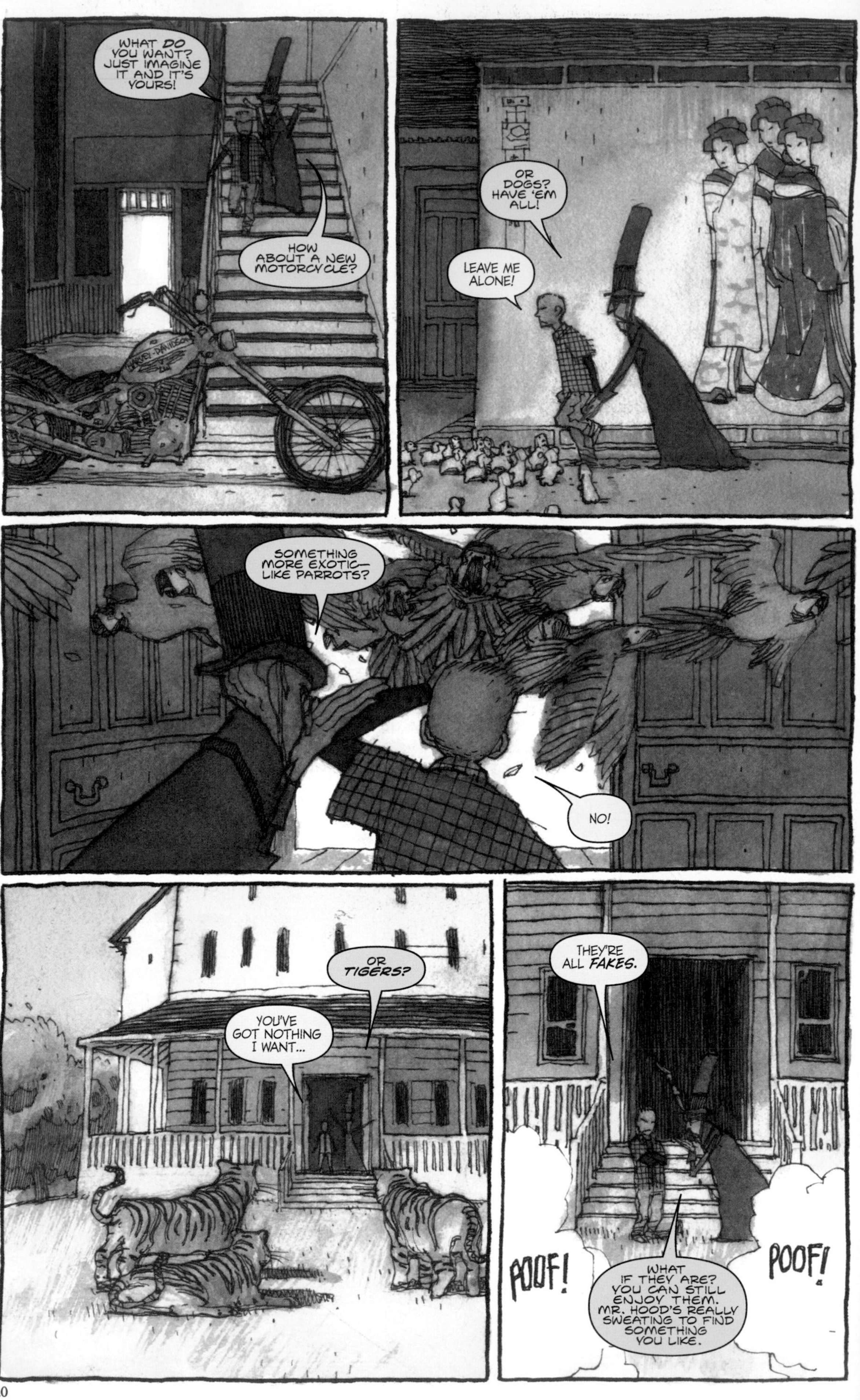
WHAT DO YOU WANT? JUST IMAGINE IT AND IT'S YOURS!
HOW ABOUT A NEW MOTORCYCLE?
OR DOGS? HAVE 'EM ALL!
LEAVE ME ALONE!
SOMETHING MORE EXOTIC— LIKE PARROTS?
NO!
OR TIGERS?
YOU'VE GOT NOTHING I WANT...
THEY'RE ALL FAKES.
POOF!
WHAT IF THEY ARE? YOU CAN STILL ENJOY THEM. MR. HOOD'S REALLY SWEATING TO FIND SOMETHING YOU LIKE.
POOF!

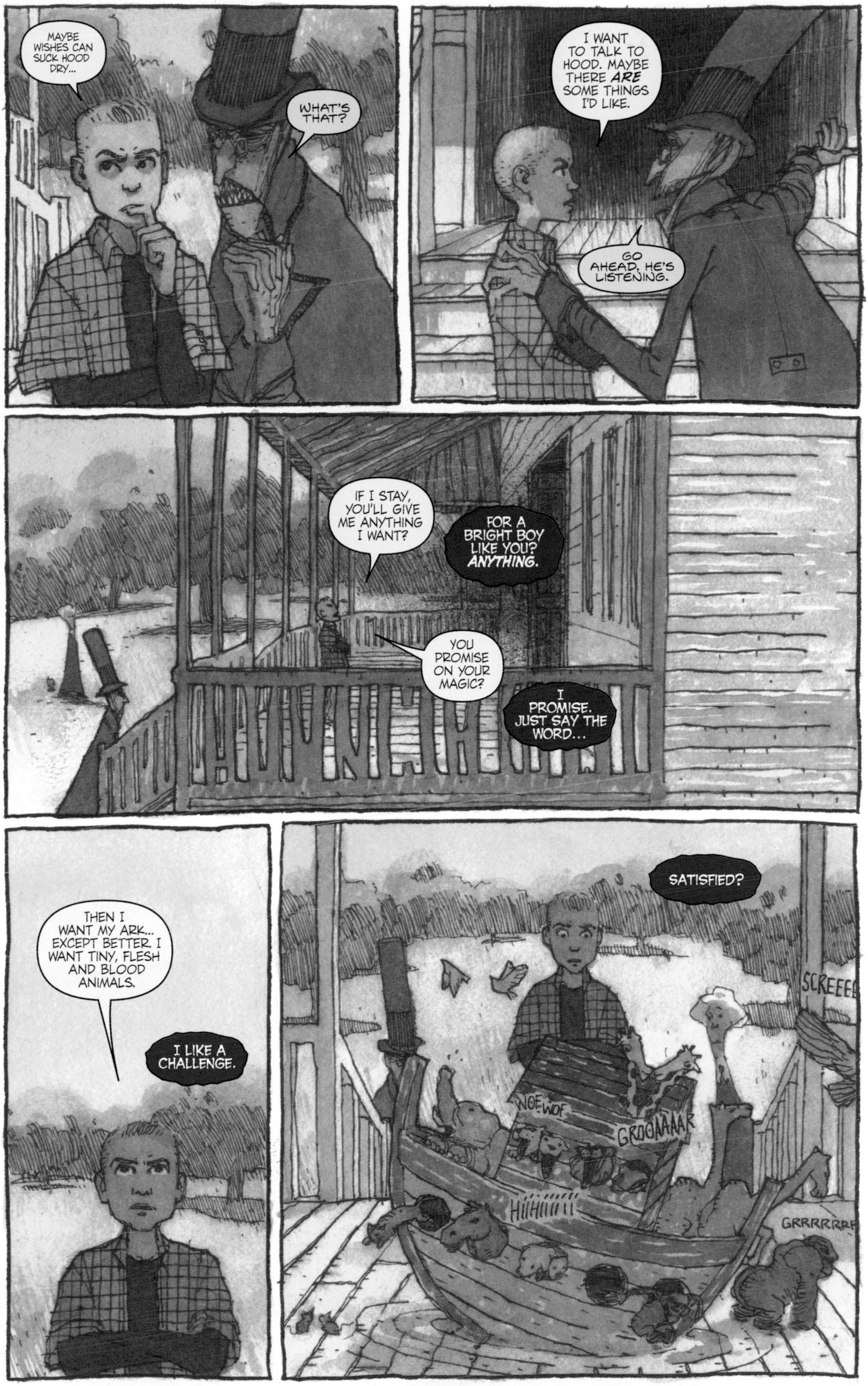

MAYBE WISHES CAN SUCK HOOD DRY...
WHAT'S THAT?
I WANT TO TALK TO HOOD. MAYBE THERE *ARE* SOME THINGS I'D LIKE.
GO AHEAD, HE'S LISTENING.
IF I STAY, YOU'LL GIVE ME ANYTHING I WANT?
FOR A BRIGHT BOY LIKE YOU? *ANYTHING*.
YOU PROMISE ON YOUR MAGIC?
I PROMISE. JUST SAY THE WORD...
THEN I WANT MY ARK... EXCEPT BETTER. I WANT TINY, FLESH AND BLOOD ANIMALS.
I LIKE A CHALLENGE.
SATISFIED?
WOF WOF
GROOAAAAR
HIIIIIII
SCREEEE
GRRRRRRR

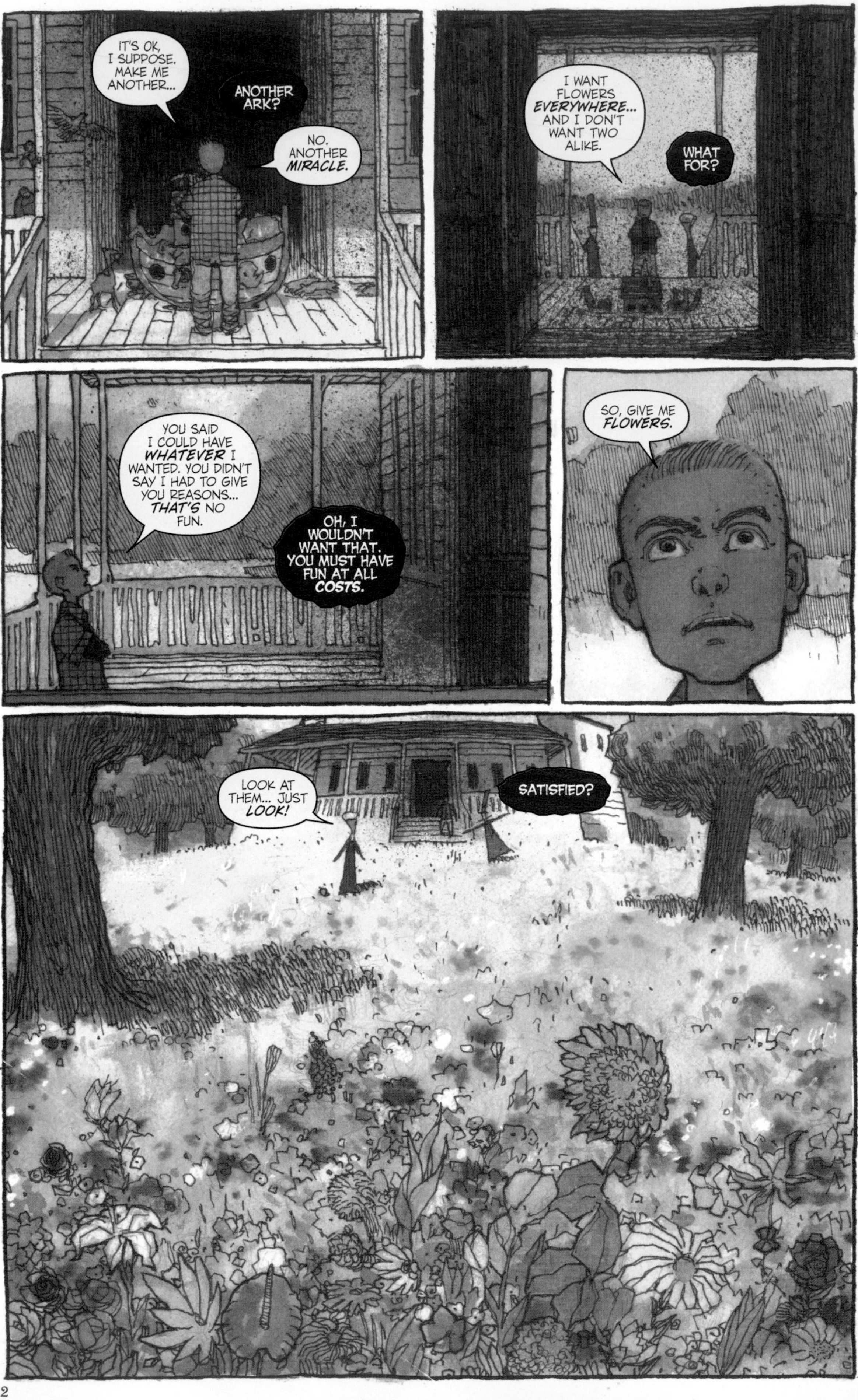
IT'S OK, I SUPPOSE. MAKE ME ANOTHER...
ANOTHER ARK?
NO. ANOTHER MIRACLE.
I WANT FLOWERS EVERYWHERE... AND I DON'T WANT TWO ALIKE.
WHAT FOR?
YOU SAID I COULD HAVE WHATEVER I WANTED. YOU DIDN'T SAY I HAD TO GIVE YOU REASONS... THAT'S NO FUN.
OH, I WOULDN'T WANT THAT. YOU MUST HAVE FUN AT ALL COSTS.
SO, GIVE ME FLOWERS.
LOOK AT THEM... JUST LOOK!
SATISFIED?

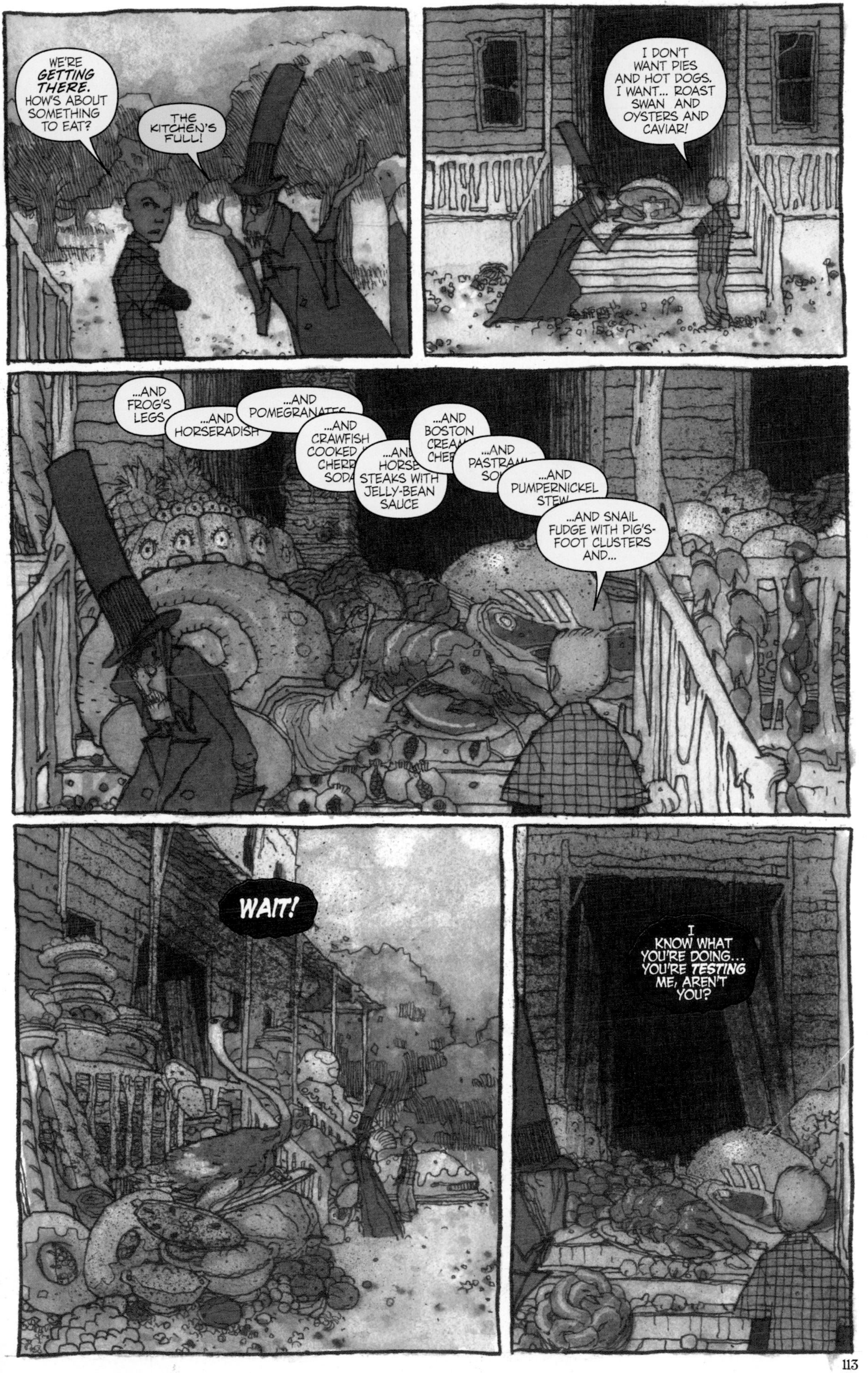
WE'RE ***GETTING THERE.*** HOW'S ABOUT SOMETHING TO EAT?
THE KITCHEN'S FULL!
I DON'T WANT PIES AND HOT DOGS. I WANT... ROAST SWAN AND OYSTERS AND CAVIAR!
...AND FROG'S LEGS
...AND HORSERADISH
...AND POMEGRANATES
...AND CRAWFISH COOKED CHERR SODA
...AN HORSE STEAKS WITH JELLY-BEAN SAUCE
...AND BOSTON CREAM CHEE
...AND PASTRAMI SO
...AND PUMPERNICKEL STEW
...AND SNAIL FUDGE WITH PIG'S-FOOT CLUSTERS AND...
WAIT!
I KNOW WHAT YOU'RE DOING... YOU'RE ***TESTING*** ME, AREN'T YOU?

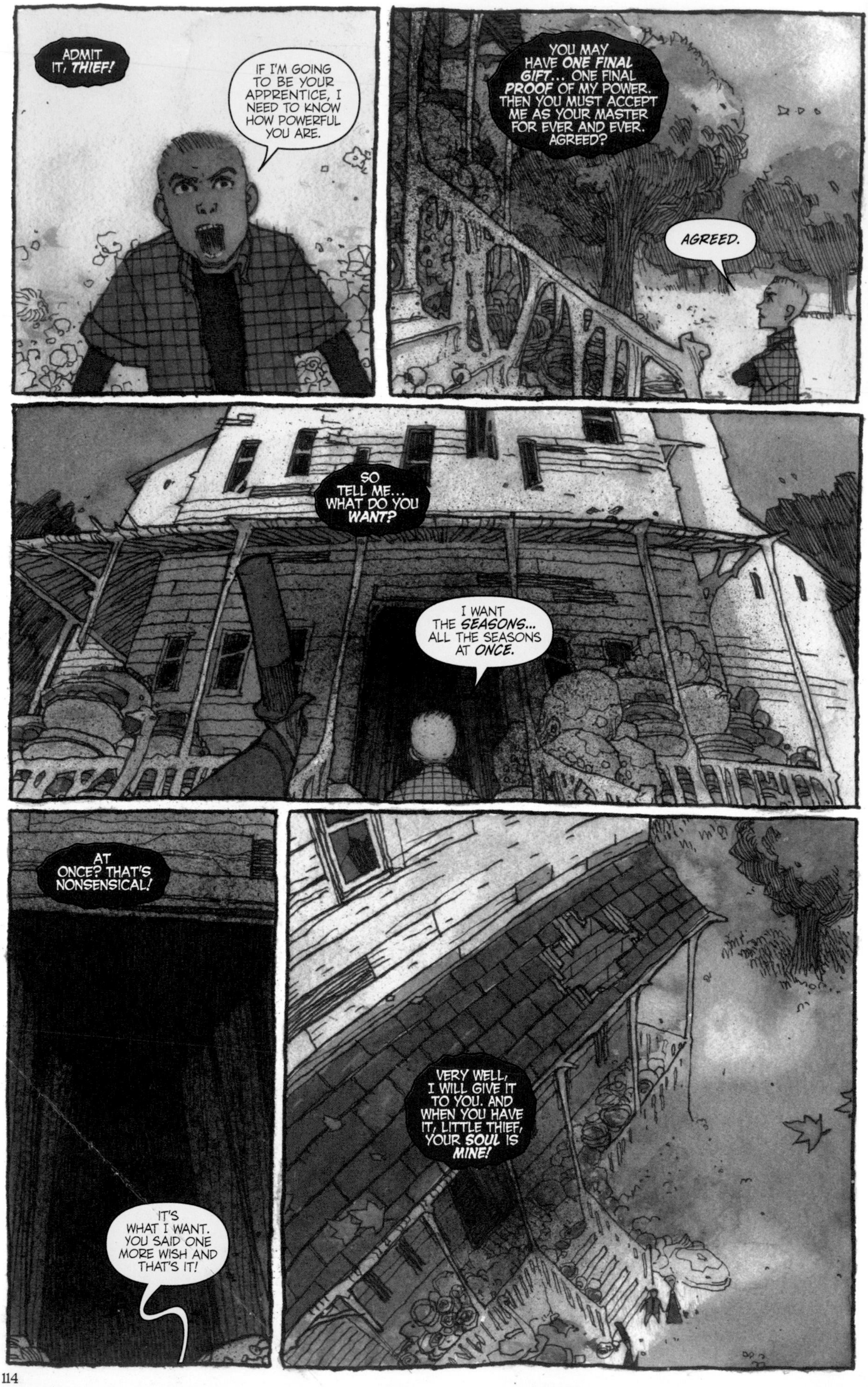
ADMIT IT, THIEF!
IF I'M GOING TO BE YOUR APPRENTICE, I NEED TO KNOW HOW POWERFUL YOU ARE.
YOU MAY HAVE ONE FINAL GIFT... ONE FINAL PROOF OF MY POWER. THEN YOU MUST ACCEPT ME AS YOUR MASTER FOR EVER AND EVER. AGREED?
AGREED.
SO TELL ME... WHAT DO YOU WANT?
I WANT THE SEASONS... ALL THE SEASONS AT ONCE.
AT ONCE? THAT'S NONSENSICAL!
IT'S WHAT I WANT. YOU SAID ONE MORE WISH AND THAT'S IT!
VERY WELL, I WILL GIVE IT TO YOU. AND WHEN YOU HAVE IT, LITTLE THIEF, YOUR SOUL IS MINE!

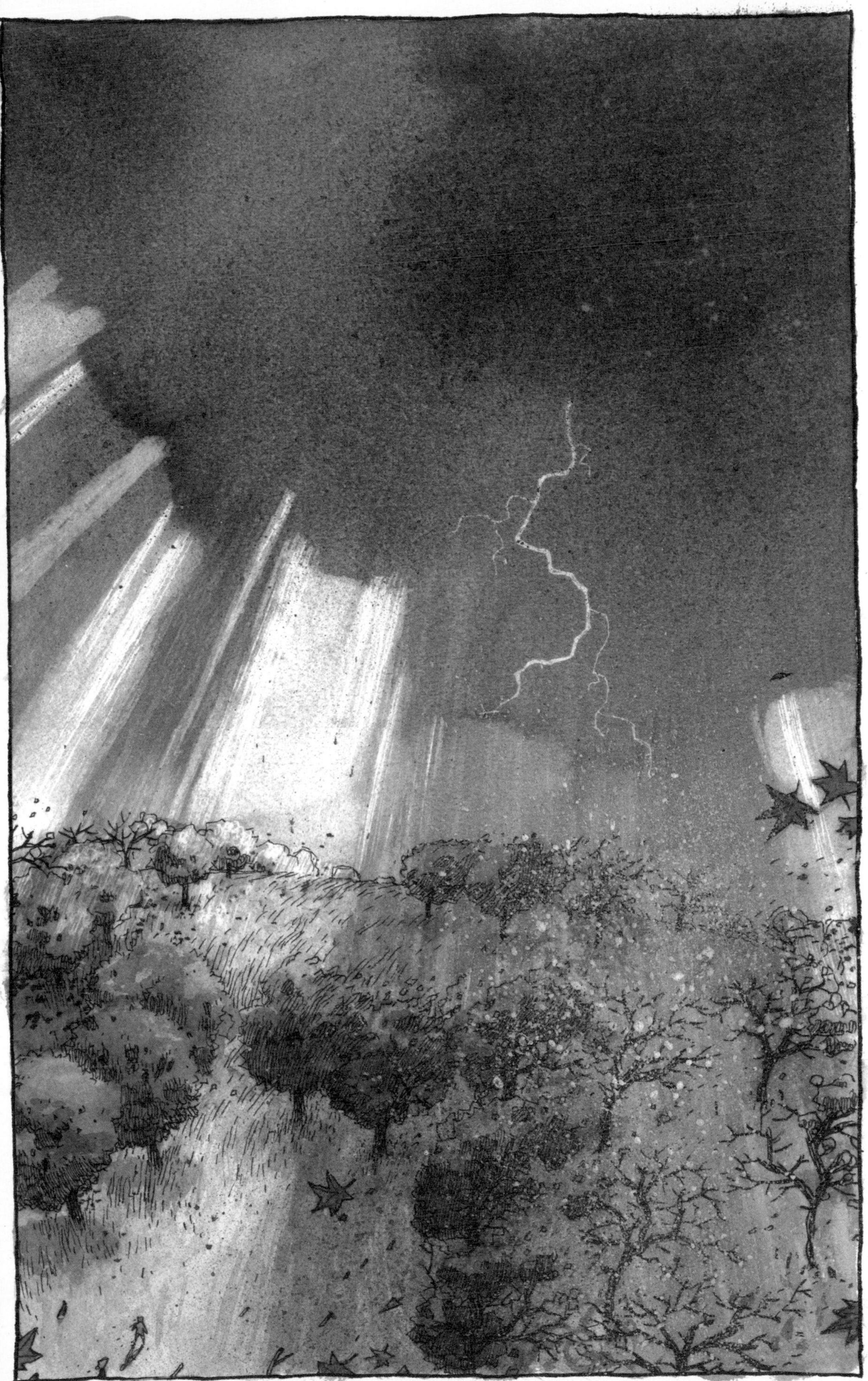

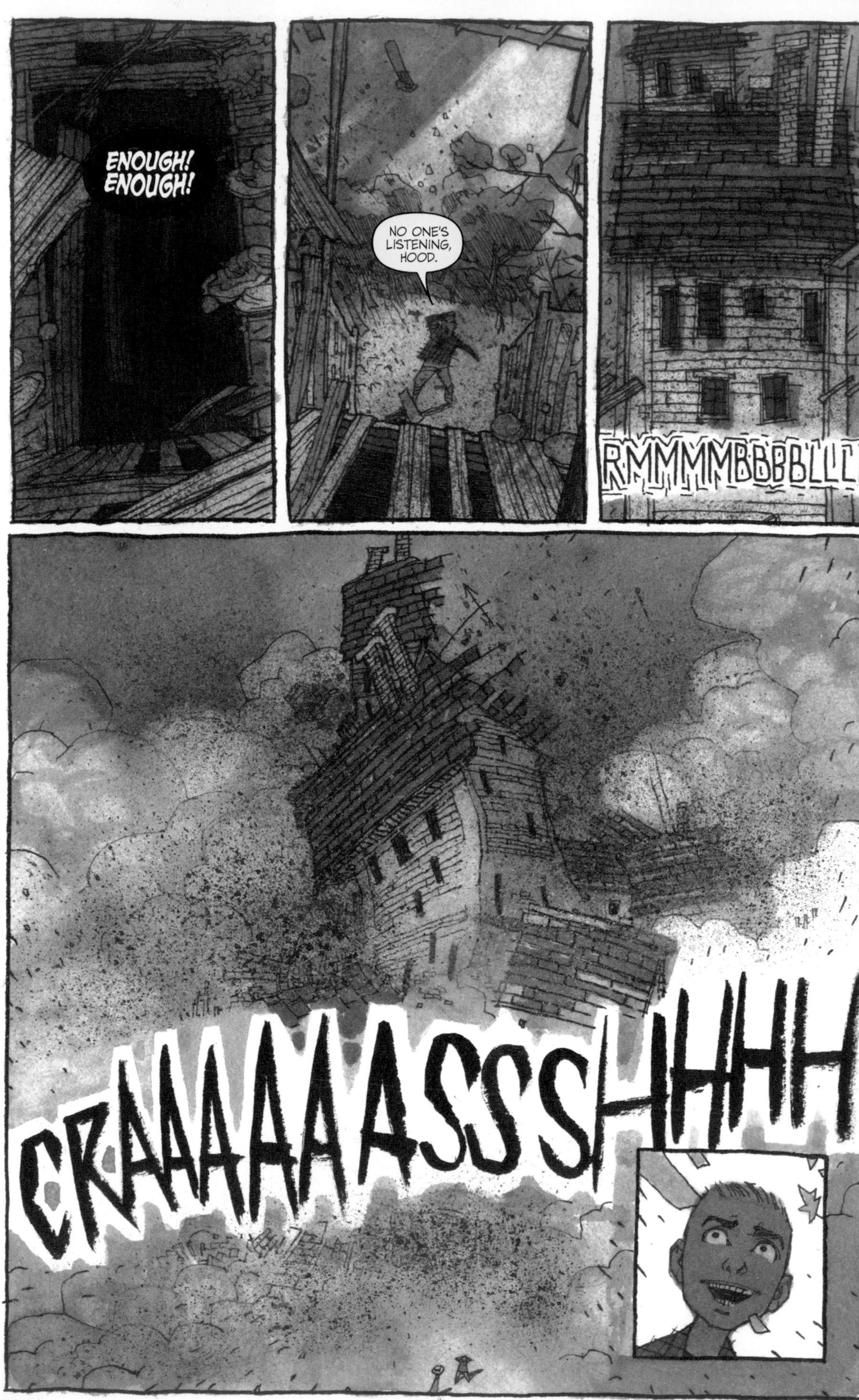
ENOUGH! ENOUGH!
NO ONE'S LISTENING, HOOD.
RMMMMBBBLLLL
CRAAAAAASSSHHHH

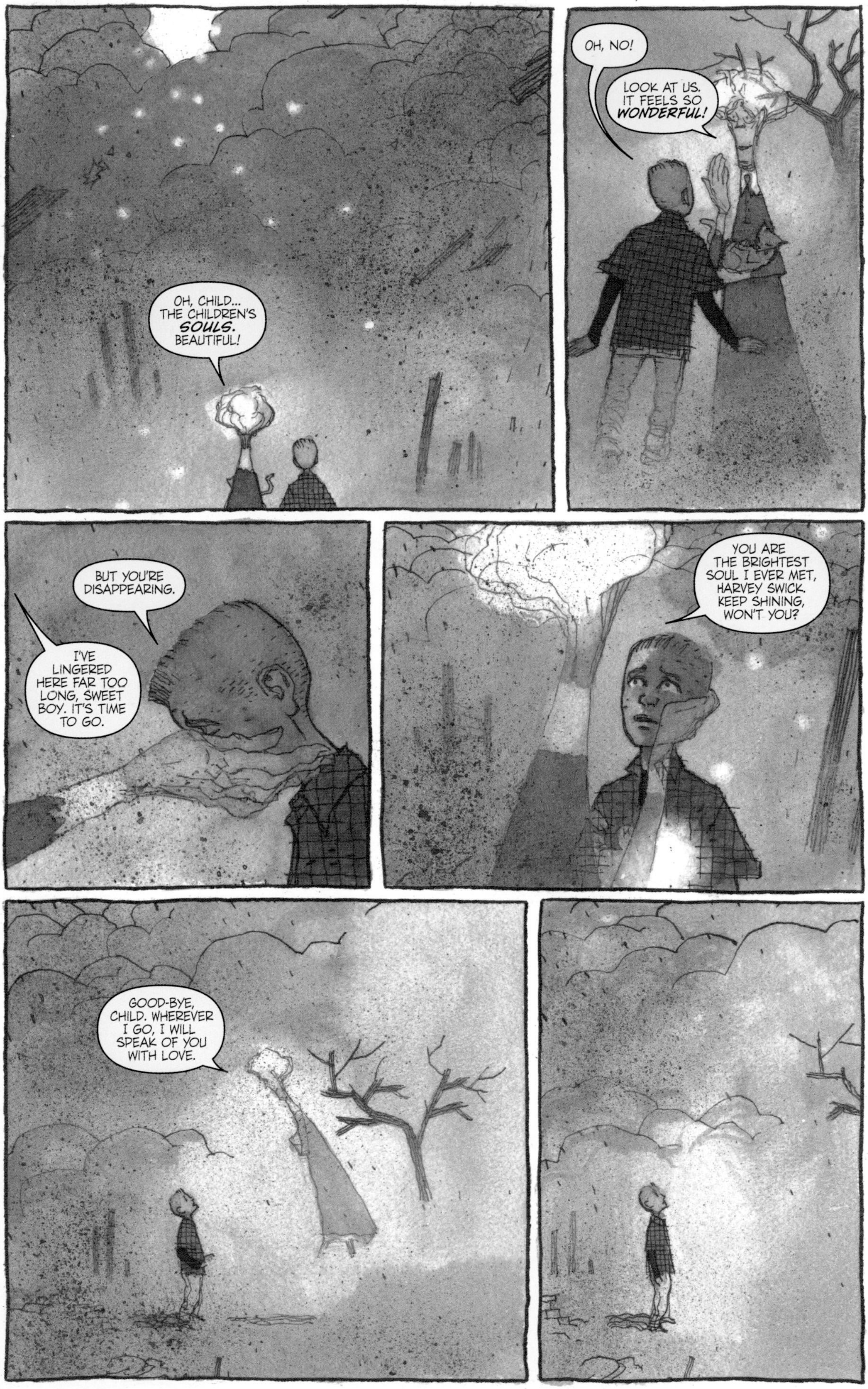
OH, CHILD... THE CHILDREN'S SOULS. BEAUTIFUL!
OH, NO!
LOOK AT US. IT FEELS SO WONDERFUL!
BUT YOU'RE DISAPPEARING.
I'VE LINGERED HERE FAR TOO LONG, SWEET BOY. IT'S TIME TO GO.
YOU ARE THE BRIGHTEST SOUL I EVER MET, HARVEY SWICK. KEEP SHINING, WON'T YOU?
GOOD-BYE, CHILD. WHEREVER I GO, I WILL SPEAK OF YOU WITH LOVE.

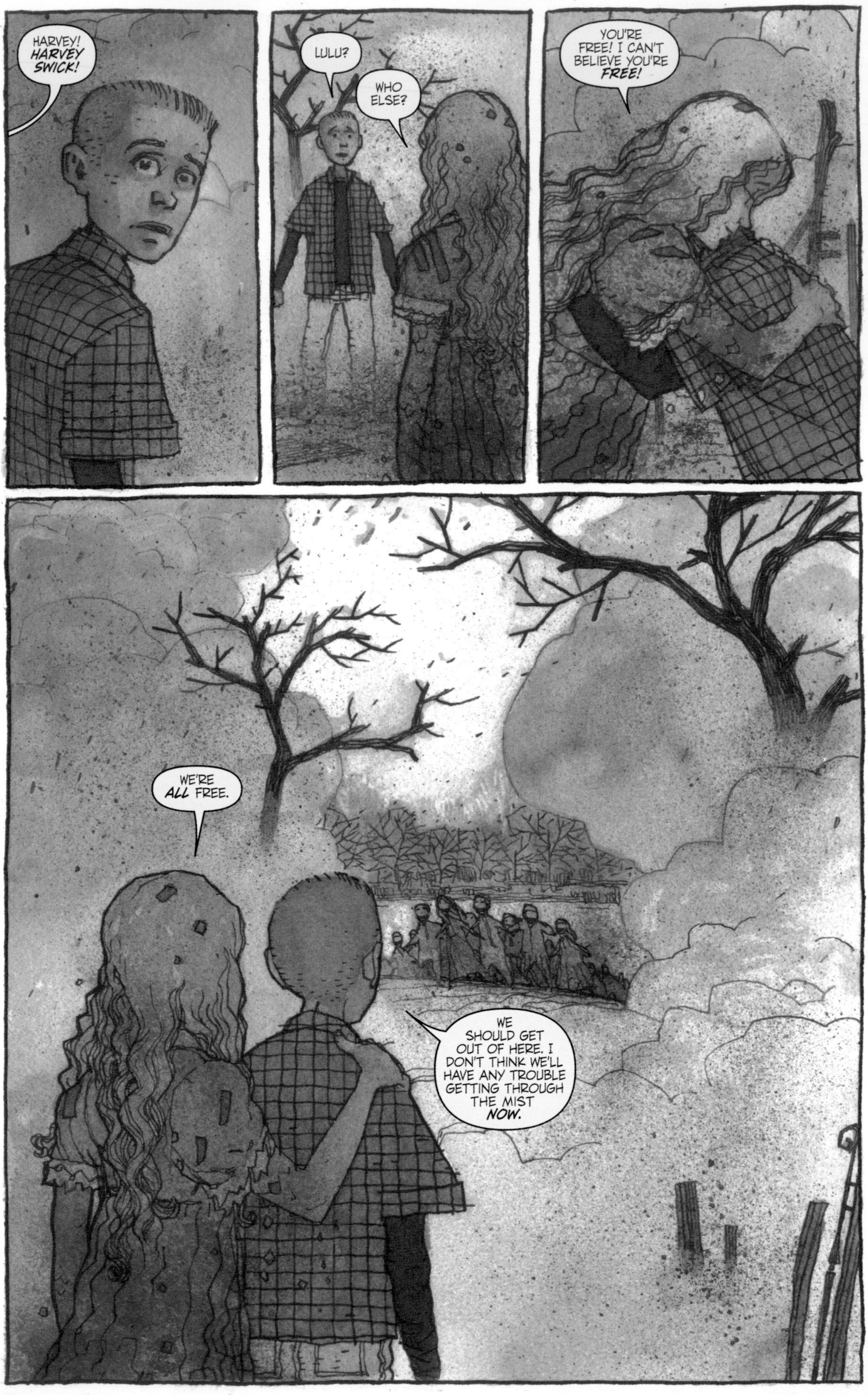
HARVEY! HARVEY SWICK!
LULU?
WHO ELSE?
YOU'RE FREE! I CAN'T BELIEVE YOU'RE FREE!
WE'RE ALL FREE.
WE SHOULD GET OUT OF HERE. I DON'T THINK WE'LL HAVE ANY TROUBLE GETTING THROUGH THE MIST NOW.

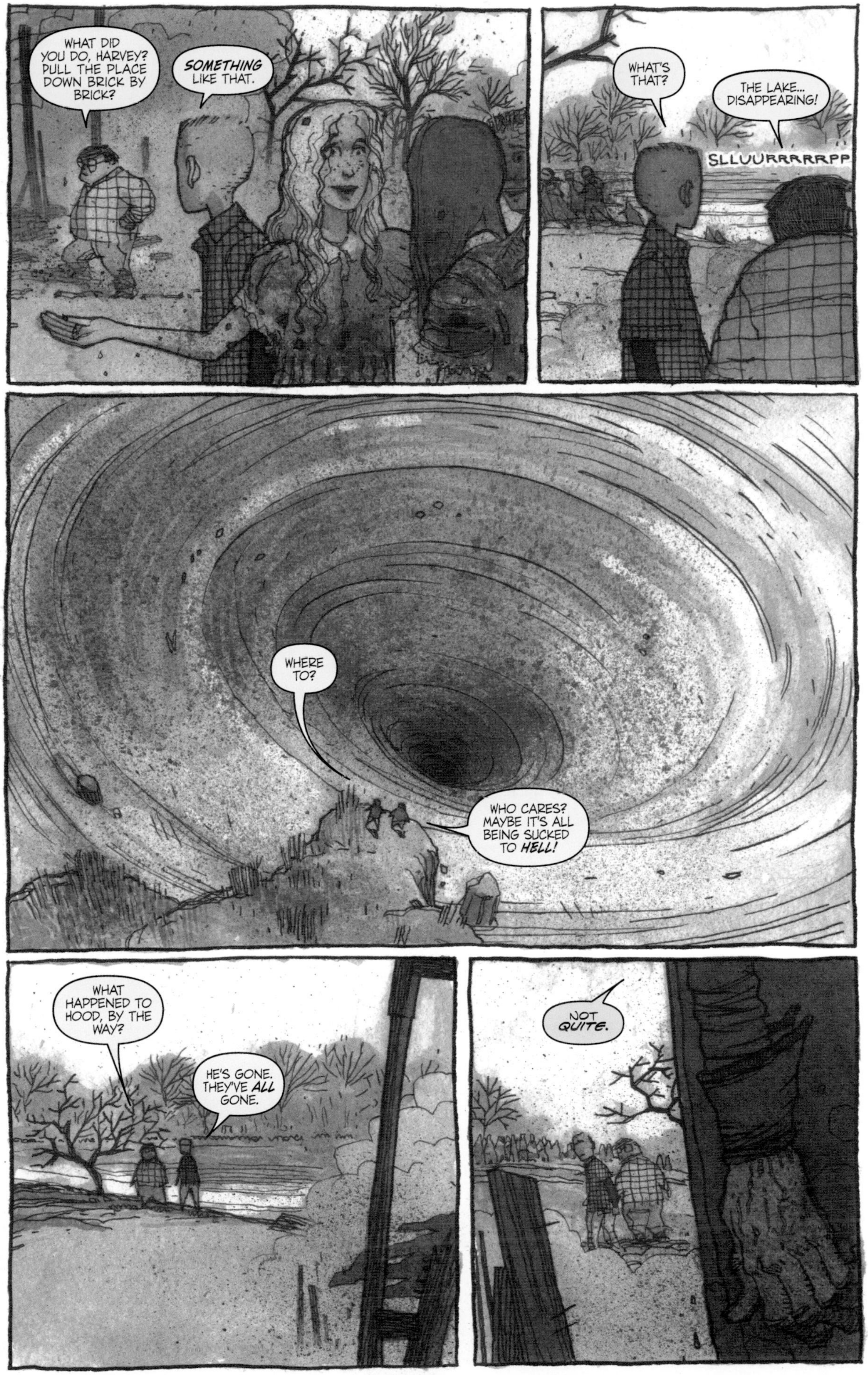

WHAT DID YOU DO, HARVEY? PULL THE PLACE DOWN BRICK BY BRICK?
SOMETHING LIKE THAT.
WHAT'S THAT?
THE LAKE... DISAPPEARING!
SLLUURRRRRPP
WHERE TO?
WHO CARES? MAYBE IT'S ALL BEING SUCKED TO HELL!
WHAT HAPPENED TO HOOD, BY THE WAY?
HE'S GONE. THEY'VE ALL GONE.
NOT QUITE.

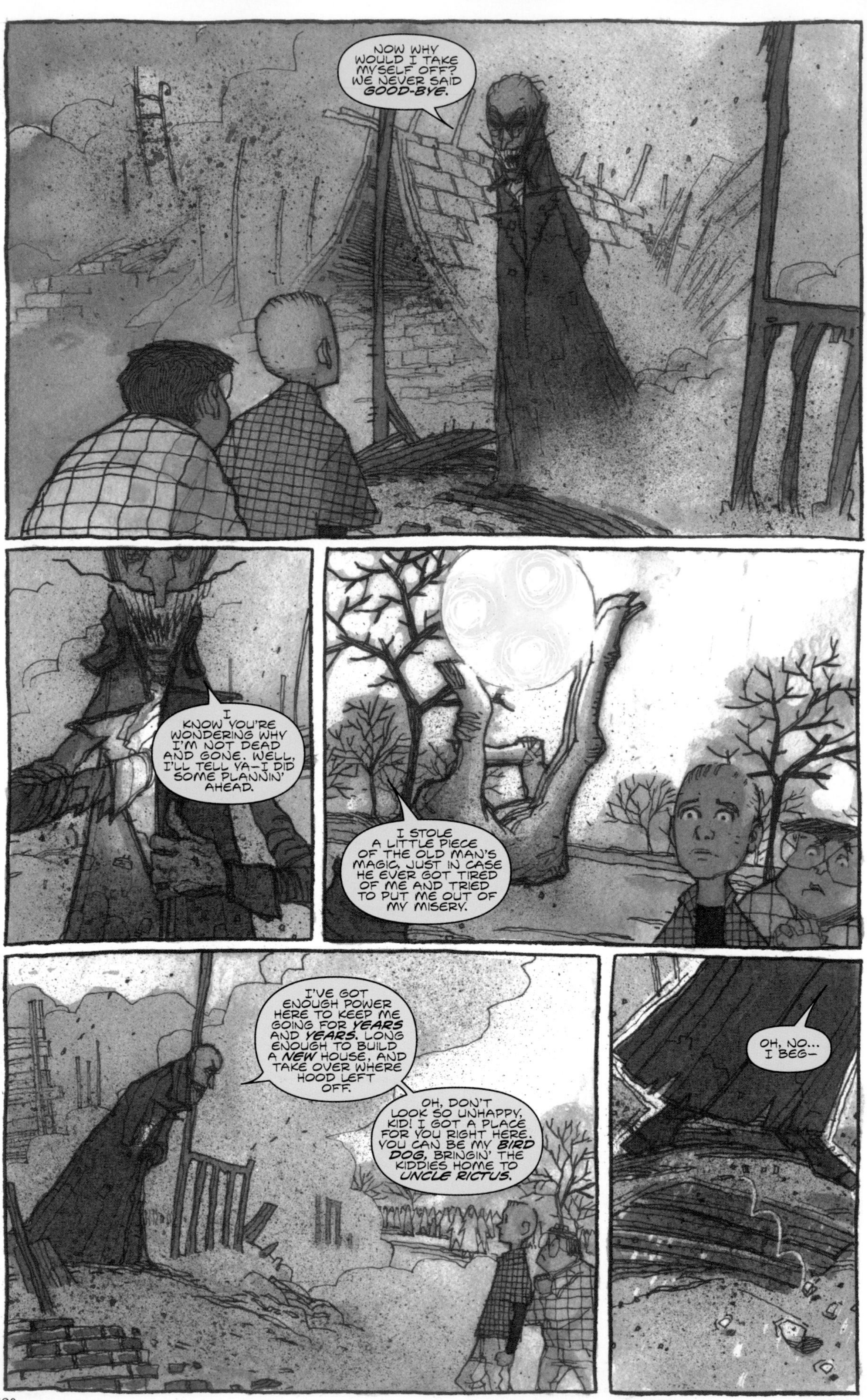
NOW WHY WOULD I TAKE MYSELF OFF? WE NEVER SAID GOOD-BYE.
I KNOW YOU'RE WONDERING WHY I'M NOT DEAD AND GONE. WELL, I'LL TELL YA—I DID SOME PLANNIN' AHEAD.
I STOLE A LITTLE PIECE OF THE OLD MAN'S MAGIC, JUST IN CASE HE EVER GOT TIRED OF ME AND TRIED TO PUT ME OUT OF MY MISERY.
I'VE GOT ENOUGH POWER HERE TO KEEP ME GOING FOR YEARS AND YEARS. LONG ENOUGH TO BUILD A NEW HOUSE, AND TAKE OVER WHERE HOOD LEFT OFF.
OH, DON'T LOOK SO UNHAPPY, KID! I GOT A PLACE FOR YOU RIGHT HERE. YOU CAN BE MY BIRD DOG, BRINGIN' THE KIDDIES HOME TO UNCLE RICTUS.
OH, NO... I BEG—

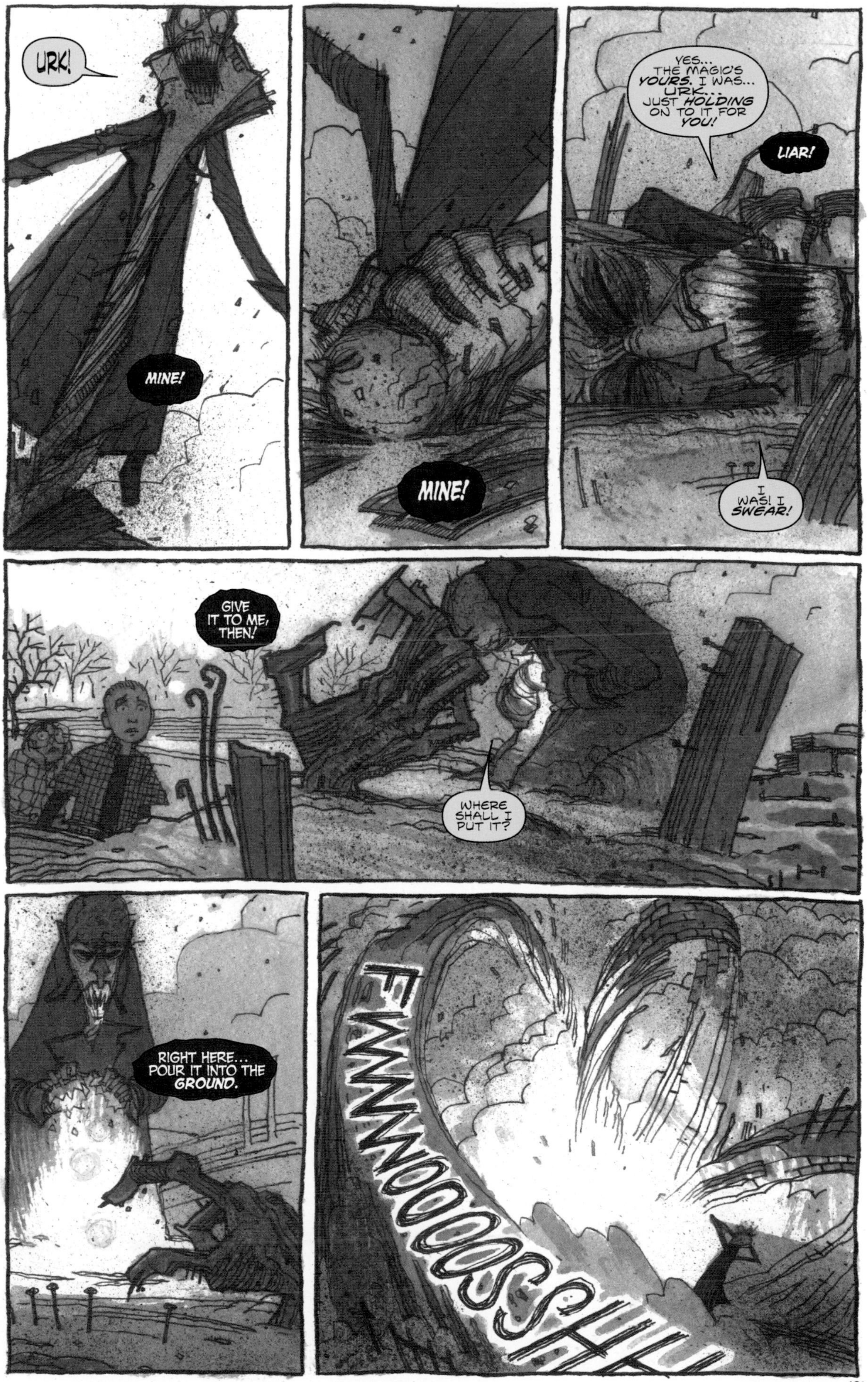
URK!
MINE!
MINE!
YES... THE MAGIC'S YOURS. I WAS... URK... JUST HOLDING ON TO IT FOR YOU!
LIAR!
I WAS! I SWEAR!
GIVE IT TO ME, THEN!
WHERE SHALL I PUT IT?
RIGHT HERE... POUR IT INTO THE GROUND.
FWWWOOOOSSHH

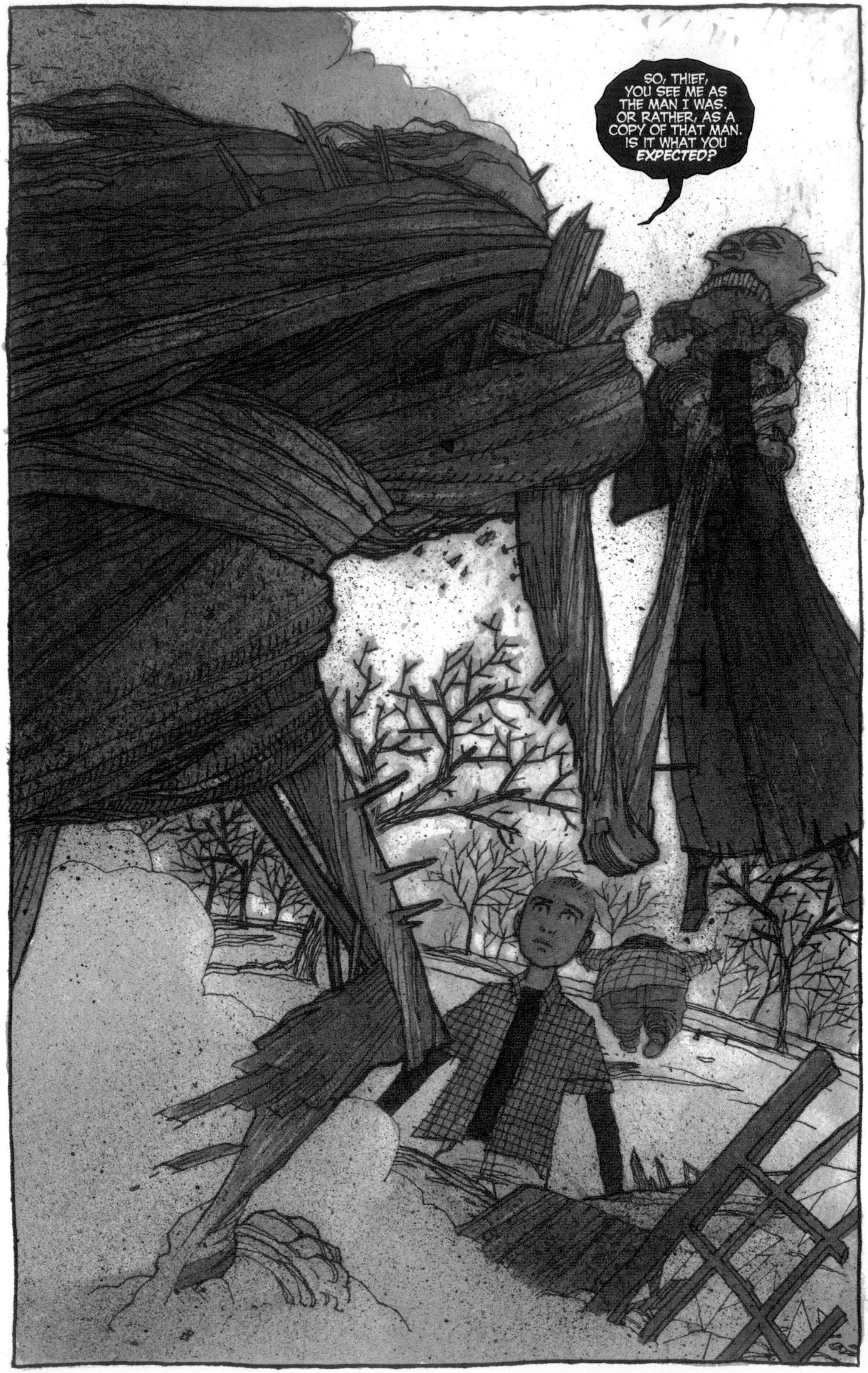
SO, THIEF, YOU SEE ME AS THE MAN I WAS. OR RATHER, AS A COPY OF THAT MAN. IS IT WHAT YOU EXPECTED?

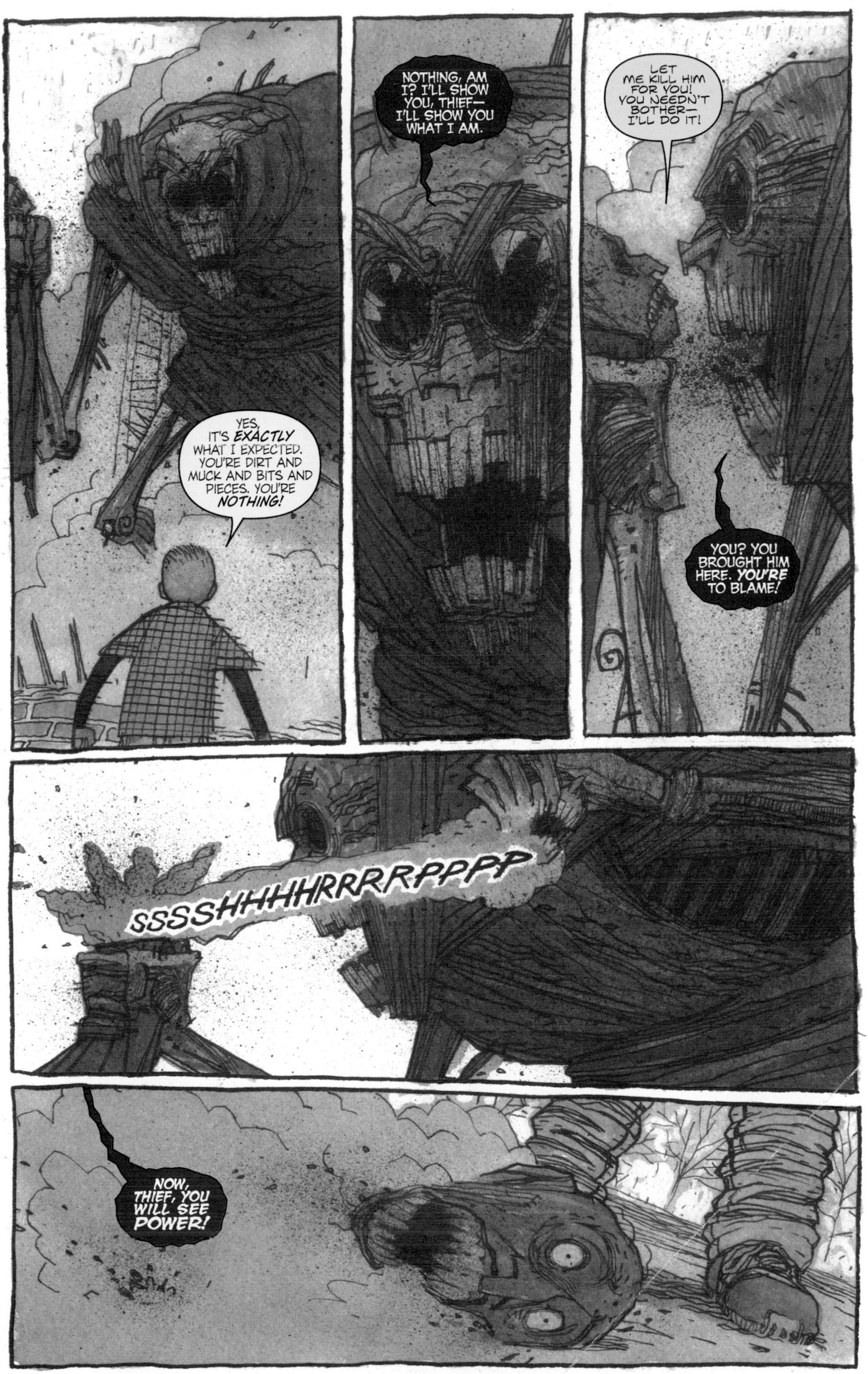
YES, IT'S EXACTLY WHAT I EXPECTED. YOU'RE DIRT AND MUCK AND BITS AND PIECES. YOU'RE NOTHING!
NOTHING, AM I? I'LL SHOW YOU, THIEF— I'LL SHOW YOU WHAT I AM.
LET ME KILL HIM FOR YOU! YOU NEEDN'T BOTHER— I'LL DO IT!
YOU? YOU BROUGHT HIM HERE. YOU'RE TO BLAME!
SSSSHHHHHRRRRRPPPPP
NOW, THIEF, YOU WILL SEE POWER!

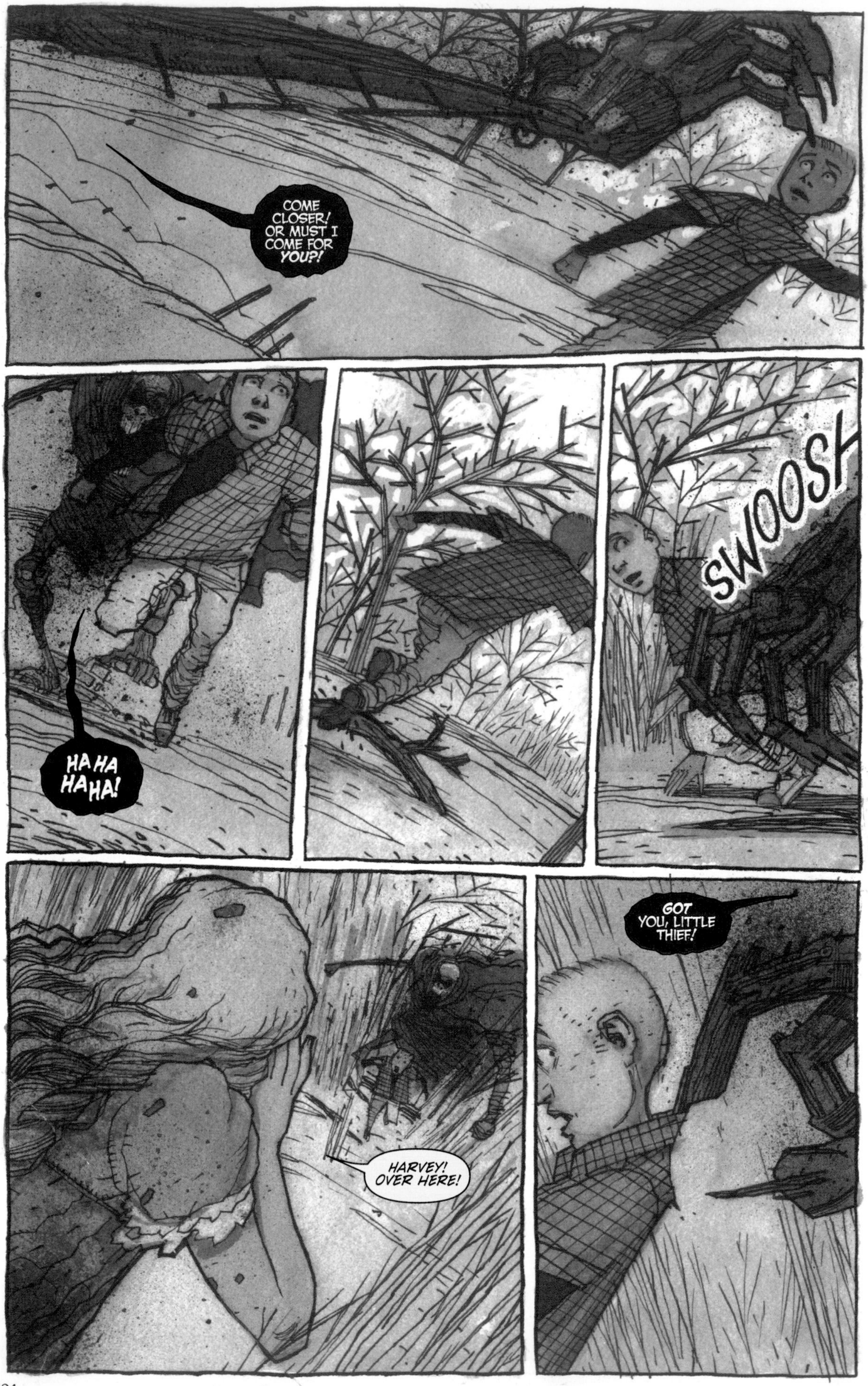
COME CLOSER! OR MUST I COME FOR YOU?!
HA HA HA HA!
SWOOSH
HARVEY! OVER HERE!
GOT YOU, LITTLE THIEF!

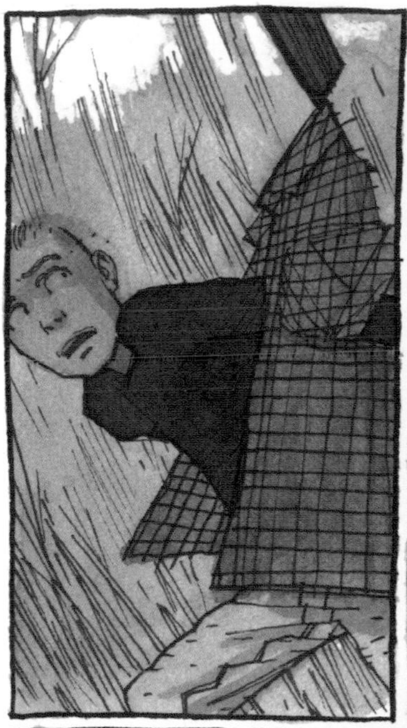

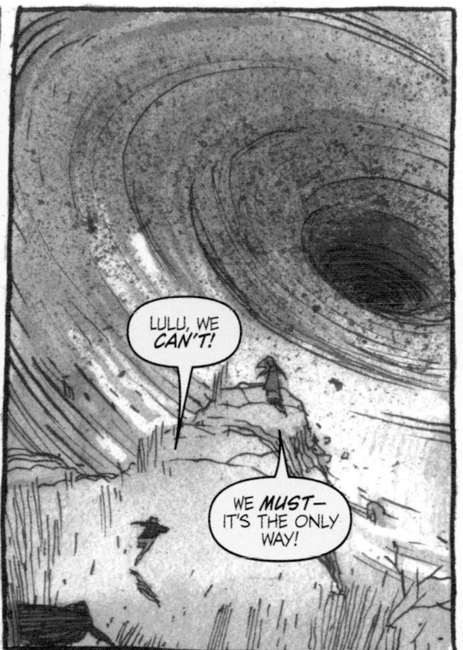
LULU, WE CAN'T!
WE MUST— IT'S THE ONLY WAY!

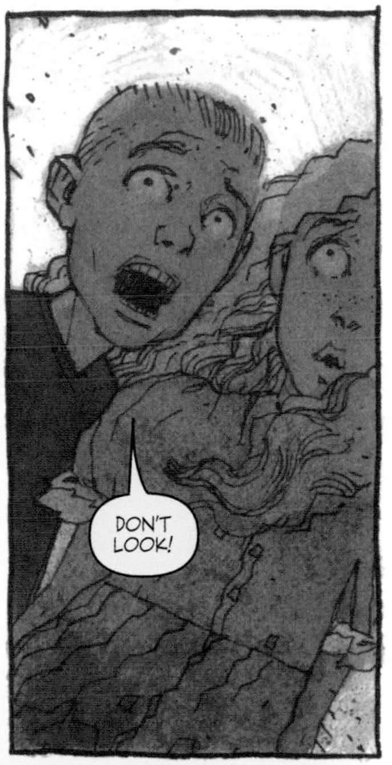
DON'T LOOK!

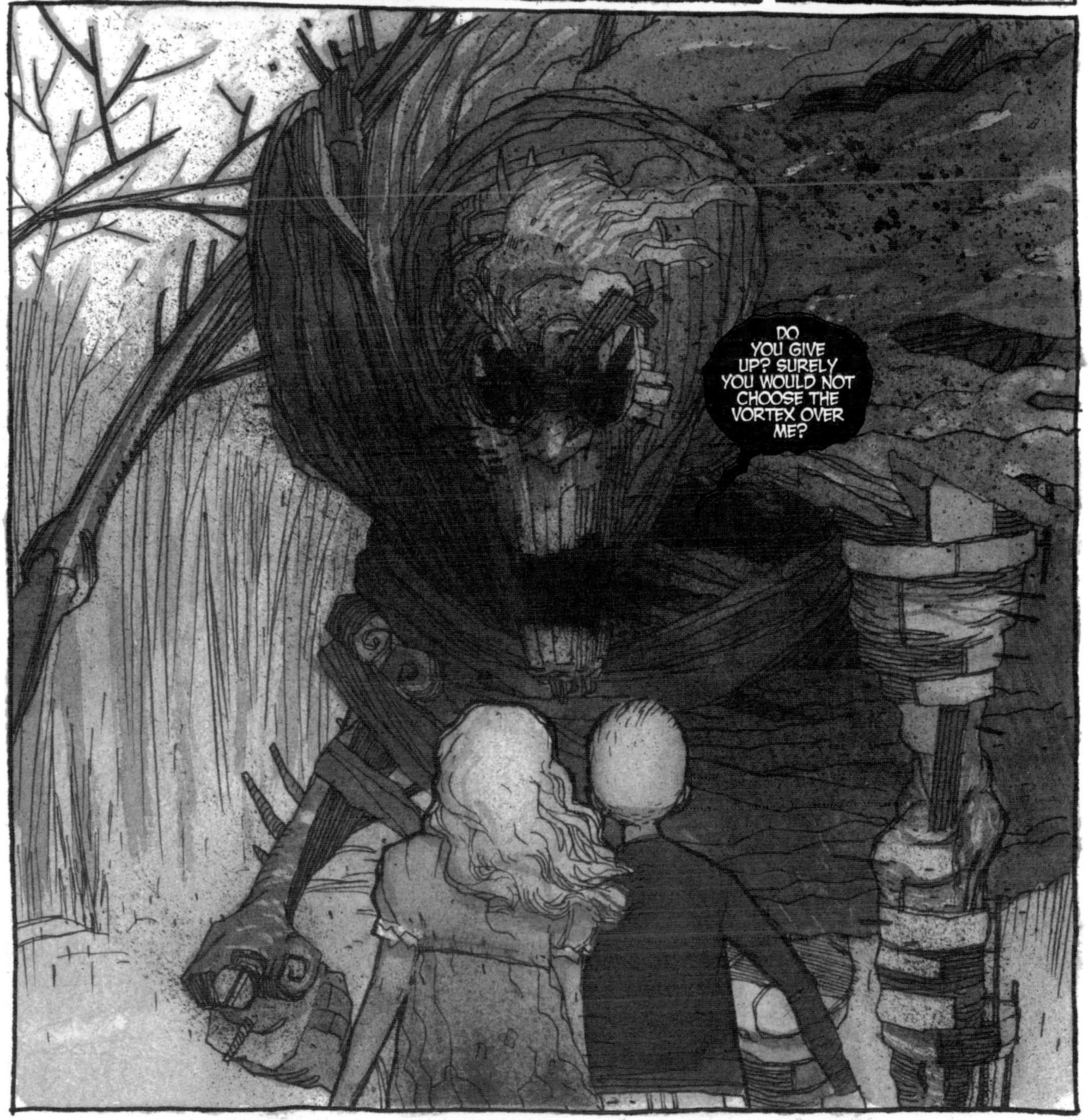
DO YOU GIVE UP? SURELY YOU WOULD NOT CHOOSE THE VORTEX OVER ME?

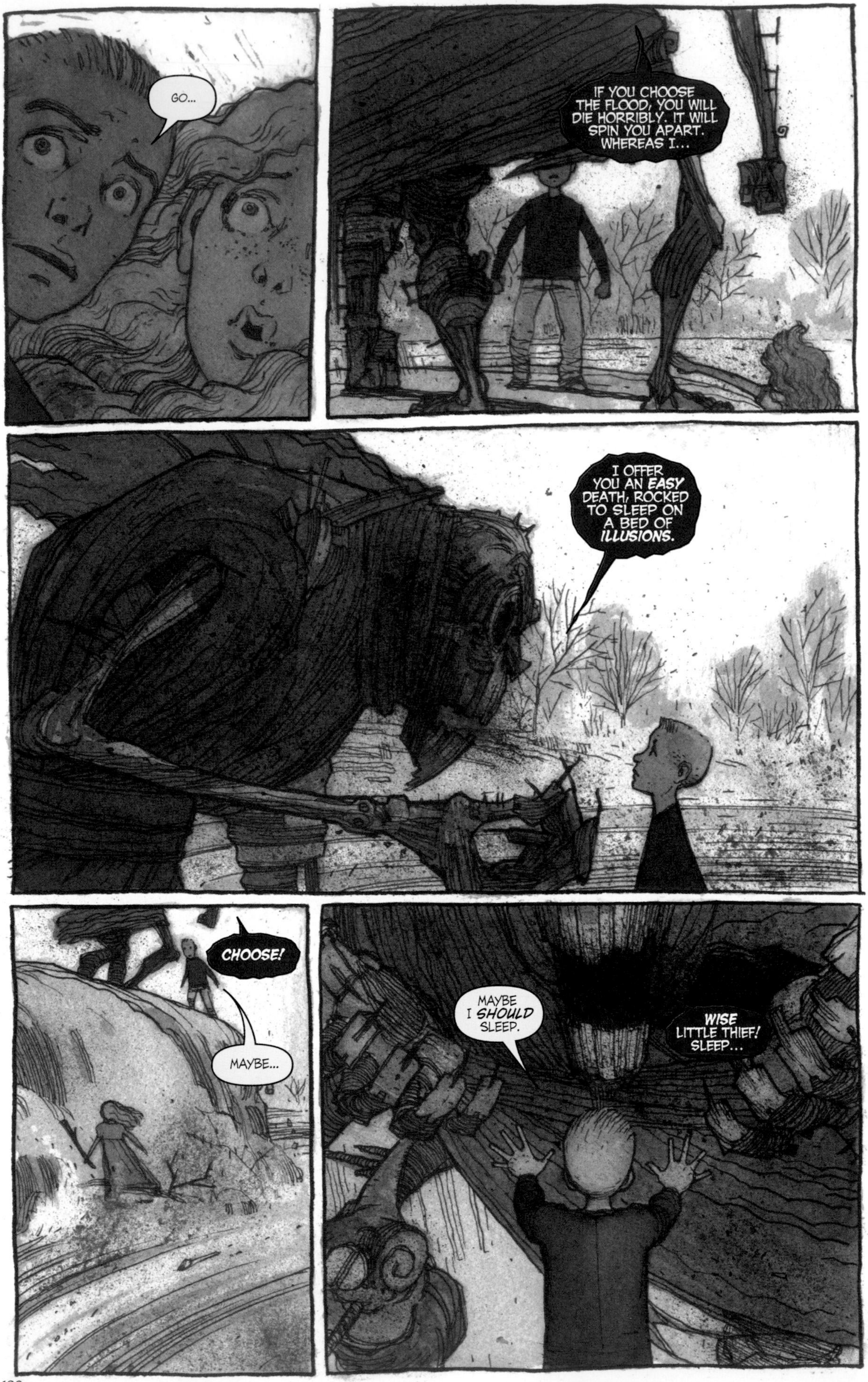
GO...
IF YOU CHOOSE THE FLOOD, YOU WILL DIE HORRIBLY. IT WILL SPIN YOU APART. WHEREAS I...
I OFFER YOU AN EASY DEATH, ROCKED TO SLEEP ON A BED OF ILLUSIONS.
CHOOSE!
MAYBE...
MAYBE I SHOULD SLEEP.
WISE LITTLE THIEF! SLEEP...

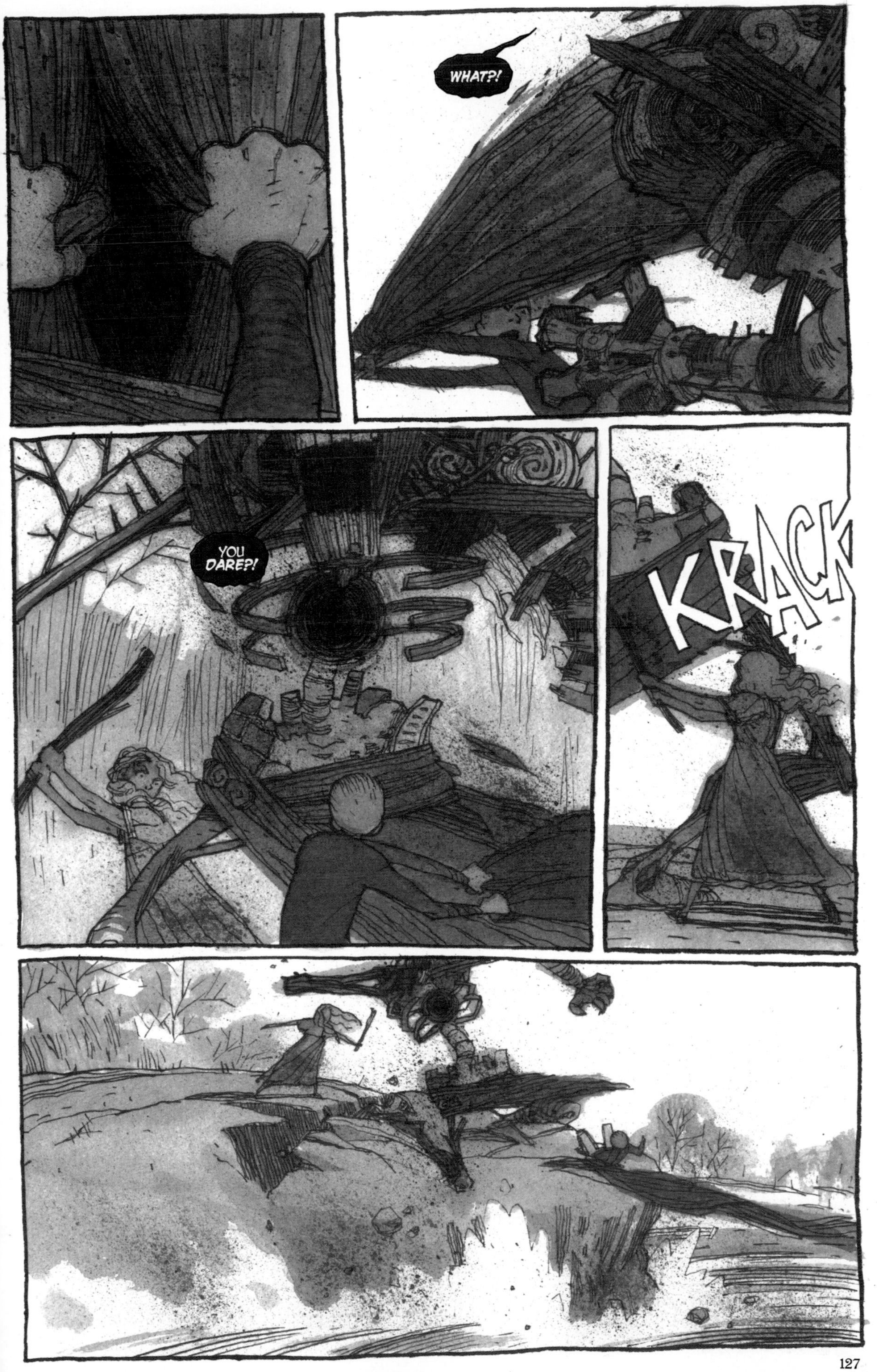
WHAT?!
YOU DARE?!
KRACK

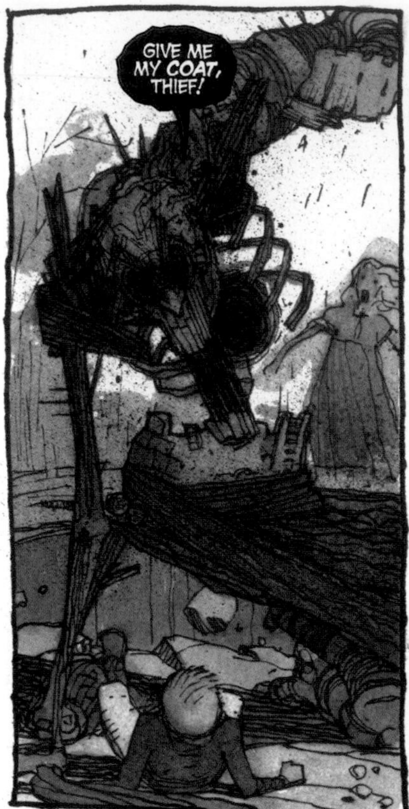
GIVE ME MY COAT, THIEF!
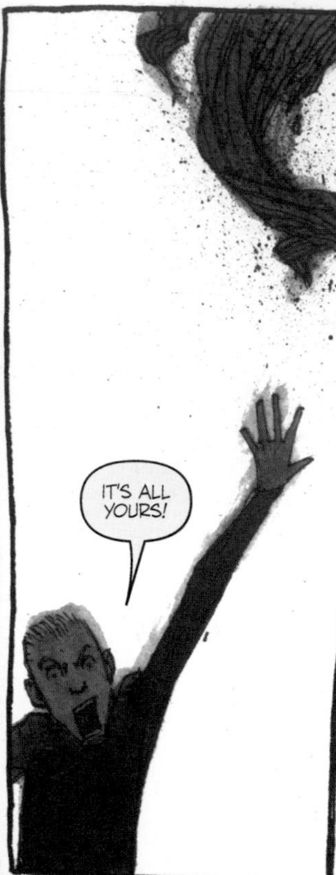
IT'S ALL YOURS!
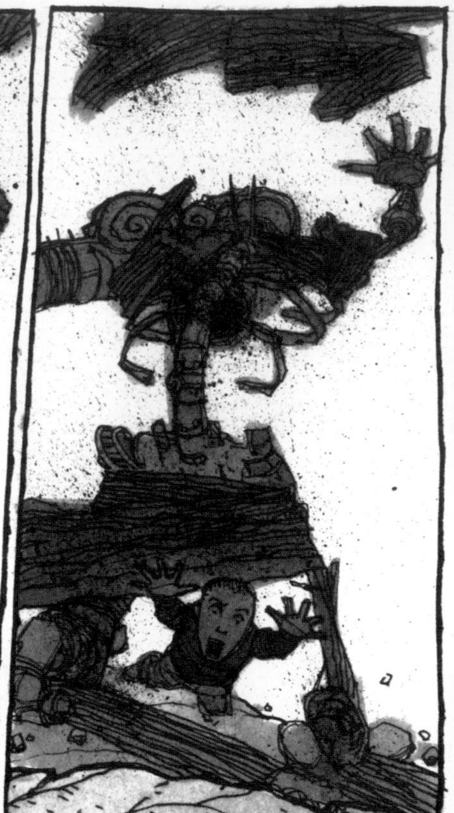
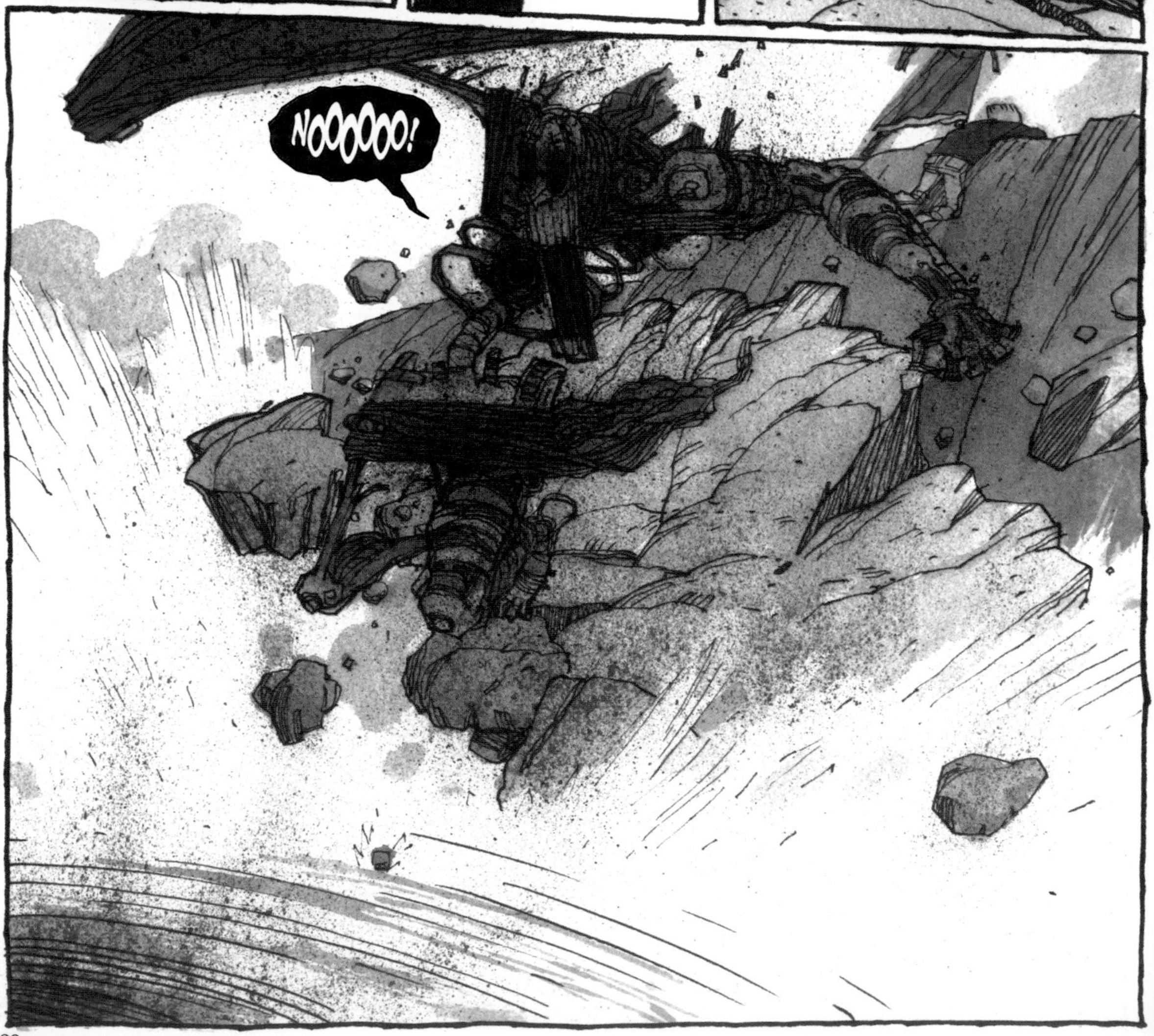
NOOOOOO!

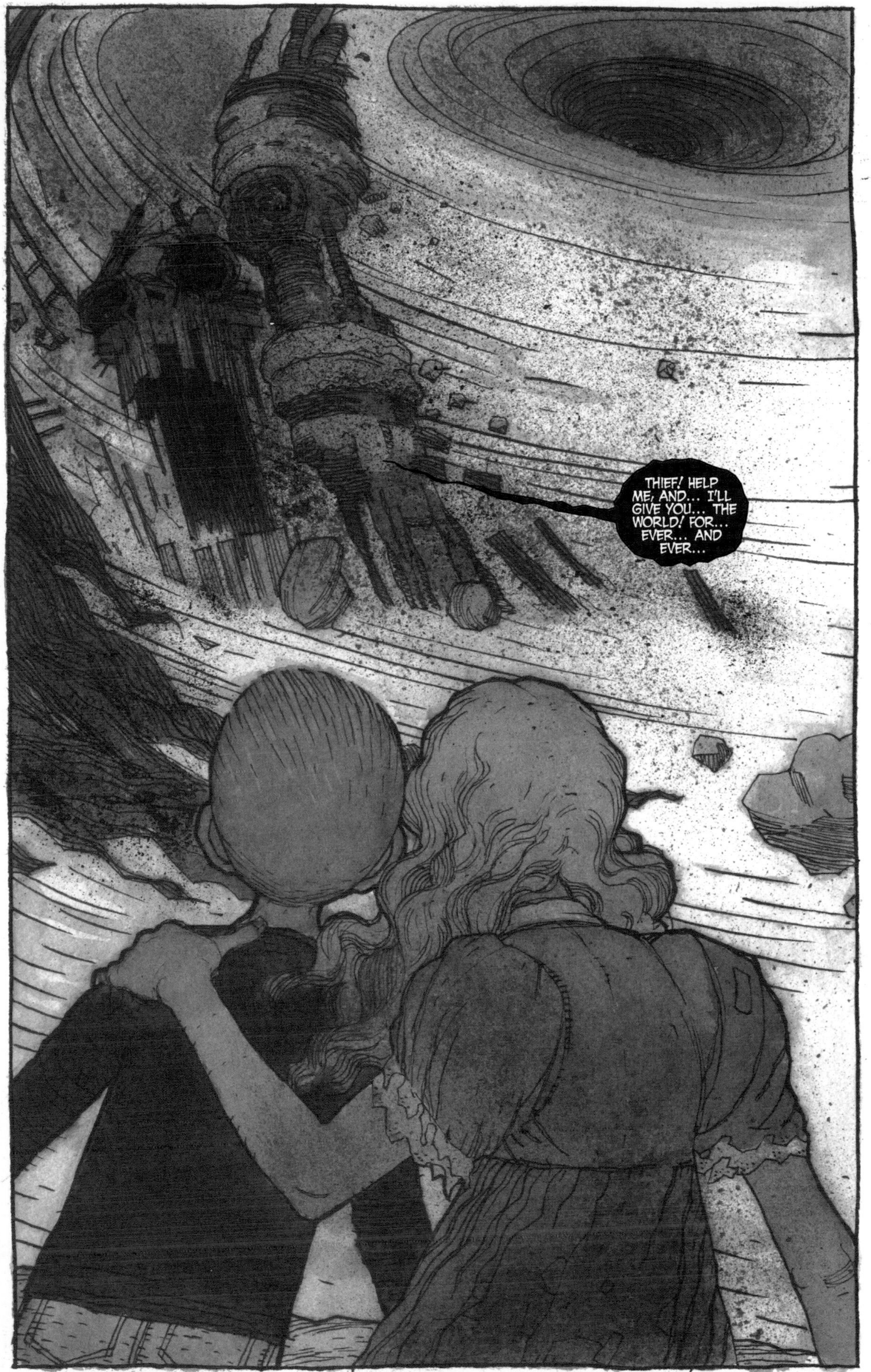
THIEF! HELP ME, AND... I'LL GIVE YOU... THE WORLD! FOR... EVER... AND EVER...

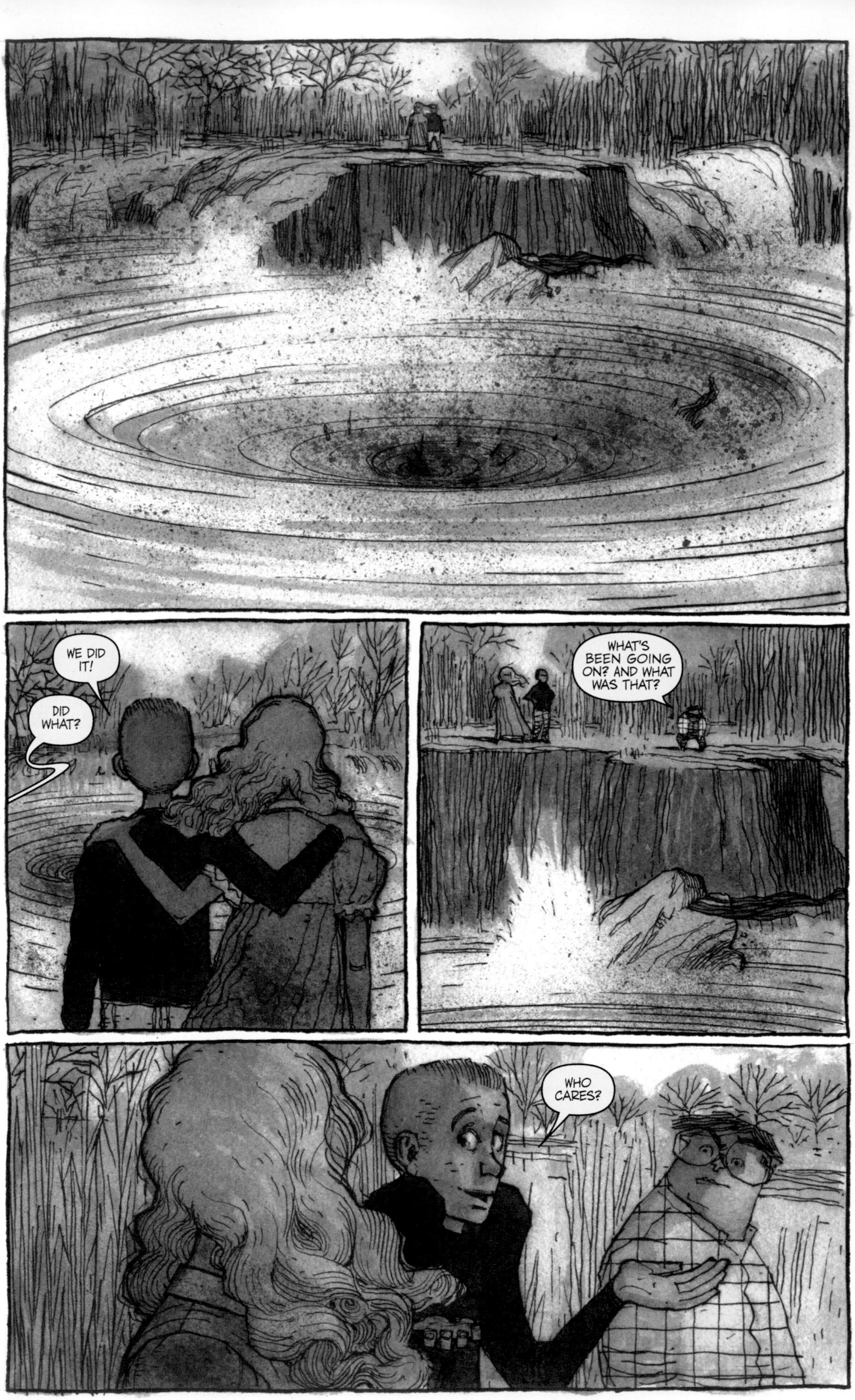
WE DID IT!
DID WHAT?
WHAT'S BEEN GOING ON? AND WHAT WAS THAT?
WHO CARES?

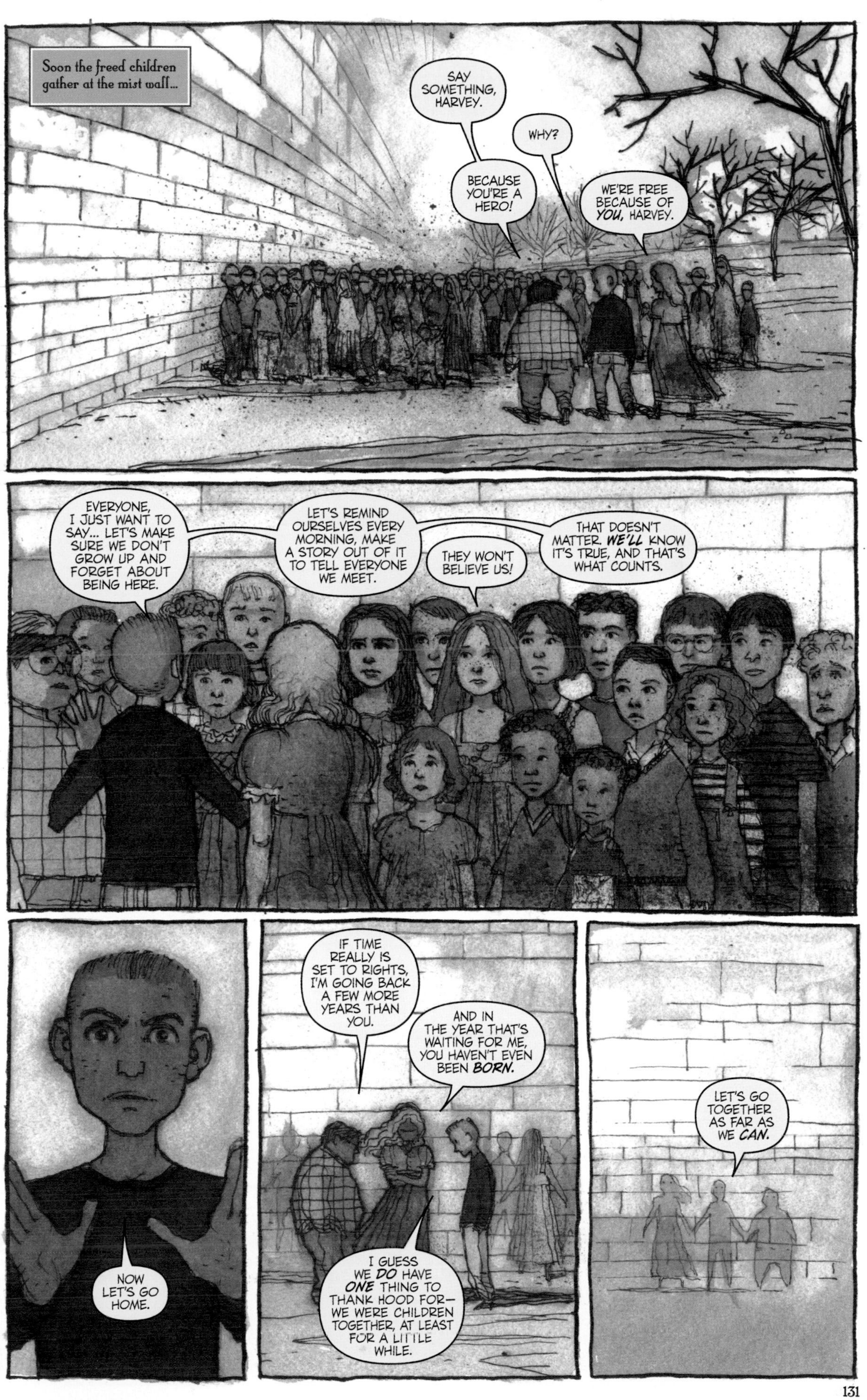
Soon the freed children gather at the mist wall...
SAY SOMETHING, HARVEY.
WHY?
BECAUSE YOU'RE A HERO!
WE'RE FREE BECAUSE OF YOU, HARVEY.
EVERYONE, I JUST WANT TO SAY... LET'S MAKE SURE WE DON'T GROW UP AND FORGET ABOUT BEING HERE.
LET'S REMIND OURSELVES EVERY MORNING, MAKE A STORY OUT OF IT TO TELL EVERYONE WE MEET.
THEY WON'T BELIEVE US!
THAT DOESN'T MATTER. WE'LL KNOW IT'S TRUE, AND THAT'S WHAT COUNTS.
NOW LET'S GO HOME.
IF TIME REALLY IS SET TO RIGHTS, I'M GOING BACK A FEW MORE YEARS THAN YOU.
AND IN THE YEAR THAT'S WAITING FOR ME, YOU HAVEN'T EVEN BEEN BORN.
I GUESS WE DO HAVE ONE THING TO THANK HOOD FOR— WE WERE CHILDREN TOGETHER, AT LEAST FOR A LITTLE WHILE.
LET'S GO TOGETHER AS FAR AS WE CAN.

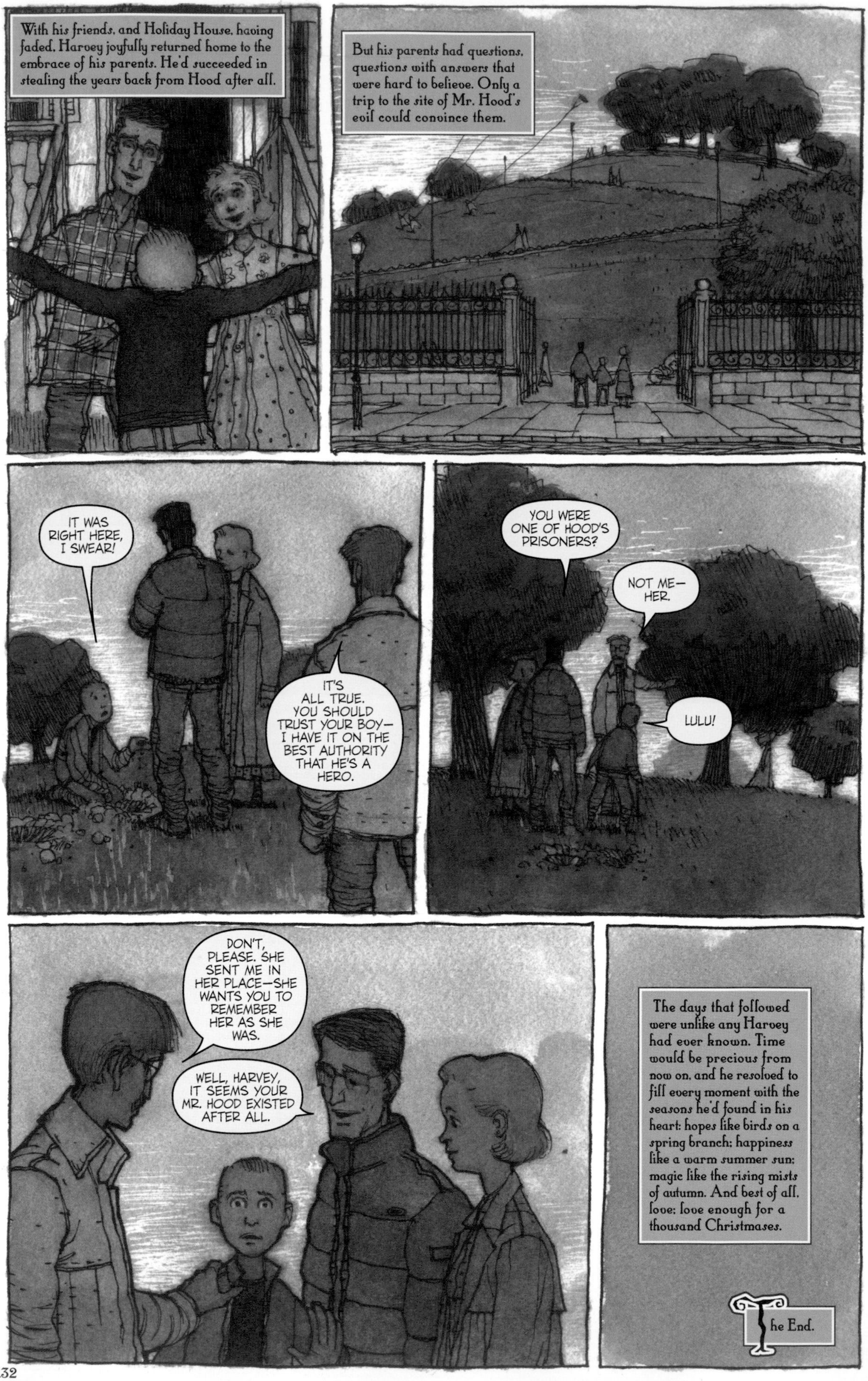
With his friends, and Holiday House, having faded, Harvey joyfully returned home to the embrace of his parents. He'd succeeded in stealing the years back from Hood after all.
But his parents had questions, questions with answers that were hard to believe. Only a trip to the site of Mr. Hood's evil could convince them.
IT WAS RIGHT HERE, I SWEAR!
IT'S ALL TRUE. YOU SHOULD TRUST YOUR BOY— I HAVE IT ON THE BEST AUTHORITY THAT HE'S A HERO.
YOU WERE ONE OF HOOD'S PRISONERS?
NOT ME— HER.
LULU!
DON'T, PLEASE. SHE SENT ME IN HER PLACE—SHE WANTS YOU TO REMEMBER HER AS SHE WAS.
WELL, HARVEY, IT SEEMS YOUR MR. HOOD EXISTED AFTER ALL.
The days that followed were unlike any Harvey had ever known. Time would be precious from now on, and he resolved to fill every moment with the seasons he'd found in his heart: hopes like birds on a spring branch; happiness like a warm summer sun; magic like the rising mists of autumn. And best of all, love; love enough for a thousand Christmases.
The End.

clive BARKER

First of all, can you tell us a bit about the genesis of _The Thief of Always_? What made you want to craft a novel aimed at a younger readership than your usual work?

Clive: This was way before Harry Potter and the re-emergence of fiction for the younger audience being so big, and I certainly did it because I wanted to tell this particular story. The story had occurred to me a while ago and I'd written it down in a short form called "The Holiday House" and I showed it to my agent, who wasn't particularly eager about it, so I went into a corner and just did it, because it was a story I wanted to write. Sometimes you've just got to do what you've got to do! It took about three months to write, probably another couple months to do fixes on, and then I gave it to HarperCollins and said, "I realize you're taking a huge risk with this, because here's a children's book coming from Clive Barker, and maybe nobody will buy it! So I'll sell it to you for a dollar." Actually, they ended up giving me a silver dollar for it. And I did the illustrations, and the thing went from there. It has since turned out to be a very successful book. It's in a lot of languages around the world and it's being taught in a lot of schools now, which is fun. I think we're at 1.5 million copies in print in America, so it wasn't bad for a book that cost them a dollar.

Was your approach to writing _The Thief of Always_ any different due to the fact that you were writing for a younger audience?

Clive: No, I mean there are things you obviously can't do—you're not going to do any sexy scenes, you're not going to do any scenes that are very violent, you're not going to use any cuss words. But storytelling's storytelling. I wanted to keep the chapters reasonably short, because I remember as a young reader I liked short chapters, but I was drawn along by the energy of the storytelling. I didn't at any point really think, "Gee, I shouldn't do that." I don't think there was anywhere in the story that I worried about content—it was a story that told itself, and it was a real pleasure to write.

Regarding the characters, is there a lot of Harvey Swick in you? Did you base any of the characters on childhood acquaintances?

Clive: It's me, it's me—it's the bored child. But I think it's every child. I think we, all of us, as children feel bored a lot of the time, waiting for adults to do whatever adults do. It's definitely less true now, but as a kid I didn't have those diversions. So there was a lot of downtime, time where you were just waiting. I used to do a lot of reading, but even reading can't take you away all the time, away from the gray reality of life in Liverpool in the '50s, which is where I was brought up, and I wanted to reflect that in Harvey. I also wanted to give Harvey some of my imaginative energy. So, yeah, I think there's something of Harvey in me.

Was the story of Holiday House based on a childhood daydream of your own, or something that occurred to you in adulthood?

Clive: It really came out of the blue. Even as a kid, I was aware that I lived from holiday to holiday. Every kid does that—you finish your summer holidays, and you think "Oh, how long is it to Thanksgiving?" (in America—in England, it was Bonfire Night). And then on Bonfire Night you thought, "OK, well, how long is it until Christmas?" I mean, you're constantly saying that. And my mother would be constantly saying, "Don't wish your life away, don't wish your life away." But the story wasn't based on anything except that there were a lot of times in my life when I wished more was going on, and I thought this would be an interesting fantasy to play with.

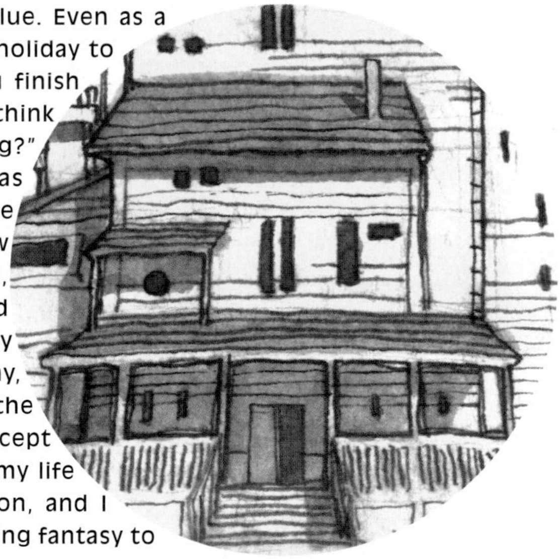

Did the basic story of the novel change at all while you were writing it? Were there any scenes or characters that didn't make the final cut?

Clive: Not that I remember. It was a neat writing experience, in the sense that I really knew what the narrative was going to be. I laid it out in chapters before writing it, I laid out what I thought the action was going to be. I had a really clear sense of it. I wish novels were always this easy, but they're not. But of all the things I've written, this was probably the simplest process.

The novel is set in a timeless era that could be taken to be anything from the 1950s to the present time. Was this a conscious decision on your part?

Clive: Yeah, I like to do that—not only the stuff for younger readers, but with all of my fiction. I don't like to be too specific about time periods. Let's make a study in contrasts: Steve—Steve King—is brilliant at using brand names and songs and particular time indicators in his stories to make you feel, "Oh, I was there. I know what it feels like to listen to Bob Dylan"—or Metallica, or whatever it is. I tend to go in the opposite direction. Almost nowhere in my novels will you find references to specific products. Unless it's really necessary, I don't even feel it's vital to tell you what the date is. If a story works, a story works. I think Harvey's world and Harvey's problem and challenge—both his boredom and his desire to fight back against the man who took time from him—those are universal ideas, and, in principle therefore, the book should be readable without any indicators as to the time period.

I know your paintings serve as inspiration for your *Abarat* book series... with certain editions of *The Thief of Always* novel also featuring your own art, was this a method of inspiration you used on this project as well?

Clive: It wasn't. It was completely the reverse. I did the entire story and then they said, "Why don't you do illustrations for it as well?" So it was the Publisher's suggestion. I thought it was a cool idea. I'd done *The Books of Blood* covers for the limited edition, so they knew I did artwork and so I thought, "Hey, why not?" And now, the *Abarat* experience is completely the reverse—I'm up to five hundred paintings here.

One of the most entertaining aspects of the story is the quartet of Hood flunkies: Carna, Jive, Rictus, and Marr. Any favorites among these? Why?

Clive: They are four faces of darkness, aren't they? The thing that smiles and won't stop smiling, the monster—Carna, the strange witch-thing which appears from nothing, and this strange little servant who's almost like the guy from *The Rocky Horror Picture Show*. And my idea was that I'm going to have these four spooky characters—and they're not going to be *scary* scary—but they're going to be spooky in a way that the audience will really enjoy. My favorite is Rictus. It was really fun to write Rictus—I mean, he's a used car salesman! There's something wonderfully sleazy about him.

With the success of *The Thief of Always*, is there any possibility that we will ever see further adventures of Harvey Swick?

Clive: I don't have any plans. Every now and then I think of something, and I think maybe there's going to be a follow-up. It needs to be completely right or I won't do it. The thing about *The Thief of Always* is that it stands on its own beautifully. So if I am going to open up the narrative again there needs to be a really

First of all, can you tell us a bit about the genesis of *The Thief of Always*? What made you want to craft a novel aimed at a younger readership than your usual work?

Clive: This was way before Harry Potter and the re-emergence of fiction for the younger audience being so big, and I certainly did it because I wanted to tell this particular story. The story had occurred to me a while ago and I'd written it down in a short form called "The Holiday House" and I showed it to my agent, who wasn't particularly eager about it, so I went into a corner and just did it, because it was a story I wanted to write. Sometimes you've just got to do what you've got to do! It took about three months to write, probably another couple months to do fixes on, and then I gave it to HarperCollins and said, "I realize you're taking a huge risk with this, because here's a children's book coming from Clive Barker, and maybe nobody will buy it! So I'll sell it to you for a dollar." Actually, they ended up giving me a silver dollar for it. And I did the illustrations, and the thing went from there. It has since turned out to be a very successful book. It's in a lot of languages around the world and it's being taught in a lot of schools now, which is fun. I think we're at 1.5 million copies in print in America, so it wasn't bad for a book that cost them a dollar.

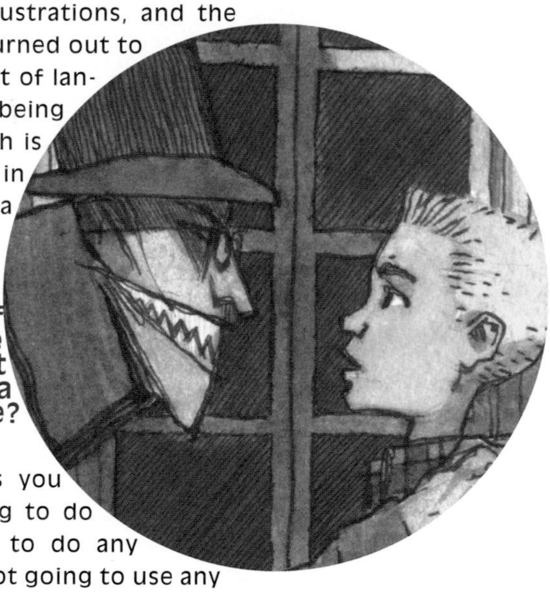

Was your approach to writing *The Thief of Always* any different due to the fact that you were writing for a younger audience?

Clive: No, I mean there are things you obviously can't do—you're not going to do any sexy scenes, you're not going to do any scenes that are very violent, you're not going to use any cuss words. But storytelling's storytelling. I wanted to keep the chapters reasonably short, because I remember as a young reader I liked short chapters, but I was drawn along by the energy of the storytelling. I didn't at any point really think, "Gee, I shouldn't do that." I don't think there was anywhere in the story that I worried about content—it was a story that told itself, and it was a real pleasure to write.

Regarding the characters, is there a lot of Harvey Swick in you? Did you base any of the characters on childhood acquaintances?

Clive: It's me, it's me—it's the bored child. But I think it's every child. I think we, all of us, as children feel bored a lot of the time, waiting for adults to do whatever adults do. It's definitely less true now, but as a kid I didn't have those diversions. So there was a lot of downtime, time where you were just waiting. I used to do a lot of reading, but even reading can't take you away all the

CLIVE BARKER'S
THE THIEF OF ALWAYS™

sketchbook & cover gallery

Character Sketches and Comments by
Gabriel Hernandez

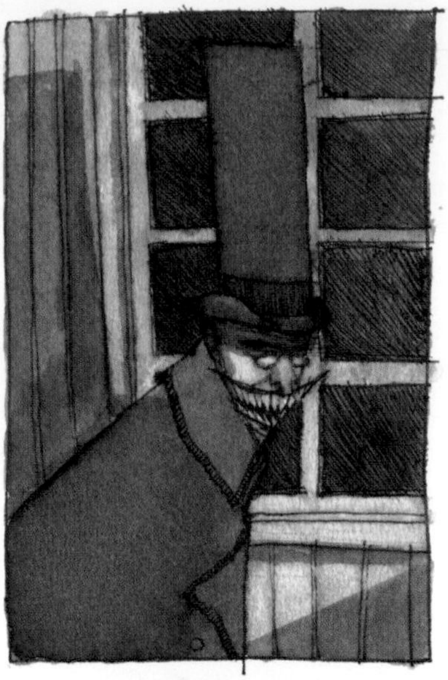

To create characters is sort of like casting a movie. The difference is, in a movie, you can cast any actor, but here, some characters are not even human and need to be created from just your imagination. Rictus and Mrs. Griffin, for example, are like puppets. Just their heads and hands have volume.

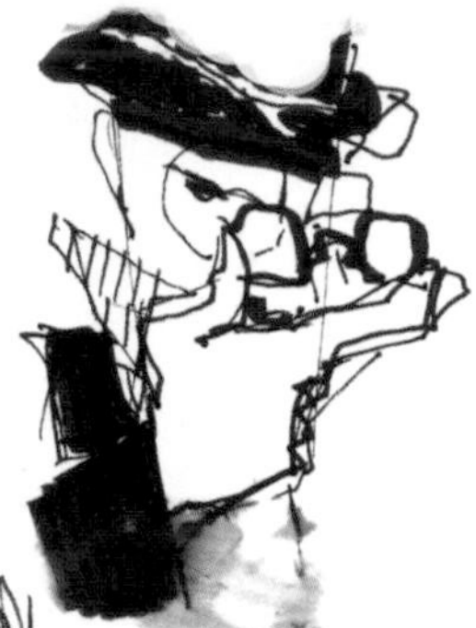

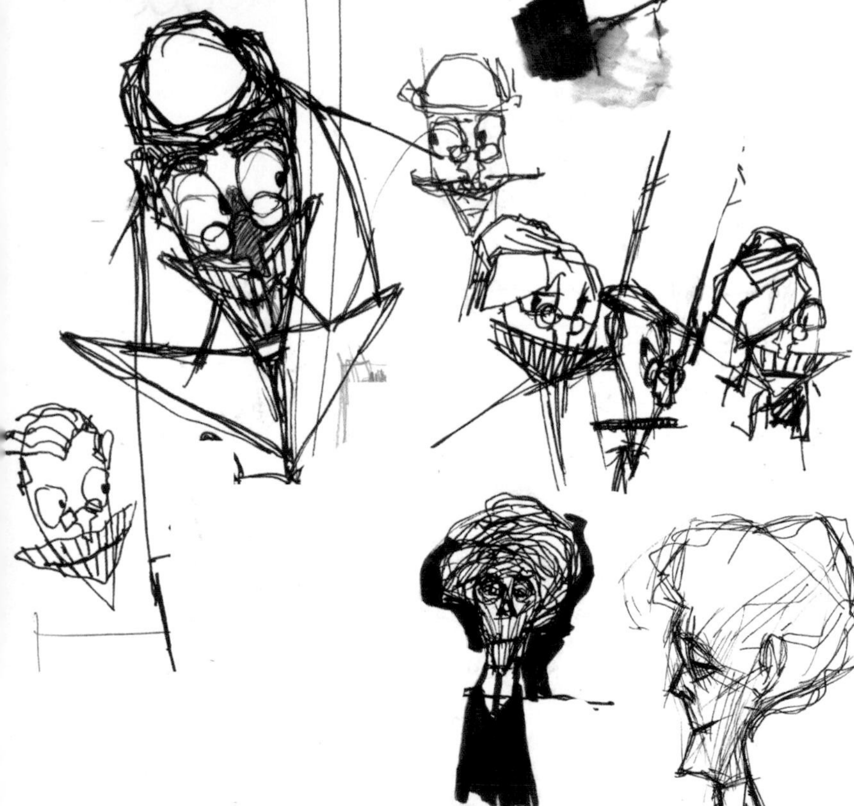

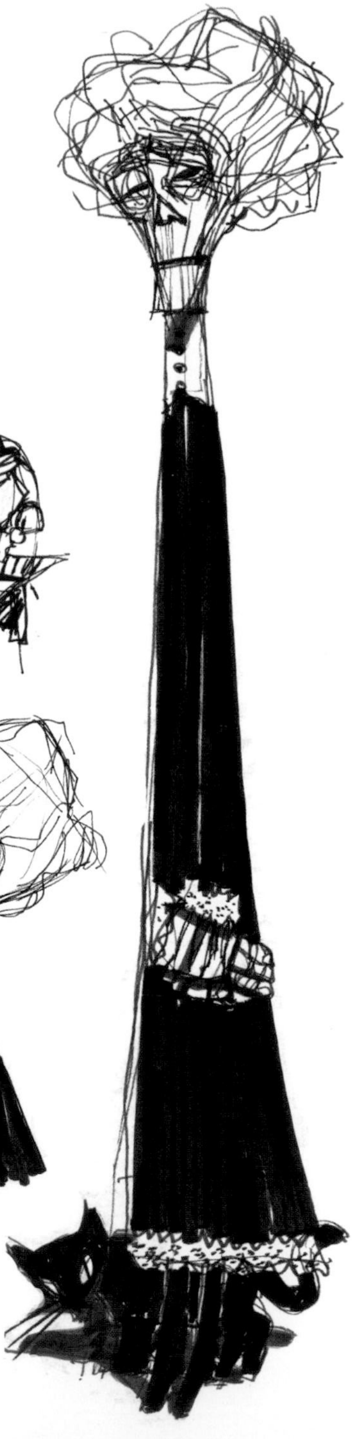

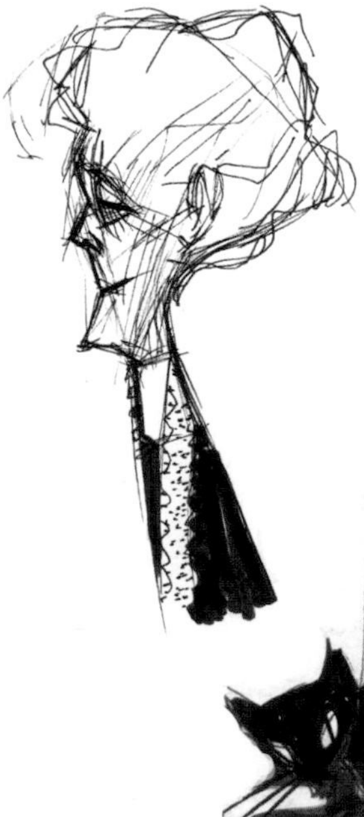

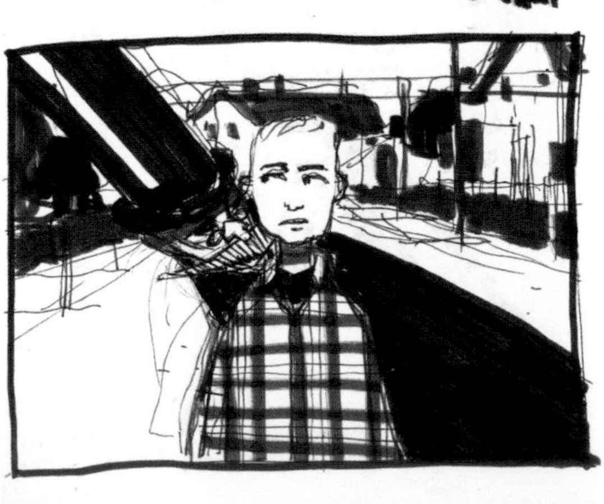

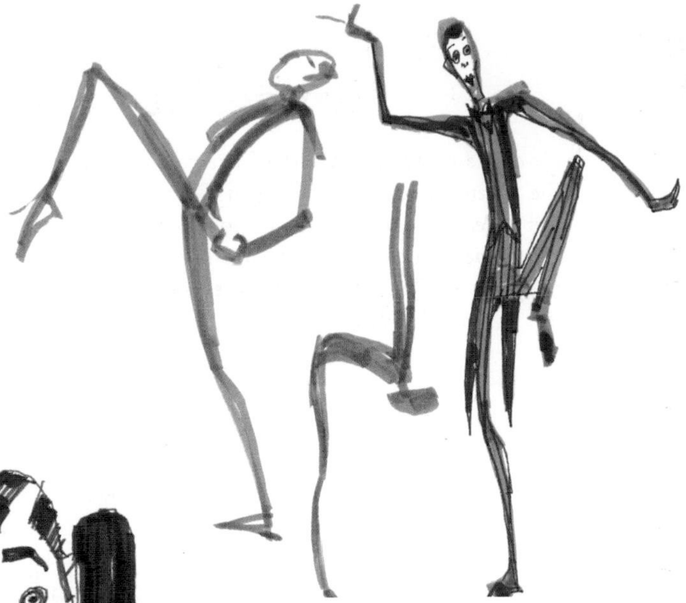

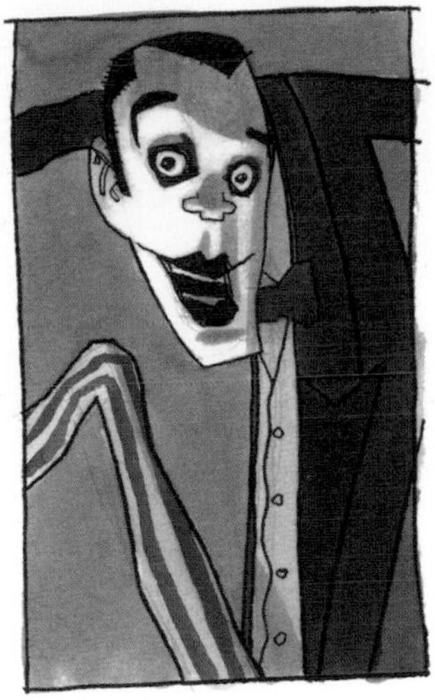

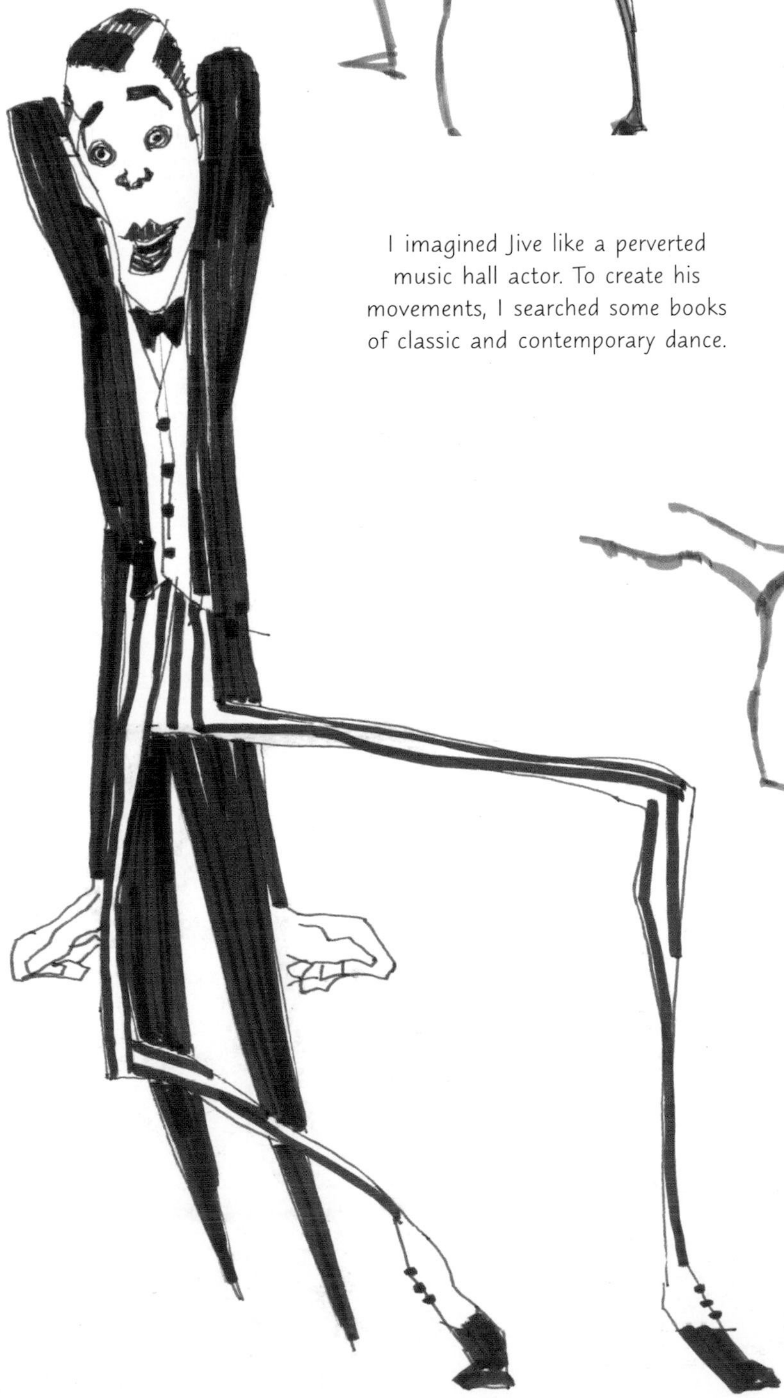

I imagined Jive like a perverted music hall actor. To create his movements, I searched some books of classic and contemporary dance.

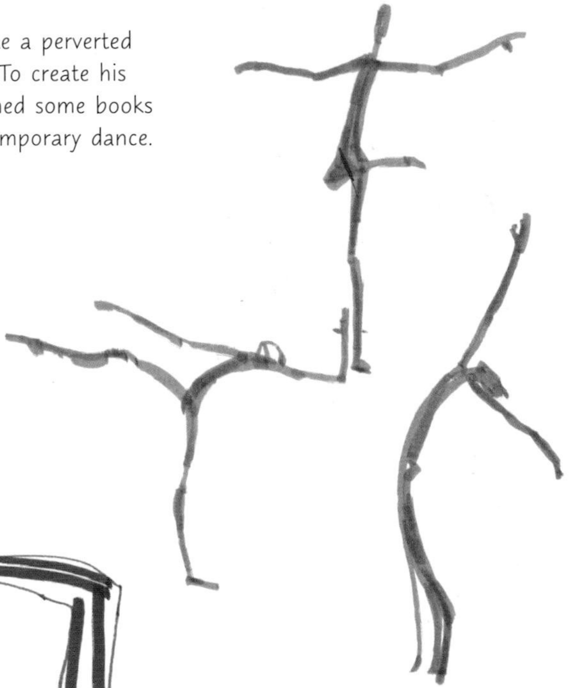

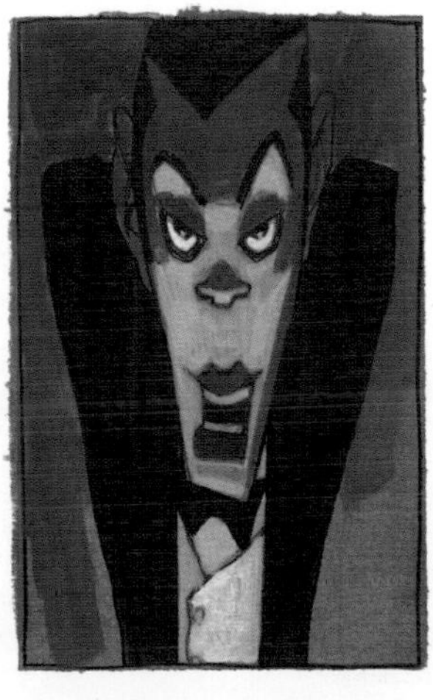

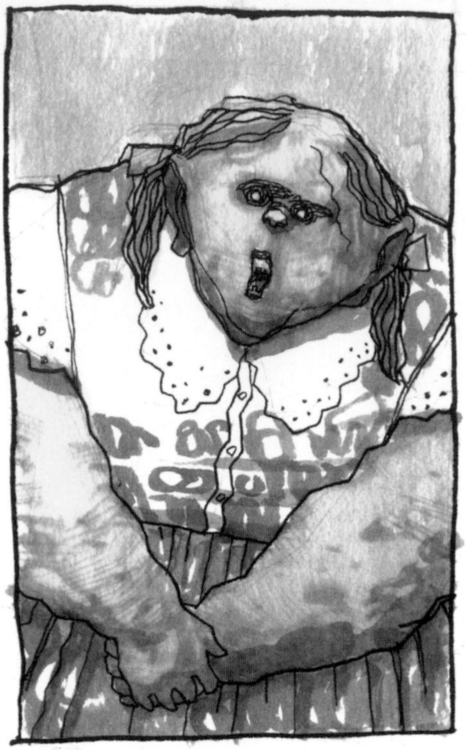

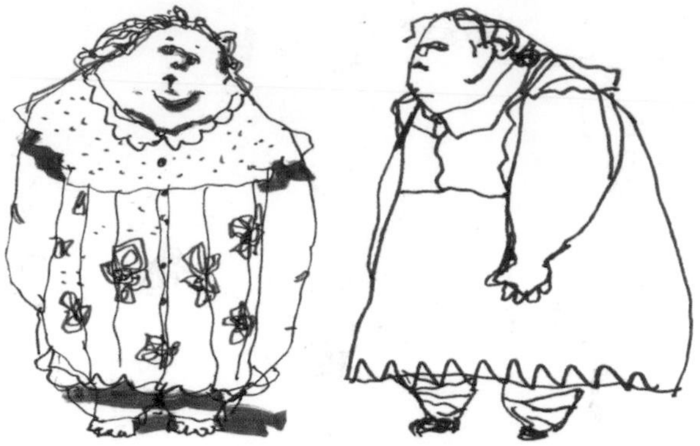

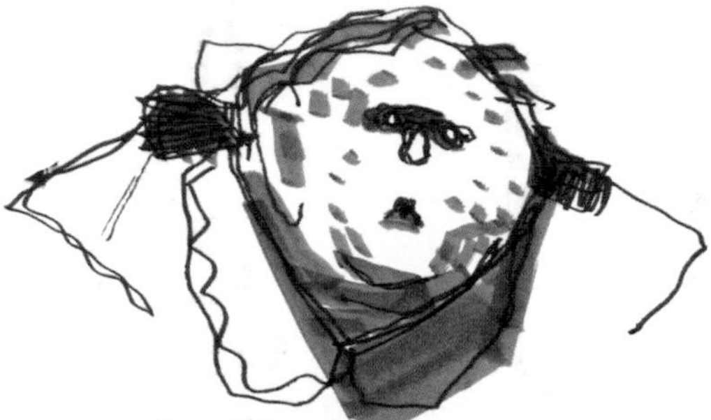

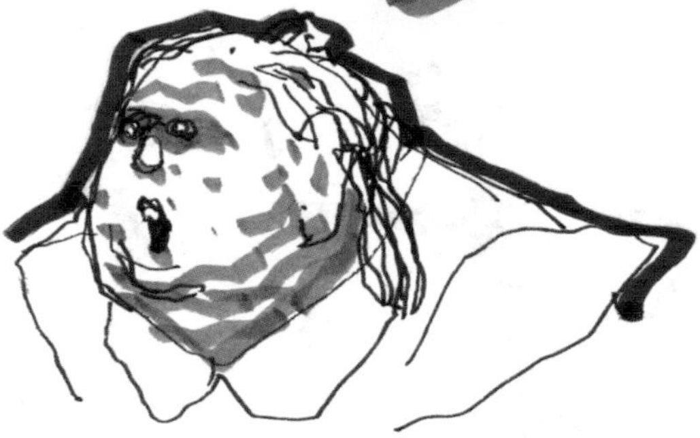

The most difficult thing about drawing Marr was to draw a slug with personality. About the Vampire Harvey, I decided to disfigure him a lot, so Wendell would be unable to recognize him.

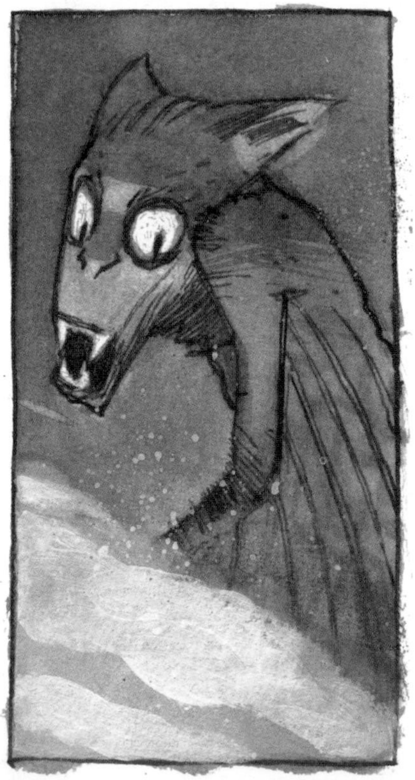

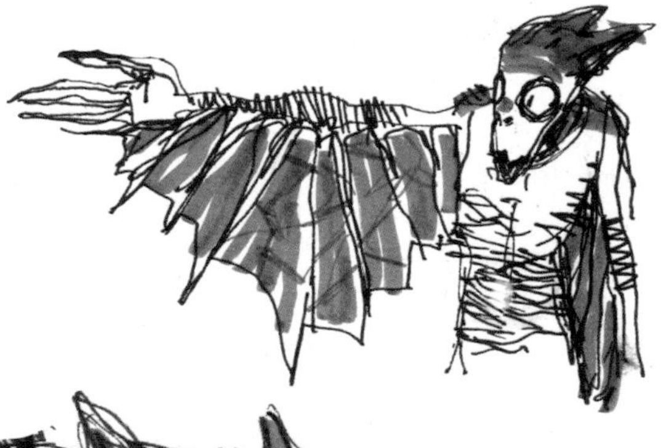

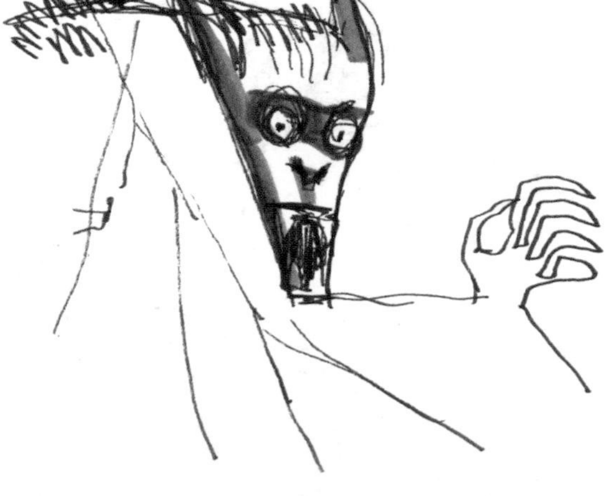

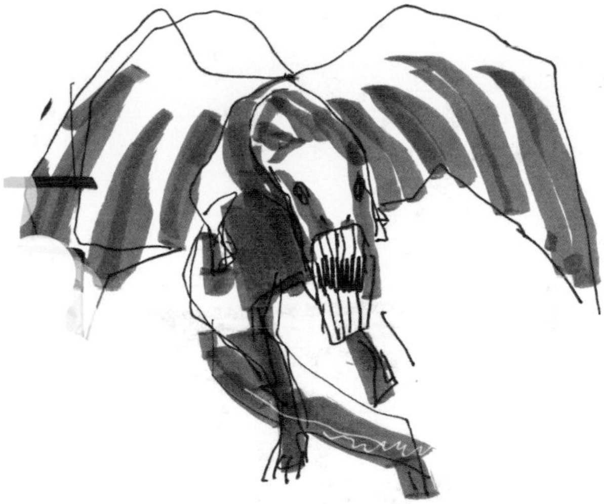

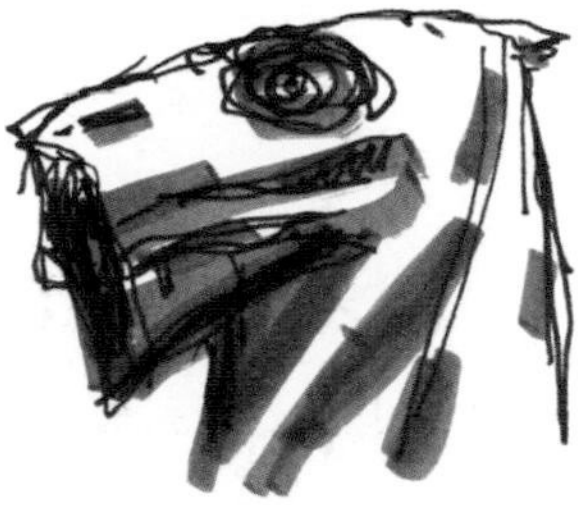

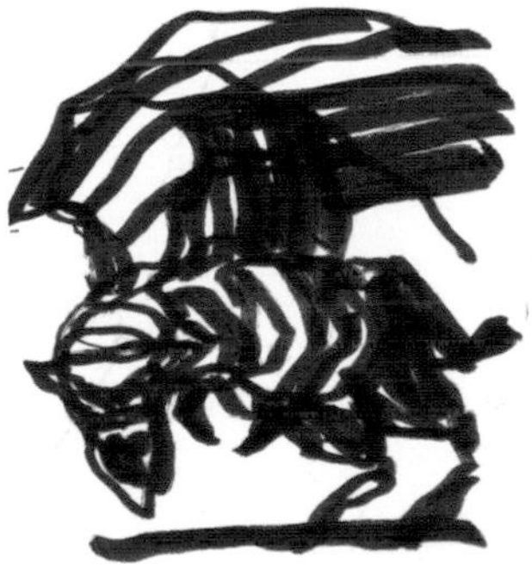

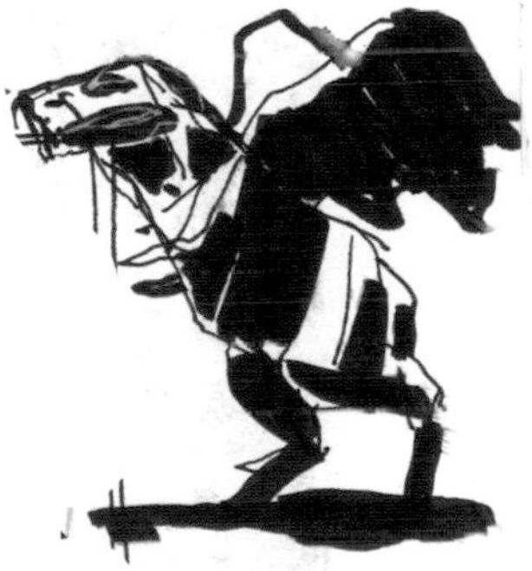

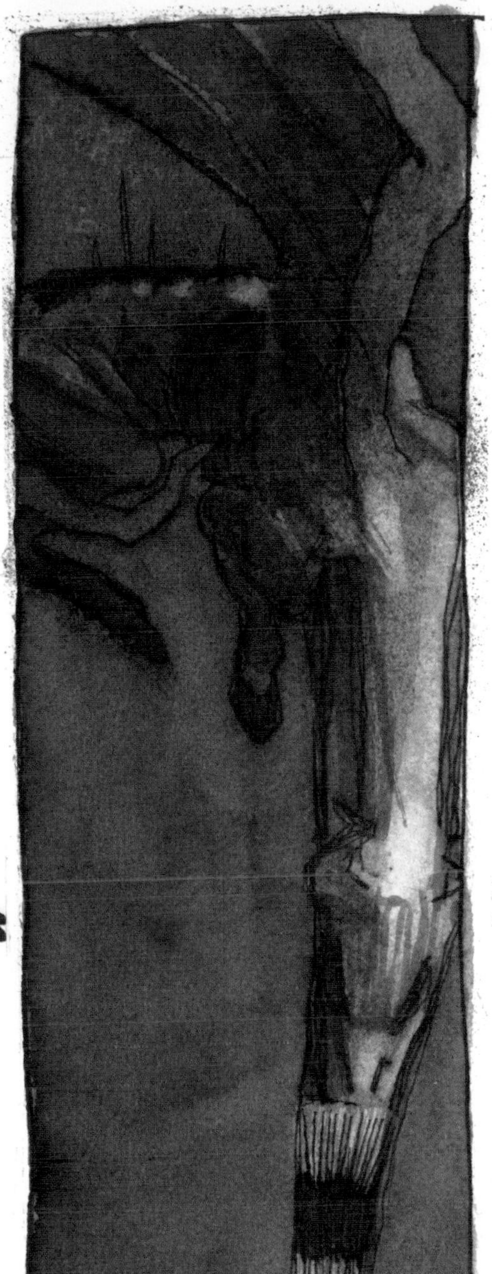

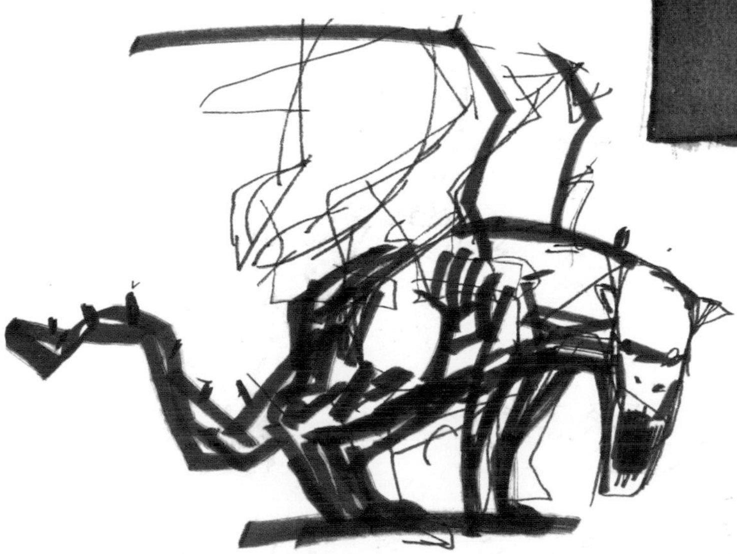

Carna was the most difficult character to create. It passed from being a Tyrannosaur-like creature to a mixture of horse, dog and a fighting bull.

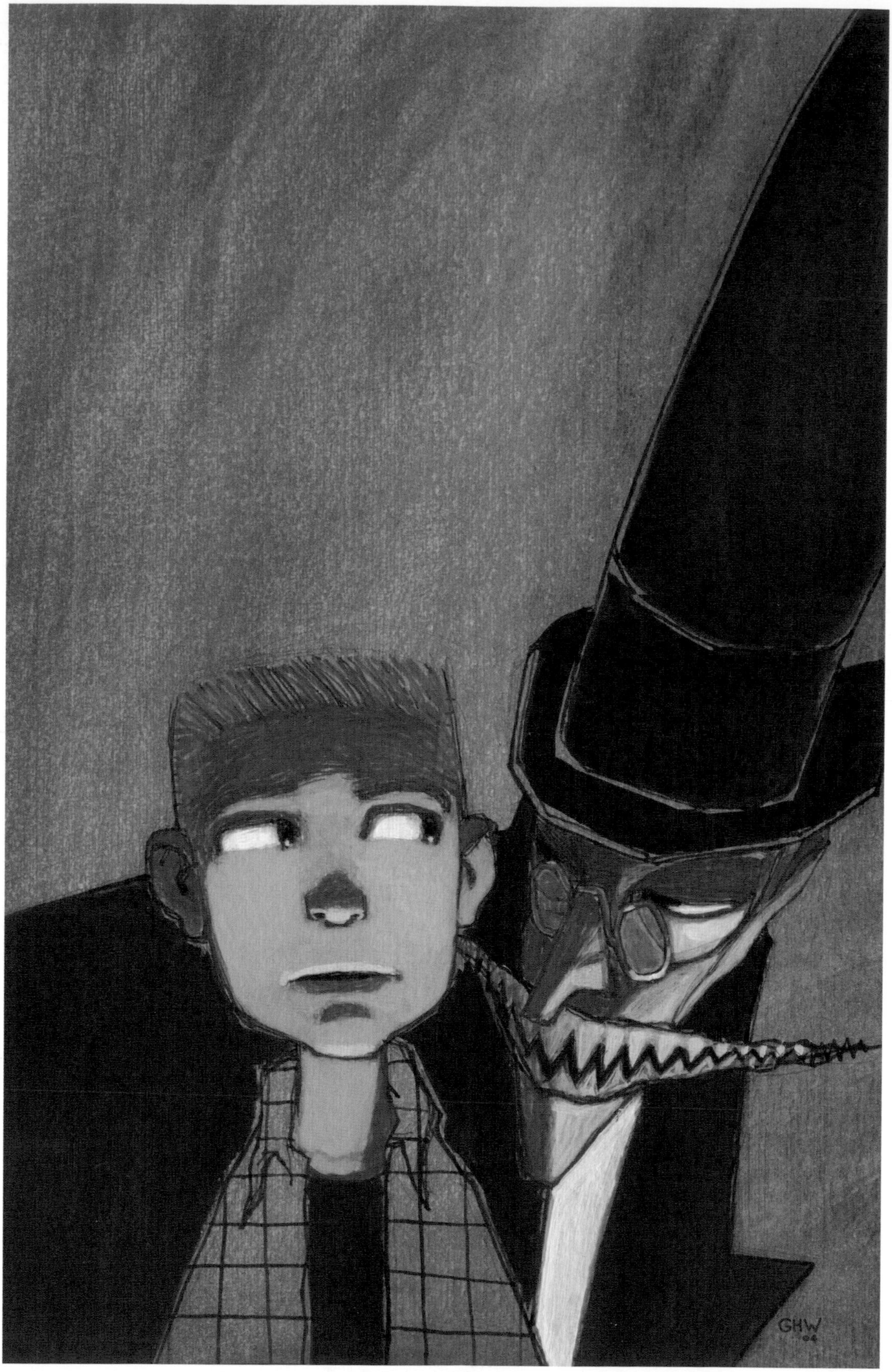
GHW
'04
this page: cover from book one
opposite page: cover from book two

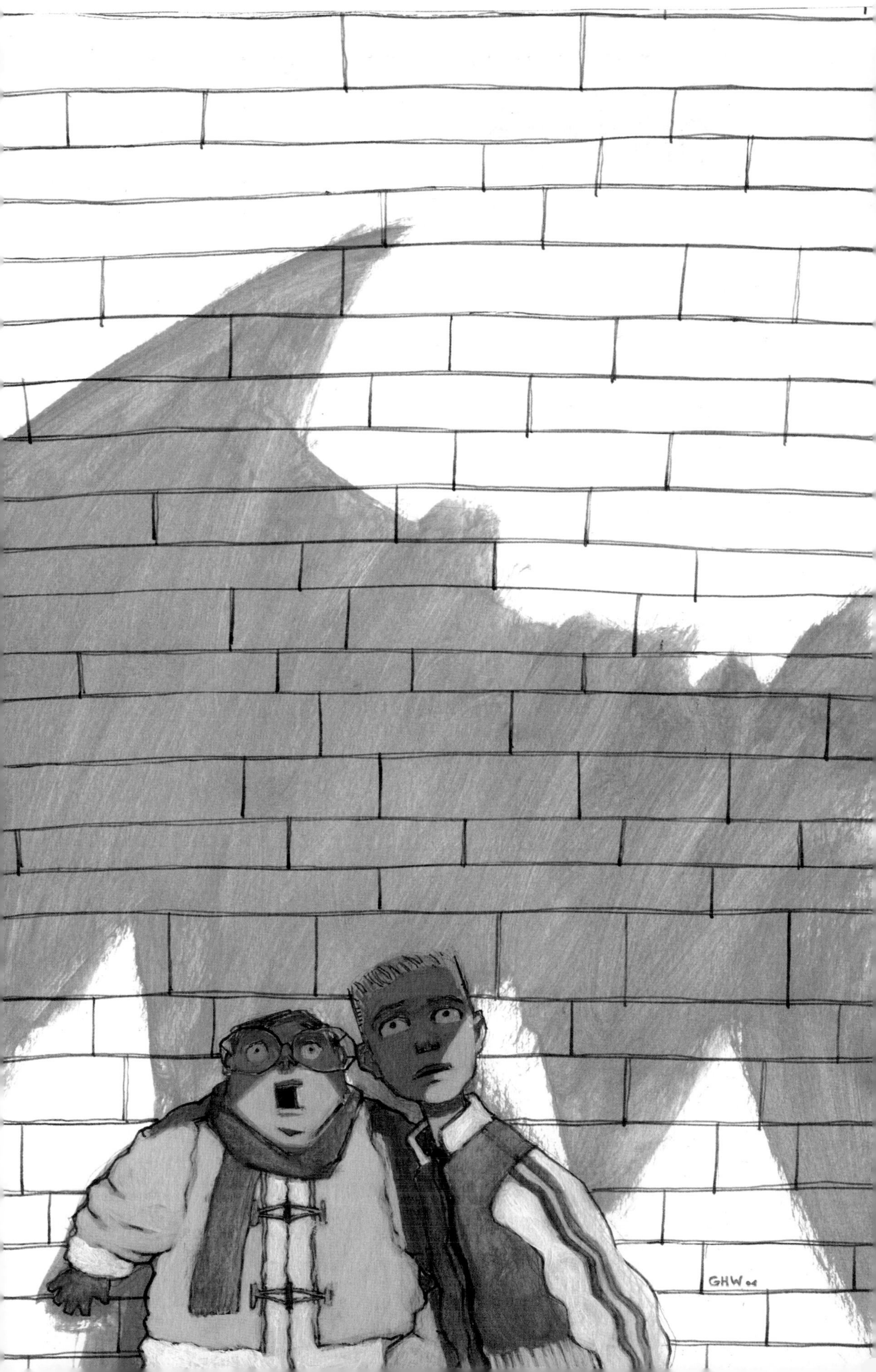
GHW 04

[redacted]

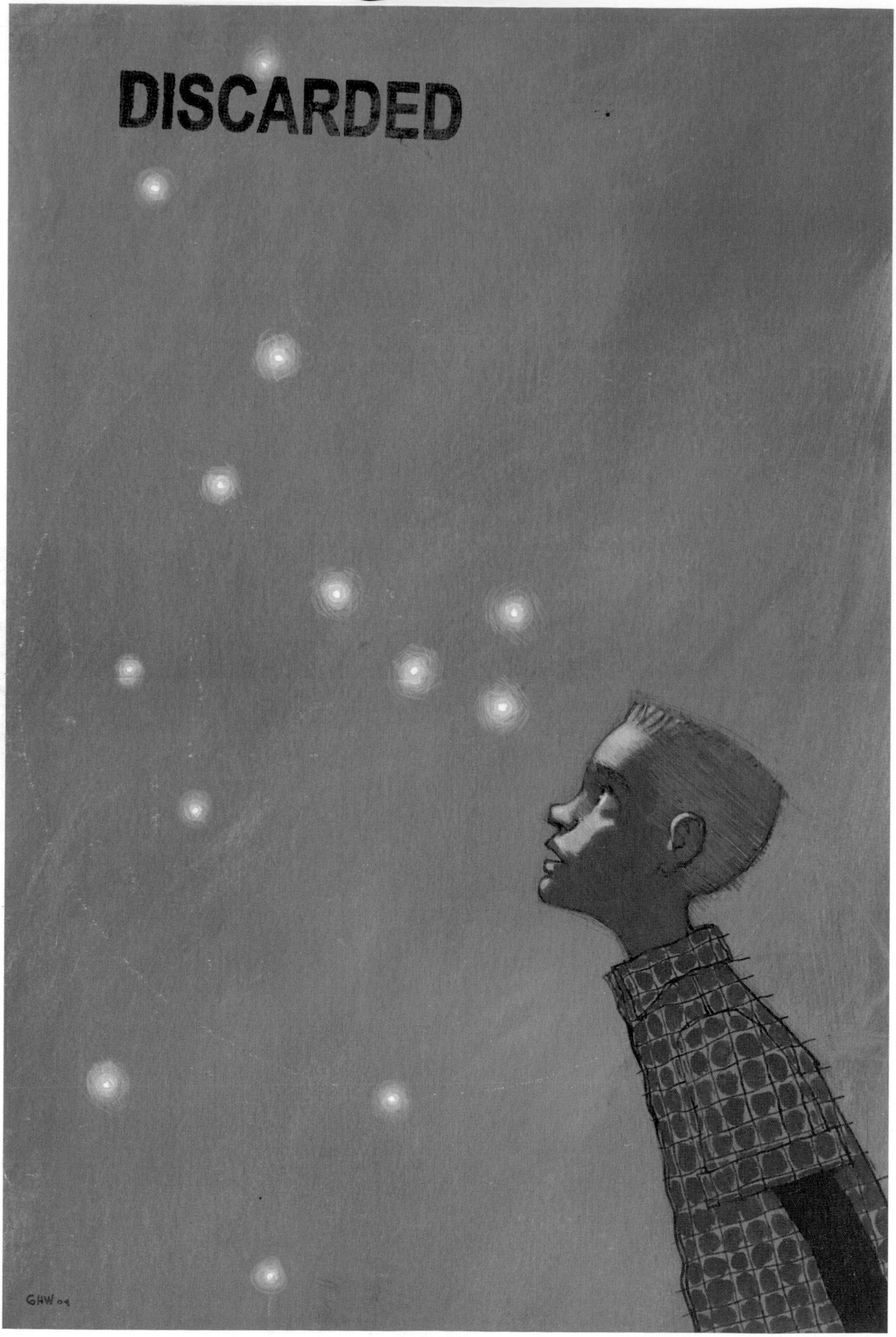
GHW 04

this page: cover from book three